PRAISE FOR *FROM ATHEISM TO CHRISTIANITY*

I am a great admirer of Joel Heck's philosophical insight and his diligence and thoroughness in research. In true form to the rest of his work, *From Atheism to Christianity* is both intellectually stimulating and spiritually nourishing and will prove to be a valuable addition to C. S. Lewis studies.

—David C. Downing
R. W. Schlosser Professor of English, Elizabethtown College

Careful in his claims and meticulous about dates, influences, and sources, Heck provides readers with an accurate, insightful, and highly readable account of Lewis's journey from cynical atheist to joyful Christian. Heck's storytelling powers illuminate and make comprehensible the winding path that Lewis took on his way to faith.

—Devin Brown
Professor of English, Asbury University
Author of *A Life Observed: A Spiritual Biography of C. S. Lewis*

Atheism is on the rise in our world, supported by a materialist world view. Nevertheless, my experience reveals that few have actually thought through the overwhelming philosophical and theological problems with atheism. Perhaps no one, in the last one hundred years, wrestled with this issue more reasonably and poignantly than C. S. Lewis as he moved from unbelief to faith. Perhaps no one has explained the route Lewis took in that process better than Joel Heck. Heck is one of the best Lewis scholars in the world and an informative guide. I highly recommend this book!

—Jerry Root
Professor of Evangelism, Wheaton College

This is a fascinatingly detailed and meticulously researched account of Lewis's slow conversion from atheism to Christianity that traces the influence of the books he read and the friends he made.

—Peter S. Williams
Co-editor of *C. S. Lewis at Poets' Corner* (Cascade, 2016)
Author of *C. S. Lewis vs. the New Atheists* (Paternoster, 2013)

Joel Heck has made a meticulous, detailed study of C. S. Lewis's journey from Christianity to atheism and back, providing clear and concise information about all the friends, authors, and texts that influenced him on the way. This book will be particularly invaluable to students who have to study Lewis but have little or no knowledge of philosophy or of the intellectual climate in Britain in the first half of the twentieth century.

—Suzanne Bray
Professor of English, Lille Catholic University

Drawing from an abundance of primary and secondary sources, Dr. Heck has provided us with the most thorough and meticulous account available of C. S. Lewis's journey into, and then out of, atheism. Heck is the foremost authority on the chronology of Lewis's life, tracing month by month the books and conversations that influenced Lewis's shifts in thought. He discovers many new, heretofore overlooked sources of influence on Lewis during his fifteen-year journey to Christianity, including idealist philosophers George Berkeley and F. H. Bradley, poets Wordsworth and Herbert, and works on mysticism by Jacob Boehme, Henry More, and William James. Heck draws masterfully from Lewis's letters, diaries, poems, and autobiographies (including *The Pilgrim's Regress*). This book is an indispensable resource for any Lewis scholar and for any serious reader seeking to understand Lewis's conversion from the inside out.

—Robert C. Koons
Professor of Philosophy, University of Texas at Austin

Perhaps no life story communicates the path from doubt to faith better than that of C. S. Lewis. Dr. Heck has written a masterpiece about Lewis's journey. Not only does this work reference the best scholarship on the life and work of Lewis, it also shares the heart of the author that no one should live and die without hope for salvation.

In my pastoral ministry, I have watched many struggle with faith and doubt. Dr. Heck embraces that tension and uses the story of Lewis to weave the reader to a God of love. There are far too many Christian books that shame atheists for their lack of faith. Finally we have a book that is a safe and intelligent read that you can offer friends and family whom you love.

—Rev. Jim Mueller
Senior Pastor of Peace Lutheran Church, Hurst, Texas

Joel Heck's splendid book is rich with fresh insights into the events, people, books, and ideas that influenced C. S. Lewis's journeys to and from atheism. Never patronizing, it should be widely read by both atheists and theists who want a deeper understanding of the dynamics of belief and unbelief.

—Angus Menuge

Professor and Chair of Philosophy, Concordia University Wisconsin

President of the Evangelical Philosophical Society

C. S. Lewis told the story of his fifteen-year journey from atheism to Christianity in his autobiographical books *The Pilgrim's Regress* and *Surprised by Joy*. With careful chronology and an examination of a wide range of writings, Joel Heck brings greater clarity to this important period. His use of Lewis's poetry and letters, among other works, fills in details and gives greater understanding of Lewis's many influences. The resulting enhanced account of Lewis's conversion underscores the compelling authenticity of his Christian apologetics in the context of his own faith and understanding.

—Steven P. Mueller

Dean of Christ College, Concordia University Irvine

Author of *Not a Tame God: Christ in the Writings of C. S. Lewis*

(CPH, 2002)

FROM ATHEISM TO CHRISTIANITY

THE STORY OF C. S. LEWIS

Peer Reviewed

JOEL D. HECK

CONCORDIA PUBLISHING HOUSE • SAINT LOUIS

To my wife, Cheryl,
my companion, my partner, my love
on this journey through life together.

Published by Concordia Publishing House
3558 S. Jefferson Ave., St. Louis, MO 63118–3968
1-800-325-3040 • cph.org

Copyright © 2017 Joel D. Heck

Manufactured in the United States of America

Library of Congress Cataloging-in-Publication Data

Names: Heck, Joel D., 1948- author.
Title: From atheism to Christianity : the story of C.S. Lewis / Joel D. Heck.
Description: St.Louis : Concordia Publishing House, 2017. | Includes
  bibliographical references and index.
Identifiers: LCCN 2016051046 (print) | LCCN 2016057360 (ebook) | ISBN
  9780758657237 (alk. paper) | ISBN 9780758657244
Subjects: LCSH: Lewis, C. S. (Clive Staples), 1898-1963. | Anglican
  converts—England—Biography. | Christian biography—England. |
  Christianity and atheism. | Authors, English—20th century—Biography.
Classification: LCC BV4935.L43 H43 2017 (print) | LCC BV4935.L43 (ebook) |
  DDC 230.092--dc23
LC record available at https://lccn.loc.gov/2016051046

3 4 5 6 7 8 9 10 11 12   27 26 25 24 23 22 21 20 19 18

CONTENTS

Acknowledgments

This book began at the Central Texas C. S. Lewis Society, which has met monthly in Austin, Texas, since 1999 and has provided much helpful critique of the manuscript in progress. Those individuals include especially Margaret Humphreys, Johnny Humphreys, Rob Koons, George Musacchio, Bill Laughlin, Claire Ducker, Karen Jordahl, Dorothy Kraemer, Patricia Youngdale, and Larry Linenschmidt, along with other occasional visitors. My heartfelt thanks and appreciation go to each of them for their comments and encouragement.

In addition to this group, I am grateful to a group of people who are either students of Lewis or students of writing or both, have written about Lewis, and read much of the manuscript during its development, making many helpful suggestions, nearly all of which I adopted. My thanks go to Jeffrey Utzinger, Devin Brown, Gene Edward Veith, Suzanne Bray, David C. Downing, Diana Glyer, Andrew Lazo, Angus J. L. Menuge, Adam Barkman, Peter S. Williams, and Stephen Thorson, but also to George Musacchio and Rob Koons once again. And I am grateful to one of my neighbors, Solana Wooldridge, who read this manuscript from the atheist's point of view and made many additional, helpful suggestions.

PREFACE

One of the world's most famous atheists of the twentieth century was C. S. Lewis. Although he did not become famous *for* his atheism, he became famous, in part, *because of* his atheism. Many other atheists of the twentieth century are well-known both for their expertise in their fields and for being atheists, people like philosophers Bertrand Russell, Gilbert Ryle, A. J. Ayer, P. F. Stawson, Antony Flew, writer Philip Pullman, and others, but none of them has captured the minds and imaginations of people like C. S. Lewis, whose influence far surpasses any of these individuals, and perhaps even all of them combined.

What journey did Lewis travel on his way to atheism? How was it that he left his atheism behind, first for theism and then for Christianity? What were the attractions of atheism for him, and then, much later, what were the attractions of theism and Christianity? Why did his journey from atheism to theism and Christianity take fifteen years? How did his thinking change as those years went by and what stages did he pass through? Who influenced his thought during that time? Who were the authors he read, the teachers and students with whom he interacted, and the friends he made? What did he mean when he once wrote about the "good atheist"?[1]

This book attempts to answer those questions, and, in the answering, offers clues to the meaning of life for the contemporary atheist and theist alike from the perspective of one who knew both atheism and Christianity from the inside. In fact, one of the reasons why the BBC invited Lewis to give the talks that later became the book we know as *Mere Christianity* was because he had been an atheist for many years.

---

[1] C. S. Lewis, "De Futilitate," in *Christian Reflections* (Grand Rapids: Eerdmans, 1967), 70.

Three major events in the recent past have made this book possible.

First, over the past five decades since his death, we have come to understand Lewis's life better as people have studied his life and writings. Chief among the studies of Lewis's journey to faith is David C. Downing's book, *The Most Reluctant Convert.* The publication of three volumes of Lewis's letters (*The Collected Letters of C. S. Lewis*), edited by Walter Hooper, has greatly aided such study, as has the publication of other helpful works, including the diary of C. S. Lewis, the diary of his brother Warren, *The Lewis Papers*;[2] the recently published "Early Prose Joy" (an early attempt by Lewis at writing an autobiography); his allegorical autobiography, *The Pilgrim's Regress*; and his actual autobiography, *Surprised by Joy.* As a matter of fact, Lewis's own Preface to *Surprised by Joy* states that he had received requests to tell how he traveled the road from atheism to Christianity.

Lewis once stated that ink was "the great cure for all human ills."[3] One major assumption guides this book: when Lewis drew a significant conclusion or took an important step in his thinking, he wrote about it. Lewis was a voluminous writer, both in his work as a scholar and in his personal life. He expressed his major ideas in books and essays, sometimes long after he drew those conclusions, in his tens of thousands of letters, and in his on-again-off-again diaries. Often his writing was therapeutic, enabling him to express his thoughts and emotions, drawing strength, understanding, and clarity from doing so. If an idea was important enough to change his thinking, it was important enough to write about in his diary, in an essay or book, or in a letter to one of his close friends. He may have spoken about important changes without writing about them, and certainly he was a great talker, but we can probably never know what he said about those changes.

---

[2] *The Lewis Papers* are a collection of family papers in the Lewis family from 1850–1930, compiled by Warren Lewis and consisting of letters, diaries, poems, brief essays, and various other documents.

[3] On May 30, 1916. See *The Collected Letters of C. S. Lewis: Volume I, Family Letters 1905–1931*, edited by Walter Hooper (London: HarperCollins, 2000), 187.

Second, in 2013, three major biographies of the life of C. S. Lewis were published during the fiftieth anniversary year of his death, one by Devin Brown, which connects the writings of Lewis more closely to the changes in his spiritual life than ever before, another by Alister McGrath, and a third by Colin Duriez. Each of these has made important contributions to our understanding of C. S. Lewis, building on many previous biographies, especially George Sayer's *Jack*.

Third, my own work has resulted in the compilation of a massive amount of information about the life of Lewis in chronological order, which is available through the online resource "Chronologically Lewis." We now have more information about Lewis than we have ever had, even more information in some places than Lewis himself had. This book stands on the shoulders of those who have studied Lewis. Its goal is to provide greater insight into one fifteen-year phase of his life and to enable readers to better understand both atheism and Christianity—Lewis's own specific versions of atheism and Christianity—as a result.

Before we move to the introduction, an explanation about Lewis's use of the word *Joy* is in order for those unfamiliar with his writings. By the word *Joy*—which he distinguished with a capital letter—Lewis did not mean delight or happiness or pleasure, whether due to outward circumstances or an inner state of mind. Joy is delightful, bringing happiness, but not delight itself. Joy is pleasurable, but not pleasure itself. He used several other terms as near synonyms for Joy, among them *longing, desire*, and the German word *Sehnsucht*. He once defined Joy as an "inconsolable longing"[4] for something beyond human experience, and he described it as thoughtful wishing that began for him at least by age 6.[5] This Joy was fleeting, and it included a desire to have that longing again just as soon as it was gone. For Lewis, Joy was a longing that is perhaps best expressed in Ecclesiastes 3:11, where Solomon writes about God, "He has put eternity into

---

[4] C. S. Lewis, *Surprised by Joy: The Shape of My Early Life* (San Diego: Harcourt Brace Jovanovich, 1955), 72.
[5] C. S. Lewis, *Dymer* (London: J. M. Dent & Sons Ltd., 1950), Preface, xi.

man's heart." Joy was a longing for something beyond this world, ultimately a longing for God that was put inside us by God Himself.[6] At times before his conversion, he mistook the beauty of art, nature, or music (as well as other things) as the source of longing, not looking behind those objects for their source or even believing that there was anything behind them.

One of the enduring images C. S. Lewis left for readers involves the game of chess. When he was four, Lewis went on vacation with his mother and brother to nearby County Down in Ireland. Before leaving, Lewis had asked his father for a chess set. While in County Down, Lewis asked if his father would remember to buy him that chess set. For many years afterward, the two brothers played chess. Little did he know at age 4 what impact the game of chess would have on both his life and his autobiography.

Lewis described his intellectual and spiritual development as a chess game in which God made four major moves. We can now identify the first two moves to the day, month, and year; the third one within a few months (with a great deal of certainty to the right year); and the fourth move to a six-day period. That was previously not possible. All other change in Lewis's thinking leads up to or follows those four moves, which serve as the major changes in his pre-Christian thinking. The four major chess moves were the loss of his first bishop, the loss of the second bishop, Check, and Checkmate. The books he was reading, the people to whom he was talking, his personal aspirations, and the changes in his living conditions or his career clarify those four moves. The reader should know that Lewis was an

---

[6] Many have written about Lewis's concept of Joy, including Jerry Root and Mark Neal in the recent *The Surprising Imagination of C. S. Lewis: An Introduction* (Nashville: Abingdon Press, 2015). See also Stephen Thorson's *Joy and Poetic Imagination: Understanding C. S. Lewis's "Great War" with Owen Barfield and its Significance for Lewis's Conversion and Writings* (Hamden, CT: Winged Lion Press, 2015). In Lewis's writings, see especially "The Weight of Glory," *The Weight of Glory and Other Addresses* (New York: Simon & Schuster, 1980), but also *Surprised by Joy* and *The Pilgrim's Regress: An Allegorical Apology for Christianity, Reason, and Romanticism* (Grand Rapids: Eerdmans, 1958).

intellectual, and that means that most of his spiritual development was the result of much thinking, much reading, and deep conversations. Although few people travel a similar path, our tracing of his mental footsteps will reward us, and we will find most of his thinking within our reach. However, as J. R. R. Tolkien once said of Lewis, "You'll never get to the bottom of him."[7] And we won't, certainly not in this book.

The opening chapters in this book describe how Lewis became an atheist, as well as discuss some of the influences both toward and away from atheism. Then chapters 3 through 7 trace the steps in Lewis's belief between 1916 and 1931 year by year in some detail, providing insight into skepticism, agnosticism, atheism, Realism, Idealism, pantheism, theism, and Christianity in the process. The concluding chapters provide closure, offering a summary of his return to theism; what Lewis in retrospect thought about atheism; and some conclusions about Lewis, atheism, and God.

Joel D. Heck
Summer 2016

---

[7] George Sayer, *Jack: A Life of C. S. Lewis* (Wheaton, IL: Crossway, 1994), xvii.

INTRODUCTION

"You can't start with God. I don't accept God!"

—C. S. Lewis to Leo Baker,
C. S. Lewis at the Breakfast Table

On October 12, 1916, the seventeen-year-old C. S. Lewis wrote a strident letter to Arthur Greeves, his boyhood friend. In this letter, he explained a position he had adopted about religion nearly four years earlier. At the time, Lewis was living and studying with William T. Kirkpatrick, a private tutor, in the hope of being successful enough on his scholarship exams to be admitted to Oxford University. Kirkpatrick, the former Headmaster of Lurgan College in Ireland, was living in retirement. He had privately tutored Albert Lewis as a student at Lurgan College, later Warren Lewis, and now the younger Lewis.

Lewis had recently read Sir James Frazer's *The Golden Bough*, which had convinced him that Christianity was just one of many mythologies. By this time in his life, Lewis had already rejected Christianity, but Frazer gave him a platform on which to base his atheism. *The Golden Bough: A Study in Comparative Religion*, published as a series of twelve books, compares Christianity to the mystery religions, arguing that Christianity is an imitation of those other religions, including those that held to a dying and rising god. Today scholars regard that viewpoint as invalid.[1] As Michael Licona has noted, "There were *no* dying and rising gods that preceded Christianity. They all post-dated the first century."[2] Consequently, Ronald Nash has stated

---

[1] Michael Green, *Lies, Lies, Lies! Exposing Myths about the Real Jesus* (Nottingham: IVP, 2009), 59f. Cited in Peter S. Williams, *C. S. Lewis vs. the New Atheists* (Milton Keynes, UK: Paternoster, 2013), 195.

[2] Michael Licona in Lee Strobel, *The Case for the Real Jesus* (Grand Rapids: Zondervan, 2007), 161. Cited in Williams, *C. S. Lewis vs. the New Atheists*, 196.

that "the tide of scholarly opinion has turned dramatically against attempts to make early Christianity dependent on the so-called dying and rising gods of Hellenistic paganism."[3] Most of the rest of Frazer's book has also been set aside, and today it is remembered largely for its literary influence on authors T. S. Eliot and James Joyce.[4]

At this time, Frazer's book series convinced him so much that he wrote an extensive defense of his thinking to Arthur Greeves, stating,

> I believe in no religion. . . . and . . . Christianity is not even the best. All religions, that is, all mythologies . . . are merely man's own invention . . . great men were regarded as gods after their death . . . thus after the death of a Hebrew philosopher Yeshua (whose name we have corrupted into Jesus) he became regarded as a god, a cult sprang up, which was afterwards connected with the ancient Hebrew-Jahweh-worship, and so Christianity came into being—one mythology among many.[5]

This was the position of Sir James Frazer. Lewis drew on Frazer's works, comparing the various religions of the world with Greek and Norse mythology. For Frazer, human belief evolved from an initial stage of primitive magic to religion and finally to the scientific stage. Although Frazer's position has since been discarded as contrary to the evidence,[6] many held to this position in the first two decades of the twentieth century. For the young Lewis, religion was a product of superstition and a result of a lack of education and clear thinking.

---

[3] Ronald H. Nash, *The Gospel and the Greeks*, 2nd ed. (New Jersey: Phillipsburg, 2003), 162.

[4] David C. Downing, *The Most Reluctant Convert: C. S. Lewis's Journey to Faith* (Downers Grove, IL: InterVarsity Press, 2002), 52.

[5] *Collected Letters of C. S. Lewis,* I, 230f.

[6] Paul C. Vitz, *Faith of the Fatherless: The Psychology of Atheism* (Dallas, TX: Spence Publishing, 2000), 131ff. Vitz cites ethnologist Wilhelm Schmidt, who has shown that all of the earliest humans and the most primitive tribes that we know have had monotheistic beliefs from the start. In fact, the history of the development of religion has been shown to be one of devolution rather than evolution, i.e., a movement from one god to few gods to many gods.

When he entered Oxford University a year later as an undergraduate, Lewis made numerous friends among his fellow students. One of those friends was Leo Baker. Early in their friendship, probably during their first term together, Lewis yelled at Baker, "You take too many things for granted. You can't start with God. I don't accept God!" [7] Stunned into silence, Baker quickly learned that assuming the existence of God was unacceptable for Lewis.

How did C. S. Lewis, the grandson of a clergyman and the child of active church members, come to adopt atheism and what were his reasons for doing so? Why did he adopt atheism so easily, even after being raised in a Christian home? Why then, many years later, did he set aside his atheism in favor of the Christianity he had previously rejected as bondage and become the author of so many best-selling books, especially the Chronicles of Narnia, *Mere Christianity*, and *The Screwtape Letters*? To these questions we now turn.

---

[7] Leo Baker, "Near the Beginning," in James Como, *C. S. Lewis at the Breakfast Table* (San Diego: Harcourt Brace & Company, 1992), 4.

Chapter 1

The Causes of Lewis's Atheism

"I had very definitely formed the opinion that the universe was, in the main, a rather regrettable institution."

—C. S. Lewis, *Surprised by Joy*

In *Surprised by Joy*, Lewis condemns himself in the strongest terms for what he calls one of the worst acts of his life. He allowed himself to be confirmed and to make his first communion in his Belfast church—St. Mark's, Dundela—at age 16, in total disbelief of the teachings that the church asked him to confirm.[1] The rift between father and son helped to create this awkward situation, and Lewis's cowardice—his unwillingness to tell his father what he actually believed—drove him to hypocrisy, and the hypocrisy, he explains, drove him to blasphemy. His brother was serving in the war effort in France, unavailable for counsel, and the few friends he had were not ones he could confide in. An entire complex of factors combined to create this regrettable situation.

C. S. Lewis's atheism began early in life while living in his parents' household, where the family practiced a superficial form of Christianity. Lewis was a bright and precocious child, and he knew just enough about the Christian faith to think he understood it. Lewis later wrote that during those early years, aesthetic experiences—such as his later

---

[1] Lewis, *Surprised by Joy*, 161.

love of music, art, and nature—were rare and that religious experiences were non-existent. He learned what most people learn from their church: how to pray, how to gather for worship, and how to act in church. He tells us that he accepted what he was told, but he had little interest in it.[2] He remembered no emotion that could qualify as truly religious.[3] He also confesses that he recalled almost nothing about his mother's religion and that he could recall nothing otherworldly about his childhood.[4] Although she was the daughter of a Church of Ireland clergyman, his mother, Flora Lewis, seems not to have modeled, taught, or encouraged personal spirituality, offering instead what Warren once called "the dry husks of religion" that came from the semi-political churchgoing of Northern Ireland.[5] It may only be that Flora ceded too much of the development of her children's spiritual life to Annie Harper and other maids or that her poor health prevented her from doing more. Either that or Jack—the name his friends called him—may simply have been too young to develop a genuine faith of his own before his mother's death when he was nine. Their Christianity seems to have been more formal than heartfelt; a church attendance, rather than meaningful, positive relationships with a living God; more a religion of the head than a religion of the heart.[6]

This formal spiritual focus in his early life explains why Lewis later wrote about the difficulty in feeling about God and the sufferings of

---

[2] Lewis, *Surprised by Joy*, 7.

[3] C. S. Lewis, "Early Prose Joy," 28. The page numbers here and throughout this book refer to the page numbers in *VII*, Journal of the Marion E. Wade Center at Wheaton College, where there appears " 'Early Prose Joy': C. S. Lewis's Early Draft of an Autobiographical Manuscript," *VII* 30 (2013): 13–49.

[4] Lewis, *Surprised by Joy*, 8.

[5] Warren Lewis, "Memoir of C. S. Lewis," in *Letters of C. S. Lewis* (Revised Harvest edition, 1993), 39.

[6] The skepticism of Lily Suffern, Flora's sister, provides a window into the Hamilton family, when Aunt Lily spoke to young C. S. Lewis about the cardinal error of all religions, i.e., the assumption that God existed and cared for us. She also claimed that the importance of Christ lay not in what He said (C. S. Lewis, *All My Road Before Me: The Diary of C. S. Lewis, 1922–1927* [New York: Harcourt Brace, 1991], 128).

Christ as one was supposed to feel. His effort to present these ideas in the imaginary world of Narnia enabled others to see them—as he put it—in their real potency, stripped of their stained-glass and Sunday School associations. The message of the Gospel, as presented to him in his childhood, did not communicate its truth effectively, but rather paralyzed his religious development for many years.[7] Warren's diary confirms this, describing the sermons of Rev. Gerald Peacocke—Rector of St. Mark's, Dundela, from 1900 to 1914—as unintelligible during his childhood attendance at St. Mark's.[8]

Those early years—from age 6 to 12—were also lonely years for Jack, especially after Warren crossed the Irish Sea to attend school in England. Deprived of his brother, the younger Lewis was lonely. He stated that solitude became the chief characteristic of that period in his life.[9] Because he had been born with only one joint in each of his thumbs, he was inept at sports; this limited for him the possible companionships of athletes and athletics and encouraged him toward the solitary activities of reading and writing. Instead of finding companions in his classmates, he developed a sense of companionship with the characters he was reading or writing about. In spite of the companionship of his brother, he once stated of this period in life that he and his brother had no friends.[10] In late 1913, he wrote to his father about the rare blessing of solitude while recuperating in the sanatorium.[11] Later, while a student at Cherbourg House, Lewis called himself "the orphan,"[12] a hint of the alienation he felt toward his father,

---

[7] C. S. Lewis, "Sometimes Fairy Stories May Say Best What's to Be Said," *On Stories and Other Essays on Literature* (New York: Harcourt Brace & Company, 1982), 47.

[8] The unpublished diary of Warren Lewis, April 19, 1931.

[9] Lewis, *Surprised by Joy*, 11.

[10] Lewis, *Surprised by Joy*, 46. In *Collected Letters of C. S. Lewis*, I, 95, a letter dated November 17, 1914, Lewis wrote about this time at Great Bookham that in that week he had not spoken to anyone except for Kirkpatrick and his wife, and that he did not really mind, since there were few people whose society he preferred to his own.

[11] *Collected Letters of C. S. Lewis*, I, 44, n. 44.

[12] Lewis, *Surprised by Joy*, 59.

but he also wrote that there he made his first real friends.[13] While it is odd that he was making friends for the first time at age 14, his solitary activities of reading and writing were contributing factors. His father Albert Lewis once confided in Warren that he was concerned that his younger son would be more of a hermit than ever by studying with a private tutor, W. T. Kirkpatrick, and he had reason to be concerned. Some of the poems Clive wrote during that period, especially the poem "Loneliness,"[14] expressed the solitude of one living in a world with few friends. What would become a great strength of Lewis—his friendliness and cordiality to almost anyone he met—was at this time in his life almost completely absent. And, as we will see, this solitude had an impact on Lewis's religious beliefs.

SUFFERING AND THE DEATH OF FLORA LEWIS

Just as Lewis was beginning his mornings in prayer and considering what it meant to love his neighbor as himself, a tragedy occurred that made it hard for him to believe in a loving God: in 1908, his mother, Flora Hamilton Lewis, died of cancer. That tragic death began a long journey for nine-year-old Lewis, and the primary conclusion he made was that, if such tragic events can happen, God must not exist. God is supposed to be good, and no God would have allowed such tragedy. No growth, no learning, no redemption can come from suffering. When he later discovered a quotation from Lucretius,[15] Lewis saw that quotation as representative of what he felt: "Had God designed the world, it would not be / A world so frail and faulty as we see."[16]

---

[13] Lewis, *Surprised by Joy*, 58.

[14] Written at Easter 1916. See *The Collected Poems of C. S. Lewis: A Critical Edition*, edited by Don W. King (Kent, OH: Kent State University Press, 2015), 61f.

[15] Lucretius was a Roman poet and philosopher who lived during the first century BC, from 99 to 55 BC.

[16] Lewis, *Surprised by Joy*, 65. The Lucretius quote is from *De Rerum Natura*, Book 5, 198–99. According to *Surprised by Joy*, 144, he discovered this quotation at least as early as his time with Kirkpatrick (1914–17).

The prayers that he was taught to say did not result in his mother's return to health. The world is frail and faulty when your mother dies, especially when she dies while you are in your tender years. Later Lewis would write about this early period in his life, "I had very definitely formed the opinion that the universe was, in the main, a rather regrettable institution."[17] In his thinking, the death of one's mother in such a tragic way could not possibly be part of the plan of a loving God. Lewis described his mother's death in this hopeless way: "It was sea and islands now; the great continent had sunk like Atlantis."[18]

Later he would write that Walter Hilton's warning about prayer would have provided the necessary correction, since Hilton had argued that we must never use prayer to try to extort anything from God.[19] That no one offered Hilton's warning reminds us that for much of his childhood and boyhood he lacked the kind of spiritual direction that would have helped him in his spiritual life and would have made some sense of suffering. In *The Problem of Pain*, Lewis summarized the core of the argument about suffering, "If God were good, He would wish to make His creatures perfectly happy, and if God were almighty, He would be able to do what He wished. But the creatures are not happy. Therefore God lacks either goodness, or power, or both."[20] Couple this argument with a world of nature which does not favor life;

---

[17] Lewis, *Surprised by Joy*, 63.

[18] Lewis, *Surprised by Joy*, 21. Or as one man more recently put it, "My whole world disappeared" (Lynn Davidman, *Motherloss* [Berkeley, CA: University of California Press, 2000], 32). This book is a study of sixty people who lost their mothers when they were between the ages of ten and fifteen.

[19] Lewis, *Surprised by Joy*, 62. Hilton was an English Christian mystic who lived during the fourteenth century, best known for his book *The Scale of Perfection*.

[20] C. S. Lewis, *The Problem of Pain* (New York: HarperCollins, 1996), 16. Epicurus is often cited as the first person to formulate the problem of evil, though some think Lactantius wrongly attributed this formulation to Epicurus. See Reinhold F. Glei, *Et invidus et inbecillus. Das angebliche Epikurfragment bei Laktanz, De ira dei 13, 20–21*, in *Vigiliae Christianae* 42 (1988): 47–58.

all life ends without hope, as Lewis wrote, and in the same way.[21] Then, later in his autobiography, he reflects on how he originally thought, referring to his views early in life this way: "The inexorable 'laws of Nature' which operate in defiance of human suffering or desert, which are not turned aside by prayer, seem at first sight to furnish a strong argument against the goodness and power of God."[22]

Decades later, Lewis wrote a letter to his former student (and former atheist) Alan Richard Griffiths. Walter Hooper informs us that Alan Richard Griffiths matriculated at Magdalen College in 1925 and that Griffiths read English with Lewis as his tutor from 1927 until 1929.[23] He comes into the story a great deal later on because both he and Lewis were at approximately the same stage in their spiritual lives in the late 1920s, so much so that Lewis called him his "chief companion"[24] on his spiritual journey. Lewis explained to Griffiths how he came to adopt atheism: "The early loss of my mother, great unhappiness at school, and the shadow of the last war and presently the experience of it, had given me a very pessimistic view of existence. My atheism was based on it."[25]

Beginning that sentence with the death of his mother shows the preeminence of that great loss in his life. A pessimistic view of existence that was the foundation of Lewis's atheism was based on her death as well as other tragic events; his inability to understand setback left him without the resources to make sense of such suffering. Later he wrote that his argument against God resulted from a universe that

---

[21] C. S. Lewis, "On Living in an Atomic Age," *Present Concerns* (New York: Harcourt Brace Jovanovich, 1986), 74.

[22] Lewis, *The Problem of Pain*, 19.

[23] *Collected Letters of C. S. Lewis*, I, 834, n. 82.

[24] Lewis, *Surprised by Joy*, 234. In *Collected Letters of C. S. Lewis*, I, 834, n. 82, Walter Hooper tells us, "Alan Richard Griffiths . . . matriculated at Magdalen in 1925 and read English under Lewis."

[25] *The Collected Letters of C. S. Lewis, Volume II: Books, Broadcasts, and War 1931–1949*, edited by Walter Hooper (London: HarperCollins, 2004), 747, written December 20, 1946.

seemed cruel and unjust.[26] He had seen much pain and suffering in his mother's last days, in the sometimes cruel school system, between people and nations during the First World War, and even in his own life. There is, perhaps, nothing that is more common to atheists than the shared belief that the universe is too cold, harsh, and uncaring for there to be a God.

THE EMOTIONAL LOSS OF HIS FATHER

Lewis tells us that he lost his father at the same time he lost his mother.[27] Partly because of his emotional makeup, and undoubtedly because he loved her deeply, Albert Lewis had great difficulty dealing with the death of his wife, Flora. The difficulty was compounded for several reasons. First, Flora died on Albert's forty-fifth birthday. Second, earlier that year Albert had lost his father, Richard. And, third, eleven days after Flora's death, his brother Joseph died. Albert had great difficulty coping with the accumulation of pain and loss, as anyone would.[28] After this devastating series of losses, all of them within six months of one another, Albert's two sons crossed the Irish Sea to Wynyard School for their education. They had been separated from their mother by death; they were now, both geographically and emotionally, separated from their father by their schooling. This decision brought both sons closer to each another, but it alienated them from their father.

Some of the additional reasons for alienation between father and sons are mentioned later in the letters and diaries of the two brothers. They called him the Pudaitabird, or P'daitabird or PB, a name they invented because of the way he pronounced "potato." Warren wrote about Albert's avoidance of breaking his daily routine, which is why Albert failed to see his younger son off to the First World War in France in 1917 and also would decline to visit him while Lewis was recuperating from war wounds in a London hospital almost a year

---

[26] C. S. Lewis, *Mere Christianity* (New York: HarperCollins, 1980), 38.
[27] Lewis, *Surprised by Joy*, 19.
[28] See Davidman, *Motherloss*, 20.

later. Albert's emotionalism, his frequent inability to reason to a logical conclusion, his desire to control every conversation,[29] his sense of the theatrical, and often hearing only what he wanted to hear all contributed to a growing distance between father and sons. The letters and diaries of both brothers document similar gaps in Albert's fatherly responsibilities when the boys were much younger.[30] For example, Lewis once wrote to Leo Baker, describing home as "a synonym for busy triviality, continual interruption and a complete lack of privacy."[31] These characteristics of their father explain why Warren once wrote, "My afternoon had no interior comforts to compensate for the weather, for it was spent in writing to the PB, which I think I dislike more than any of my obligations."[32] While Lewis's letter to Alan Richard Griffiths— quoted earlier—does not mention his father, it does mention his "great unhappiness at school," for which he blamed his father.

Not named by Lewis, but often a part of the adoption of atheism, is an absent, harsh, abusive, or dysfunctional father, which is a recurring feature in the biography of well-known atheists, such as Friedrich Nietzsche, David Hume, Arthur Schopenhauer, Thomas Hobbes, Jean Meslier, and many others.[33] Psychologists have developed the connection between a child's understanding of his father and his

---

[29] Joan Murphy, daughter of Joseph Lewis, Jack's cousin, said of Albert, "He was a very dominant, even domineering man" (*C. S. Lewis and His Circle: Essays and Memoirs from the Oxford C. S. Lewis Society*, Roger White, Judith Wolfe, and Brendan Wolfe, eds. [Oxford: Oxford University Press, 2015], 170).

[30] Warren Lewis, "Memoir of C. S. Lewis," *Letters of C. S. Lewis*, 30.

[31] *Collected Letters of C. S. Lewis*, I, 471, January 12, 1920.

[32] The unpublished diary of Warren Hamilton Lewis, an entry dated September 22, 1925.

[33] Vitz, *Faith of the Fatherless*, 128. There are, of course, other reasons, some mentioned by Vitz, including painful experiences with representatives of religion and painful struggles within the self. See also chapter 2, "Atheists and Their Fathers," 17–57, in its entirety, and chapter 5, "Superficial Atheism: A Personal Account," 130–38, which lists additional factors such as social unease, the desire for acceptance, personal independence, and personal convenience.

understanding of God, the so-called defective father hypothesis.[34] As a result, "an atheist's disappointment in and resentment of his own father unconsciously justifies the rejection of God."[35] This hypothesis clearly applies to the Lewis brothers, far more because of their father's emotional distance and dominating personality than for any abuse or harshness. When the Lewis brothers rejected their father, they also rejected God.[36]

EARLY SCHOOLING

The Lewis brothers suffered one of the worst educational experiences of their day at Wynyard School in Watford, a city located just northwest of London, under Headmaster Robert Capron. Warren had enrolled there in 1905, and Jack started at Wynyard three years later, less than a month after his mother's death. Capron frequently used corporal punishment as a disciplinary and educational tool. Because of this, but especially because of poor instruction, the boys learned very little. Though once a reputable school, Wynyard had declined a great deal by the time the Lewis brothers arrived. Eventually Capron left the school, was later certified insane, and died at the Camberwell House Asylum in south London only a year after the younger Lewis left the school. C. S. Lewis described it as a "hole" in an early letter to his father, and Warren once admitted that for an entire term he had done the same four math problems over and over again in order to escape the watchful eye of the Headmaster.[37]

Despite the atheism of his childhood, at Wynyard, young Lewis actually went through a time of believing in Christianity.[38] He attended

---

[34] Of course this hypothesis is by no means absolute. For example, J. R. R. Tolkien, who played a major role in bringing Lewis to faith, experienced an absent father from the age 4 onwards and was never, as far as we can tell, an atheist.

[35] Vitz, *Faith of the Fatherless*, 16.

[36] Older brother Warren also became an atheist, as he indicates in his diary on the date May 13, 1931 (*Brothers & Friends* [New York: Harper & Row, 1983], 80).

[37] *Collected Letters of C. S. Lewis*, I, 7. See also George Sayer's *Jack*, 60 and *The Lewis Papers* 3:40.

[38] Lewis, *Surprised by Joy*, 33.

St. John's Church, Watford, where he heard Christian teachings from people who actually believed them with the result that he came to believe them also. That means, of course, that he had not believed them previously, largely because of the sterile atmosphere in the Lewis household in Belfast. This Watford experience resulted in Lewis beginning to pray, read the Bible, and obey his conscience. There, he wrote, he discussed religion with his school friends in a healthy and profitable way,[39] an indication that Christianity was more than a set of dogmas—it was something he actually attempted to live.

THE ADOPTION OF ATHEISM

During the years after his mother's death in 1908, Lewis attended church, held to the Christian faith while at Wynyard School, and struggled with believing in a benevolent God. Then, in 1911, he began to attend Cherbourg House, and during that time he adopted a formal belief system: atheism. He tells us that he was fourteen years old when he became an atheist.[40] He had attended church several times during his first year at Cherbourg, but he never wrote as positively about worship services at Cherbourg as he did at Watford. He stated about his time at Cherbourg that he did not have a single emotion which he would have considered religious.[41] He had tried to understand why the stories of Christianity were not sheer illusion when everyone understood that the Roman gods and goddesses were not characters from history. In his autobiography, he states that no one attempted to explain the difference, and no one showed how Christianity was a fulfillment of paganism.[42] As had been the case at home, he lacked the spiritual direction that he needed from his instructors at Cherbourg

---

[39] Lewis, *Surprised by Joy*, 33f.

[40] Lewis, *Surprised by Joy*, 63. See also Lewis, "Early Prose Joy," 28f. See also a letter to John Rowland, dated June 9, 1944, located in the Harry Ransom Center, Austin, Texas.

[41] Lewis, "Early Prose Joy," 28.

[42] Lewis, *Surprised by Joy*, 63.

House, nor did he realize how firm a historical foundation Christianity was based upon.

Pagans believed that the gods were involved in the lives of people, sometimes requiring a sacrifice in order to stop a plague and at other times creating a sense of longing for a better world through their literature. The Norse and Greek myths expressed the interest of the gods in human activity, and the presence of dryads and nymphs in their world of nature showed that pagans believed some divine presence was quite near. They did not divest the world of the divine, as the modern materialists had done, and their myths about a supreme deity, or various deities, reinforced their conviction that they were accountable to higher powers. But no one explained this sense of the divine, and its similarity to Christianity, to the young Lewis.

The beginning of Lewis's formal atheism took place at a date sometime between his fourteenth birthday and his departure from Cherbourg House the following July.[43] Lewis's letters to Arthur Greeves show him vigorously defending his atheism and pointedly ridiculing Greeves's Christianity for its alleged lack of evidence. Lewis's early poem, " 'Carpe Diem' after Horace," which he wrote in October 1913, reflects the pessimism of his newly adopted thinking. Horace was the leading Roman poet of the first century BC, writing during the time of Caesar Augustus. Horace used the phrase "carpe diem," "seize the day," as an Epicurean statement about enjoying the moment, or living for today.[44] Here young Lewis celebrated the momentary rather than the eternal and adopted the position that humans should enjoy the brief amount of time we have because soon death will end all.

---

[43] In other words, between November 29, 1912, his fourteenth birthday, and the end of that school year at Cherbourg, July 29, 1913 ("Early Prose Joy," 28). Since seven of the eight months of this period of time belong to 1913, that makes the year 1913 more likely as the year he became an atheist. However, Miss Cowie was replaced in May 1912, and his rapid decline began at that time. Therefore, December 1912 or January 1913 seems very likely.

[44] Horace, Odes, 1.11.

The poem *Quam Bene Saturno*, also written while Lewis was at Cherbourg, concludes with words that challenge authority while complaining about the human lot in life.[45] The poem, which begins with "Alas!" and concludes with the line "With grim array our path surround,"[46] demonstrates a pessimistic worldview—no peace; only famine, slaughter, fire, and sword—and an acknowledgment of the Roman gods Saturn, Neptune, and Jove.

Perhaps such expression about the Roman gods was fed by a conviction that came from Lewis's reading the ancient mythologies. As he read them, he began to wonder why Christ could not be placed on the same level as Adonis, Apollo, or Neptune. He called his turn to atheism the anthropological route to atheism,[47] apparently indicating that he saw Christ, or at least the worship of Christ, as a human invention on a par with the worship of the Roman deity Jupiter.[48]

In *Surprised by Joy*, Lewis himself suggests that the immediate cause of his atheism was Miss Cowie, the Cherbourg House matron who was dabbling with occult movements, Theosophy,[49] Rosicrucianism,[50] and Spiritualism.[51] He partially absolves her, however, stating, "Nothing was further from her intention than to destroy my faith."[52] Lewis admired many things about her, perhaps because she provided the motherly support he had lost when his mother died, but her departure from Cherbourg at the mid-point of Lewis's schooling at Cherbourg (May 1912) resulted in the departure of the good effects of her presence and the remaining of the bad. From that time on, Lewis

---

[45] June 29, 1913. See "Chronologically Lewis" at www.joelheck.com.

[46] *The Collected Poems of C. S. Lewis*, 30.

[47] Lewis, "Early Prose Joy," 28.

[48] This seems to be what Lewis meant by "the anthropological argument," as evidenced in "Religion without Dogma," *God in the Dock*, edited by Walter Hooper (Grand Rapids: Eerdmans, 1970), especially 131f.

[49] The term *theosophy* is a general word for study of the occult.

[50] A combination of occult teachings, Jewish mysticism, Gnosticism, and other teachings, claiming secret knowledge handed down from ancient times (www.britannica.com/EBchecked/topic/510019/Rosicrucian).

[51] Lewis, *Surprised by Joy*, 59.

[52] Lewis, *Surprised by Joy*, 59.

wrote, a rapid decline began.[53] He described that time as a time of faith combined with a good deal of fear, egged on by the pessimism of Shaw, Voltaire, and Lucretius, especially the latter's claim that religion drove men to evil.[54] He also states that he has little doubt that his "wishes gave wings to [his] reasoning. Hating and fearing the beliefs in which I had been brought up, I desired passionately to find them untrue."[55] While he was drawn to Miss Cowie's ideas, he remained fearful of the unknown, of spiritual forces, and of the potential for personal harm. He escaped that fear by choosing atheism.

While at Cherbourg House, Lewis gave up his Christian faith.[56] He also tells us what a relief it was to set aside his Christianity.[57] He claimed that his difficulty with mustering the right attitude toward prayer was a major factor, and that this caused him to want to shed his religion, though his attitude toward prayer was undoubtedly one of the last straws rather than a major cause.[58] He also credited his reading of the Classics, especially Virgil, and their many different religious ideas as a reason for thinking that Christianity was simply another one of the mythologies. As stated above, no one attempted to show him how Christianity fulfilled Paganism or how Paganism prefigured Christianity.[59] Years later he would conclude that such stories were divine hints in poetic and imaginative form, preparing these peoples for the Incarnation of Christ.[60] Then, Lewis asked us to remember his own long-held pessimism, which was due not only to his mother's death but also his own clumsiness and his father's conviction that life was a constant struggle against overwhelming odds.[61] With the

---

[53] Lewis, *Surprised by Joy*, 66.
[54] Lewis, *Surprised by Joy*, 171. For the quotation from Lucretius, see *De Rerum Nature*, Book 1, 101.
[55] Lewis, "Early Prose Joy," 28.
[56] Lewis, *Surprised by Joy*, 58.
[57] Lewis, *Surprised by Joy*, 60.
[58] Lewis, *Surprised by Joy*, 62.
[59] Lewis, *Surprised by Joy*, 62.
[60] Lewis, "Religion without Dogma," *God in the Dock*, 132.
[61] Lewis, *Surprised by Joy*, 63f.

accumulation of so many negative experiences, he chose to adopt atheism.

THE ATTRACTION OF IMAGINATION AND DESIRE

Although Lewis had become an atheist, other factors that contradicted his atheism were simultaneously at work in his life and had been for some years. These experiences pointed to the imaginative, almost spiritual, worlds of fantasy and music. He once stated that he did not think that the resemblance between the Christian and the imaginative experience was accidental, and he must have noticed this even in his atheistic years. He thought that all things, especially the imagination, reflected heavenly truth.[62] His earlier writing in childhood about "dressed animals" was indebted to children's author Edith Nesbit, John Tenniel—the illustrator of Lewis Carroll's *Alice's Adventures in Wonderland* and *Through the Looking-Glass*—and another children's author Beatrix Potter, specifically her story *Squirrel Nutkin*. His "knights in armor" were drawn from Conan Doyle's *Sir Nigel*, and, as a result, as early as 1908, he had written about Animal-Land. Animal-Land was set in a medieval time period, which anticipated the medieval setting of Narnia.[63] Even then Lewis loved the ancient and disliked the modern. But it was at this time an unimaginative interest, and this lack of imagination closed a door to a major portion of his mind. In the sense of imagination as daydreaming (talking animals, knights in armor, etc.), he was living very much in his imagination. But in the sense of imagination as invention or creation of other worlds, he was not.

Music had a similar attraction for Lewis, since it aroused his imagination and drew him into another world. He had discovered, and been enraptured by, the music of Richard Wagner in 1911, particularly the *Ring of the Nibelung*, a four-opera cycle about a magic ring and the murder and intrigue surrounding those who wanted it. While at Cherbourg House, in May 1912, he wrote an essay on the development

---

[62] Lewis, *Surprised by Joy*, 167.
[63] Lewis, *Surprised by Joy*, 15.

of the opera as a genre and Wagner's influence on it. For the next twenty years or so, Wagner's music would provide, first, another reason for holding to his pessimistic view of the universe, since Wagner's opera cycle was fundamentally pessimistic. Second, however, his longing for Wagner's music—and the imaginative country for which his music aroused desire—pointed to another desire for something out of this world. At the same time, great music, such as that of Wagner, created for him a standard which most church music could not match. This—for Lewis—provided a strong reason for rejecting the claims of Christianity, since most of the music closely associated with Christian worship could not compare to the compositions of Bach, Handel, Mozart, and Wagner. He once wrote, "The 'sentimentality and cheapness' of much Christian hymnody had been a strong point in my own resistance to conversion."[64]

LOKI BOUND—A PARABLE OF LEWIS'S DEFIANCE

In spite of the pleasant interior worlds of music and imagination, the world outside had a cruel message for Lewis. The start of World War I—or the Great War, as it was called—in 1914, along with Lewis's service in that war, beginning in 1917, cemented him in his atheistic position. It also disproved the axiom that there are no atheists in foxholes.

The year 1914 was also the year that Lewis wrote his opera *Loki Bound* to express his personal war with God.[65] *Loki Bound* owes its origin especially to the *Poetic Edda* and the *Prose Edda* of Nordic mythology.[66] However, the name *Loki Bound* also comes from Aeschylus's *Prometheus Bound*, a play about man's relationship to the

---

[64] See Lewis, "Christianity and Culture," *Christian Reflections*, 13.

[65] Lewis wrote other poems, and some book reviews, during his atheistic years which are not included in this book, because they tell us nothing about his thinking on the topic of atheism.

[66] *Collected Letters of C. S. Lewis*, I, 249. Lewis himself states that Loki is based on a story in the Edda.

gods, and someone who defies the gods, as well as from Percy Bysshe Shelley's lyrical drama *Prometheus Unbound.*

As Zeus and Prometheus are at odds throughout *Prometheus Bound*, so Loki and Odin, the chief god of Norse mythology, are at odds throughout *Loki Bound.* As Prometheus is chained to a mountain as punishment for giving fire to mankind and teaching them medicine, agriculture, mathematics, and other skills, so Loki is first enslaved by Odin, then bound by Thor. Likewise, in the Eddas, Loki is an unpredictable deity who both helps the gods and creates problems for them. In *Loki Bound*, Loki has a quarrel with the gods over the injustice of the creation of man.

By the time he wrote *Loki Bound*, Lewis had become familiar with Richard Wagner's Ring cycle with its attitude of despair and godlessness, having first seen Arthur Rackham's illustrations of the Ring saga in December 1911. That Lewis wrote about "the twilight of the gods" in his summary of Episode III of *Loki Bound* is not accidental—he borrowed that phrase from Wagner, who drew his heroic pessimism from Norse mythology.

In the portion of the opera that has survived, Lewis expresses his pessimistic attitude toward God in the words of Loki. In fact, Lewis once described the malicious Loki as a projection of himself in his own prideful sense of superiority[67] by which he tried to compensate himself for his own unhappiness. When he wrote his autobiography more than forty years after *Loki Bound*, Lewis stated that, given his thoughts about the universe at that time in life, he was reasonable in condemning it.[68] Loki protested against Odin, who forced souls into existence against their will and, when asked questions, Odin answered darkly without revealing his thoughts. Worse than that, Loki described Odin as a powerful criminal and the originator of injustice, the cause of sorrow and pain. Loki wanted his revenge against Odin, and in Lewis's opera Loki worked hard to get that revenge. When at the end of the story Odin offered him reconciliation and release, Loki rejected

---

[67] Lewis, *Surprised by Joy*, 115.
[68] Lewis, *Surprised by Joy*, 115. The book was published in 1955.

the offer with angry words. Although *Loki Bound* was never completed, the tragedy ends with those angry words.

At this point in Lewis's life, *Loki Bound* expressed Lewis's contradictory anger with God both for creating a world and for not existing.[69] Why should human beings be forced to exist without their consent? Lewis wrote much of this play during June 1914, but he set aside "the gods of Asgard" later that year when he went to study with W. T. Kirkpatrick, an atheist who confirmed Lewis in his atheism. Having discovered the poetry of Yeats in May 1914 and the poetry and prose stories of William Morris in November 1914, the same year that he wrote *Loki Bound*, Lewis was drawn simultaneously in two directions—toward the pessimism of a world devoid of God and toward a world of spirituality.

BEGINNINGS AT OXFORD

During these years and his early years as a student at Oxford University, the Lucretius quotation, which he probably discovered in 1914, gradually took on more importance.[70] The world was too "frail and faulty" to have been designed by God, an argument that still carries much weight today. In 1946 Lewis wrote to Alan Griffiths that he still thought the argument from design a very weak basis for theism, and that the argument from un-design was quite strong for atheism.[71] And yet, paradoxically, he also wrote that many Christians he knew were influenced by the argument from design.[72] The design argument works both ways, in favor of God because of the complex features of the world that point to purpose and against God because of the flaws in those very same features. Failing to take into account a fall into sin,

---

[69] Lewis, *Surprised by Joy*, 115.
[70] Lewis was also attending the lectures of Cyril Bailey on Lucretius during the Hilary term of 1919 (January–April).
[71] *Collected Letters of C. S. Lewis*, II, 747. The letter is dated December 20, 1946. That opinion also appears in an essay of his when he uses a line of poetry from the atheist A. E. Housman, "Whatever brute and blackguard made the world." See Lewis, "De Futilitate," *Christian Reflections*, 66.
[72] Lewis, "Is Theism Important?" *God in the Dock*, 173.

or a corruption, some think that God could not be the intelligence behind such a broken world of hurricanes, earthquakes, and a host of other tragedies.

Included in Lewis's argument against God at this time was "the inherent 'vanity' of the 'creature,' the fact that life preys on life, that all beauty and happiness are produced only to be destroyed."[73] The sorrows of the world, even apart from war and revolution, sickness and poverty, challenge belief in God. He had yet another factor that contributed to his atheism. He tells us, "Add to this that my early reading—not only Wells but Sir Robert Ball[74]—had lodged very firmly in my imagination the vastness and cold of space, the littleness of Man."[75] He had found reasons for rejecting God both near at hand and far away.

THE GOOD ATHEIST

Years later, during World War Two, Lewis saw one major problem with concluding that the hostile and apparently meaningless universe was evidence for the non-existence of God. He himself wrote, "The defiance of *the good atheist* hurled at an apparently ruthless and idiotic cosmos is really an unconscious homage to something in or behind that cosmos which he recognizes as infinitely valuable and authoritative: for if mercy and justice were really only private whims of his own with no objective and impersonal roots, and if he realized this, he could not go on being indignant."[76] Lewis's idea of the good atheist assumes at least two things—first, that some atheists argue not against God as much as their conception of what God and the universe appear to be like, and, second, that such atheists would be or should be willing to listen to someone who could offer an explanation of

---

[73] *Collected Letters of C. S. Lewis*, II, 747.
[74] Irish astronomer, later professor of astronomy at Cambridge University, and writer of popular science books (1840–1913), reflective of Lewis's love of astronomy.
[75] Lewis, *Surprised by Joy*, 65.
[76] Lewis, "De Futilitate," *Christian Reflections*, 70.

God's apparent silence and the widespread suffering in every inhabited part of the world. The good atheist is standing on principles that make no sense apart from the existence of a transcendent moral God. If morality is just a personal preference, why should there be any justice or mercy?

Lewis claims that the fact that the good atheist arraigns heaven itself for disregarding human beings means that "at some level of his mind he knows they are enthroned in a higher heaven still."[77] Lewis concludes by stating: "I cannot and never could persuade myself that such defiance is displeasing to the supreme mind," and then he states that the atheism of Shelley is holier than the theism of Paley.[78] Lewis himself had been such a person. He went on to describe this as a major teaching of the book of Job. No explanation is given in the Bible for Job's suffering, because that is not the point of the book. Lewis's point is that the person who understands justice and then criticizes divine justice because of the suffering he sees, or thinks he sees, is one whom God approves for this concern.[79] In other words, this person understands justice and cares about the apparent lack of it in the world around him, and such understanding carries an unconscious allegiance to the source of moral standards.

Years later Lewis reflected on this atheistic period in his life and wrote, "The materialist's universe had the enormous attraction that it offered you limited liabilities. No strictly infinite disaster could overtake you in it. Death ended all. And if ever finite disasters proved greater than one wished to bear, suicide would always be possible. The horror of the Christian universe was that it had no door marked *Exit*."[80] In other words, materialism appears to bring relief as well as

---

[77] Lewis, "De Futilitate," *Christian Reflections*, 70.
[78] Lewis, "De Futilitate," *Christian Reflections*, 70. William Paley was the Enlightenment-era philosopher who developed the Argument from Design as a proof for God's existence.
[79] Lewis, "De Futilitate," *Christian Reflections*, 70.
[80] Lewis, *Surprised by Joy*, 171.

the end of everything, while Christianity with its claim of eternal existence has no possibility of escape. When he adopted atheism, he wrote that he felt like Ariel, the spirit in Shakespeare's *Tempest*, set free, or—paradoxically—like John Bunyan's main character Christian with the burden rolled from his back. In *The Pilgrim's Regress*, an allegorical story explaining the journey he traveled from atheism to theism and Christianity, Lewis stated that the lifting of the burden at his adoption of atheism was such that he felt he could fly.[81]

INDIVIDUALISM

Lewis did not want people to think that every atheist was merely denying that which he most feared, i.e., an eternal God who punishes eternally. Lewis was in one sense a happy atheist, freed from the burden of what he called the transcendental interferer, preferring the observation of Dostoyevsky, "If God is dead, then everything is permitted."[82] The permanent charm of unbelief, Lewis contended, was the sense of freedom and autonomy, the ability to maintain one's privacy, supreme and unchallenged, out from under the bondage of an unseen Creator, and not having to look over the shoulder to see if God was watching.[83] At the same time that he was rejecting a heavenly Father, he was also rejecting an earthly father, which caused him some feelings of guilt, as he eventually admitted much, much later. At one point in *The Pilgrim's Regress*, the main character John states what he most wanted to avoid was being "caught into slavery again, to walk warily and on sufferance all his days, never to be alone; never the master of his own soul; to have no privacy, no corner whereof you could say to the whole universe: This is my own, here I can do as I please."[84] During

---

[81] Lewis, *The Pilgrim's Regress*, 24.

[82] Fyodor Dostoyevsky, *The Brothers Karamazov*, chapter 11. Although the exact wording is not found in this work, the idea appears here. See *Surprised by Joy*, 172, for the phrase "transcendental interferer."

[83] Lewis, "Early Prose Joy," 29.

[84] Lewis, *The Pilgrim's Regress*, 142.

his atheistic years, submission to an unseen God was something Lewis very much desired to avoid.

While the chronic lack of real spiritual guidance during his formative years seriously hampered him, at the core of Lewis's rejection of Christianity was his individualism. More important than the loss of his mother, his unhappy experiences at school, or the cruelty of the war was the desire to be his own person, subject to the authority of no one else, either human or divine. He stated that "what mattered most of all was my deep-seated hatred of authority, my monstrous individualism, my lawlessness. No word in my vocabulary expressed deeper hatred than the word *Interference*."[85] Years later he would write that he had always wanted not to be interfered with; he had wanted to call his soul his own.[86] This is probably the emotional need, about which he later wrote, that needed to be satisfied, because he wanted nature to be independent rather than one created by God.[87]

When Lewis was confronted with the occult, first in the matron at Cherbourg and later in the poetry of Yeats, that occultism had appealed to the rebel in him.[88] Early in his life, he may himself have been the sort of person he once described as one who deliberately tried not to know whether or not Christianity was true, because he foresaw endless trouble if it turned out to be true.[89] Certainly he admitted that during his search he entertained "some willful blindness."[90]

Lewis also stated in "Early Prose Joy"[91] that his adoption of atheism was in part wish fulfillment, claiming that his wishes gave wings to his atheism. He rejected his formal, church-going Christianity partly because he very much wanted it to be untrue.[92] Paul Vitz has

---

[85] Lewis, *Surprised by Joy*, 172.
[86] Lewis, *Surprised by Joy*, 228.
[87] Lewis, *Surprised by Joy*, 209.
[88] Lewis, *Surprised by Joy*, 176.
[89] Lewis, "Man or Rabbit?" *God in the Dock*, 111.
[90] Lewis, *Surprised by Joy*, 209.
[91] An early attempt, dated to 1930, to write his autobiography, only recently published in *VII*.
[92] Lewis, "Early Prose Joy," 28.

argued that wish fulfillment works both ways, stating that illusion has become for many the psychological basis for rejecting God, that is, that atheists are projecting their theory that there is no God, which originates with their desire that God not exist.[93]

THE NEW LOOK AND GOOD COMPANY

In 1921, halfway through his undergraduate program, Lewis met the Rev. Dr. Frederick Macran, an atheist priest and Irish parson, a man whom Lewis mentions in his autobiography who had lost his faith but retained his clerical living.[94] Macran was part of what Lewis calls the New Look, the belief that there is only one kind of reality, a materialistic reality.[95] This view, which Lewis had already adopted before they met, was very commonly held at this time in Oxford. Macran had a strong desire for immortality, but he also turned his back on anything that might make that immortality possible. In reaction to this inconsistency, Lewis tried to avoid anything that might smack of such an overactive desire for immortality.

On May 11, 1921, Lewis spent part of the morning in the Oxford Union[96] with Macran and others, while Macran expounded on various topics, including the Christian claim of the divinity of Christ. On that point, Macran insisted that Christ was only a man.[97] His position, as Lewis puts it later in *Mere Christianity*, was a willingness to recognize Jesus as a good teacher, but not as God.[98] A few years later, Macran wondered whether Christ was a great teacher or simply a fanatic.[99]

---

[93] Vitz, *Faith of the Fatherless*, 9.

[94] Lewis, *Surprised by Joy*, 201. See also *Collected Letters of C. S. Lewis*, I, 547.

[95] The philosophy of the "New Look" was what Lewis called "Stoical Monism" (*Surprised by Joy*, 205).

[96] A debating society made up primarily of people from the University of Oxford. It includes the Goodman Library and a debating chamber, dining room and bar, as well as other facilities.

[97] *Collected Letters of C. S. Lewis*, I, 548. Macran definitely expressed that opinion on April 19, 1922 (Lewis, *All My Road Before Me*, 22).

[98] Lewis, *Mere Christianity*, 52.

[99] Lewis, *All My Road Before Me*, 183. The date in Lewis's diary is Jan. 22, 1923.

Harry Emerson Fosdick once said to an atheist, "Tell me what kind of God you don't believe in. Perhaps I don't believe in that kind of God either."[100] At one time, Lewis viewed God as a rule-setter, ready to condemn anyone who breaks one of those rules. The Steward in Lewis's *Pilgrim's Regress* is that sort of person, telling the main character, John, what will happen if he breaks any of the rules: John will be shut up in a black hole that is full of snakes and scorpions. Then, in an admission that the rules could not truly be kept by anyone, the Steward tells John that he should lie about whether or not he had broken any rules.[101] During his atheistic years, Lewis had no conception of a loving God who desired a relationship with those whom He created and established protective rules for running the human machine.[102] John saw God only as Judge, the dispenser of law and judgment but not grace and forgiveness. This picture had been reinforced early in Lewis's life by legalistic images of God in human parents and authority figures, and it had encouraged his later rejection of God's existence. It's no wonder that he wrote to Arthur Greeves about being content to live without believing in someone who was prepared to torture him forever if he failed to live up to an almost impossible ideal.[103]

SUMMARY

The story of Lewis's shift from his vague and uninterested boyhood belief in God into atheism shows some of the major motivations that have led many people to adopt atheism. He argued for atheism *first* because of the pain and suffering he saw in the world, *partly* because of the lack of order he saw in the universe, *partly* because of

---

[100] The quotation has also been attributed to Harvard chaplain George Buttrick. On Fosdick, see, for example, George N. Marshall, *Challenge of a Liberal Faith* (Boston: Skinner House, 1988), 101.

[101] Lewis, *The Pilgrim's Regress*, 5.

[102] Lewis, *Mere Christianity*, 69.

[103] *Collected Letters of C. S. Lewis*, I, 235. The date of the letter is October 18, 1916.

his father's type of parenting, *very much* because of his personal rebellion against divine interference, *in part* because it was common to
view Christ as just another one of the many corn gods (harvest deities
who die and return to life again, even as the seed is planted in the earth
to rise in the new life of a plant), and *possibly* in order to deal with the
problem of personal guilt in his life, which partly explains the relief he
felt when he adopted atheism. His atheism was not simplistic, but
multi-faceted and complex, not shallow, but deep. He also described
his pre-Christian life as a series of wrong turnings.[104] Later, he
described the move from atheism to Christianity in reverse, stating
that faith resulted from historical events that have a moral character,
which itself is linked to paganism. These pagan stories themselves
presuppose a Supreme Being.[105] In other words, faith is not a purely
intellectual matter. It begins with historical events that clearly
happened, it continues with a sense that there is something else, and it
speaks to one's sense of right and wrong, which cannot be explained
as coincidence.

At the core of his atheism, however, was his hatred of authority,
monstrous individualism, and lawlessness.[106] He did not yet realize
that everyone has that same individualism inside.

---

[104] Lewis, *Surprised by Joy*, 177.
[105] Lewis, "Is Theism Important?" *God in the Dock*, 175.
[106] Lewis, *Surprised by Joy*, 172.

CHAPTER 2

LITERARY INFLUENCES
IN TWO DIRECTIONS

"God is, if I may say it, very unscrupulous."

—C. S. Lewis, *Surprised by Joy*

Having adopted atheism, Lewis found many writers whose works confirmed his atheism. Some of those writers include the Irish playwright George Bernard Shaw (1856–1950), the German philosopher Arthur Schopenhauer (1788–1860), the social anthropologist Sir James Frazer (1854–1941), German philosopher and cultural critic Friedrich Nietzsche (1844–1900), the English writer H. G. Wells (1866–1946),[1] and, of course, the Roman poet Lucretius.

Other writers, however, raised the issue of other worlds, arousing a longing for something he could not yet identify. Writers like William Morris, Sir Thomas Malory, and W. B. Yeats attracted him with the power of their stories and their poetry. By the mid-1920s, he had identified that attraction as an other-worldly attraction, a spiritual longing; but during his years with Kirkpatrick (1914–17), this had not yet occurred. A full appraisal of all the authors who influenced Lewis

---

[1] Wells is especially known as the author of science fiction books *The Time Machine, The War of the Worlds, The Invisible Man*, and *The Island of Doctor Moreau*. He wrote in a wide variety of literary genres. Lewis learned to enjoy Wells at Wynyard School. These are the years 1908–10. See Lewis, *Surprised by Joy*, 35.

during this period would fill a huge volume, so this chapter will examine primarily a handful of the important romantic writers who caused Lewis to think that there was more to life than meets the materialistic eye. Lewis mentions all of these writers in his autobiography *Surprised by Joy* as influential in his spiritual journey.

These romantic writers offered something that his parents had not; Lewis once stated that neither of his parents listened for "the horns of elfland,"[2] by which he meant the best kind of romanticism that authors such as Spenser, Coleridge, Morris, and Malory offered. These authors drew out an intense longing in Lewis for something beyond the world of the senses, even something from another world.

CONFIRMED IN ATHEISM

In the first category—those who confirmed Lewis's atheism—is Frazer's multi-volume *The Golden Bough* and the works of Schopenhauer, both of which Lewis's private tutor Kirkpatrick greatly appreciated.[3] Kirkpatrick undoubtedly had recommended Arthur Schopenhauer's *The World as Will and Idea*, which Lewis was reading in November of 1915 in the midst of his time with Kirkpatrick. That book, the central work of Schopenhauer, argued that nothing was behind human life, that human intelligence was a tool evolved for meeting needs, and that ideas such as God, immortality, and free will were simply illusions. Schopenhauer, who was known as the great pessimist, no doubt confirmed Lewis in the pessimistic worldview that had been caused by the death of his mother, his negative school experiences, his physical clumsiness, and other factors.

Five poems written during this same year, 1915, echo the pessimism Lewis had absorbed from Frazer's and Schopenhauer's worldview. In the first, "The Wood Desolate (near Bookham),"[4] Lewis describes the wooded areas near Kirkpatrick's home in Great

---

[2] Lewis, *Surprised by Joy*, 5.
[3] Lewis, *Surprised by Joy*, 139.
[4] The dates used for these poems are those suggested by Don W. King in *The Collected Poems of C. S. Lewis*.

Bookham as dark, cold, dread, and desolate. A second poem, "Yet More of the Wood Desolate," written at Christmas 1915, continues these themes, speaking of the winter season with the cold and deadness of that time of year, concluding with the wish that the speaker might go into the darkness when his days are over. The third poem is entitled "Against Potpourri." Here Lewis describes someone who is gathering flowers to create a potpourri. Although the flowers are beautiful, they cannot truly capture beauty or recapture the past. With the war going on, Lewis's pessimism came through. Lewis wrote the fourth poem, "A Prelude," just before going to bed. Here, perhaps the very process of writing dispelled the dreary chill of the winter's night and his own pessimism, expressing his love of the world of faery and the ancient stories, such as those of William Morris and Sir Thomas Malory, which he had only just discovered the previous year. The last of five pessimistic poems, "New Year's Eve," was also written at Christmas time. This poem bemoans the past year, which has smothered our laughter and groans, sometimes because of bloodshed and sometimes because of mourning, both products of the war. Lewis wonders how to cry out to the Thing that guides the years, and he ends the poem on a despairing note.

These five poems contrast with two more optimistic poems, the first, "The Hills of Down," written at Easter. This poem idealizes the hills of Down, that is, County Down in Ireland, compared to the dreary world, the Arthurian Avalon, or the world of faery. To search for one of them would be to lose the hills of Down. "The Hills of Down" expresses the warmth of Lewis's homeland which provided him with life, longing, and belonging. The other poem written that year at Christmas is entitled "Sonnet to John Keats." This poem praises Keats for his enchanted lyrics, simultaneously describing two Christian authors, Alexander Pope and Samuel Johnson, as writers who slaughtered poetry. Lewis later came to appreciate both Pope and Johnson, but in his "Sonnet to John Keats" he looks in another direction for the fulfillment of a longing that seems not able to be met in mere earthly objects or events.

INFLUENCE IN TWO DIRECTIONS

Other writers, like H. G. Wells and William Morris, actually influenced Lewis in two directions, both toward theism and away from it. From 1916 onward, while Lewis was studying with Kirkpatrick, two competing forces vied for supremacy in Lewis's mind: the imaginative—or the "many-islanded sea of poetry and myth"—and a "glib and shallow"[5] rationality. He began to see that the intellect was not the only vehicle for truth. The imagination slowly began to bubble up toward the surface of truth through several important writers.

Owen Barfield, Lewis's lifelong friend whom he met first as an undergraduate, had suspected that Lewis had great appreciation for the imagination, but he thought that Lewis had considered it to have nothing to do with truth and so guarded his imagination.[6] For the next decade-and-a-half, Lewis gradually learned to lower his defenses and see that imagination could offer both truth (in the sense of spiritual realities beyond the five senses) and meaning.[7]

WILLIAM MORRIS (1834–96)

The books of William Morris[8] were among the most important writings Lewis read during his years with Kirkpatrick and later as an Oxford undergraduate—they not only appealed to Lewis's imagination by the power of their stories, but they were written from a non-Christian point of view. Lewis considered the discovery of Morris alongside his first discoveries of George MacDonald, G. K. Chesterton,

---

[5] Lewis, *Surprised by Joy*, 170.

[6] G. B. Tennyson, ed., *Owen Barfield on C. S. Lewis* (Barfield Press, UK, 2011), 98–103.

[7] Once he made peace with his imagination, he wrote, "For me, reason is the natural organ of truth; but imagination is the organ of meaning. Imagination, producing new metaphors or revivifying old, is not the cause of truth, but its condition" ("Bluspels and Flalansferes: A Semantic Nightmare," *Rehabilitations* [London: Oxford University Press, 1939; republished St. Clair Shores, MI: Scholarly Press, Inc., 1979], 157).

[8] Morris founded the Socialist League in 1884, a league that was encouraged by Engels and Marx, and he also later founded the Hammersmith Socialist Society.

and Charles Williams as major literary events in his life.[9] Morris used religious and powerfully evocative language in his books. Lewis later commented on an essay he had written on Morris that it was the one essay about which he cared the most.[10] Lewis's essay on William Morris in *Rehabilitations*, though panned by critics as a poor essay, shows his enthusiasm for Morris.

Years later, Lewis probably read that very same essay to the Martlets, an Oxford undergraduate literary society, defending Morris against negative reactions to Romanticism.[11] In the essay, he defends Morris by discussing Northernness—the stories and legends of Norse mythology, which created in him a longing for such ideas—Morris's "matter-of-factness in expression," Morris's treatment of love, and his theological paganism. Morris, he argues, exemplifies in his writings the internal struggle between the love for mortal life and the longing for immortality, a struggle Lewis himself had experienced when he was reading Morris during his atheistic years.[12]

Lewis first discovered William Morris in November 1914. He read Morris's book *The Well at the World's End* at least three times.[13] In May 1915, he read Morris's *The Roots of the Mountains*, one of Morris's first romances. Paradoxically for an atheist, Lewis reports that the book disappointed him because it had nothing supernatural or other-worldly about it. However, the supernatural element hovered on the margin of the plot all the time, and he delighted in such names as The Dusky Men, The Shadowy Vale, The Shivering Flood, and The

---

[9] *Collected Letters of C. S. Lewis*, II, 183. Since Lewis first read Charles Williams in 1936, beyond the date of his conversion to Christianity, Williams is not included in this chapter.

[10] The essay appears both in *Rehabilitations and Other Essays* and in *Selected Literary Essays*, Walter Hooper, ed. (Cambridge: Cambridge University Press, 1969). See C. S. Lewis, "On Criticism," *Of Other Worlds: Essays and Stories*, edited by Walter Hooper (New York: Harcourt Brace & Company, 1966), 53.

[11] Roger Lancelyn Green and Walter Hooper, *C. S. Lewis: A Biography* (New York: HarperCollins, 1974), 61. The date is November 5, 1937.

[12] MS. Top. Oxon. d. 95/5, fos. 99–100.

[13] In 1914, 1915, and 1926.

Weltering Water.[14] In January 1917, he read Morris's 10,000-line epic poem *The Story of Sigurd the Volsung and the Fall of the Niblungs*,[15] a story of heroic battles and mighty warriors, of bravery and treachery, love and desire.

Lewis's first two readings of *The Well at the World's End* took place at Great Bookham while Lewis was under Kirkpatrick's tutelage, and while at Great Bookham he ordered and read nearly all of Morris.[16] In his later autobiography, he would echo that book title when he wrote about the plain of Down in Northern Ireland and the Mourne Mountains beyond it as the way to the world's end, "the land of longing. . . ."[17] Shortly thereafter, he wrote that his favorite author during this period of time was William Morris.[18] That Morris is mentioned frequently in *Surprised by Joy* tells us of Lewis's own assessment of the importance of Morris for his own thinking. Morris seems to have supplied for Lewis the semi-religious experience he had shut out of his life by adopting a secular view of life. It is here that Lewis writes about his first encounter with *The Well at the World's End*:

> In Arthur's bookcase, I found *The Well at the World's End*. I looked—I read chapter headings—I dipped—and next day I was off into town to buy a copy of my own. . . . After that I read all the Morris I could get. . . . The growth of the new delight is marked by my sudden realization, almost with a sense of disloyalty, that the letters WILLIAM MORRIS were coming to have at least as potent a magic in them as WAGNER.[19]

Throughout most of 1915 and early 1916, the writings of William Morris became what the music of Richard Wagner's *Ring* cycle had

---

[14] *Collected Letters of C. S. Lewis*, I, 122.

[15] One could argue that Morris's supernatural beings in that poem, the Norns, were the source of Lewis's Sorns in *Out of the Silent Planet*, even if only in the sound of the name.

[16] Lewis, *Surprised by Joy*, 147.

[17] Lewis, *Surprised by Joy*, 155.

[18] Lewis, *Surprised by Joy*, 163.

[19] Lewis, *Surprised by Joy*, 164.

been—the most frequent medium through which he experienced longing.[20] It was not always so when Lewis read Morris, since at times he slipped into daydream, at other times he longed for another world, and at still other times he felt a very un-mysterious "wanting" in need of clarification.[21] Lewis later learned that it was neither Morris nor Northernness that caused the Joy.[22]

A decade and a half later, Lewis wrote to Arthur Greeves about changes in Lewis's library,[23] specifically about adding Morris and getting rid of some Kipling.[24] At that time, Lewis also wrote about William Morris's *The Well at the World's End*, longings, and Morris's love and eternal values. Lewis had recently read Morris's play *Love is Enough*. Having just become a theist the previous month,[25] Lewis found Morris affirming his longing for another world.[26]

Although few readers know *The Well at the World's End* apart from the mention of it in Lewis's writings, it significantly influenced both Lewis and J. R. R. Tolkien. Lewis seems to have borrowed from *The Well at the World's End* ideas and names such as King Peter, a final coronation scene, and a stone table, while Tolkien may have been influenced by a major character named Gandolf,[27] Black Riders, a fast, white horse named Silverfax,[28] and the use of the occasional poem in the midst of the story. In the third Chronicle of Narnia, *The Voyage of the Dawn Treader*, Lewis writes about the World's End as the place

---

[20] Lewis, *Surprised by Joy*, 169.

[21] Lewis, "Early Prose Joy," 20f.

[22] Lewis, *Surprised by Joy*, 168.

[23] The date was July 1, 1930.

[24] *Collected Letters of C. S. Lewis*, I, 910.

[25] See, for example, Andrew Lazo, "Correcting the Chronology: Some Implications of 'Early Prose Joy,'" *VII* 29 (2012): 13–49.

[26] *Collected Letters of C. S. Lewis*, I, 910f.

[27] Gandalf is also mentioned in one of the Icelandic Eddas, a more direct source than Morris for Tolkien. Still the use of the name Gandolf by Morris, though less direct and with a different spelling, is noteworthy.

[28] The Middle English word *fax* means "hair, head of hair" or "mane." Silverfax, therefore, apparently means that the horse had a silver mane.

where Reepicheep desires to go.[29] In *The Pilgrim's Regress*, he writes that "a world beyond the world's end" was in some sense real.[30] Certainly the concept of the world's end intrigued Lewis, leading him to think both of the world's end geographically and chronologically, as well as what lay beyond it.

In his essay "On Stories," C. S. Lewis doubted whether anyone could write a story to fit the title, *The Well at the World's End*.[31] Lewis was enthralled with the title of the book, but he also loved its content which suggested to him other worlds beyond the physical world and satisfied in some way his longing for that other world.

Morris's *The Wood Beyond the World* had almost as much influence on Lewis as *The Well at the World's End*. The title itself suggests the wood between the worlds from the Chronicle of Narnia known as *The Magician's Nephew*. The Lady of the story is similar to the Green Lady of *The Silver Chair* (the fourth Chronicle of Narnia), and Morris uses the phrase "son of Adam," which Lewis used in *The Lion, the Witch and the Wardrobe* to refer to a male human by connecting it to the biblical creation story. The desire of the main character Walter to pursue the adventure in front of him (as did Reepicheep in *The Voyage of the Dawn Treader*, not only pursuing the adventure in front of him, but also longing for Aslan's country) and his longing for the maid when they were separated also show Morris's influence on Lewis. The idea of a wood beyond the world, or the phrase itself, appears six times in "Early Prose Joy," reflective of his longing, beginning in 1914, for that other world that his materialistic atheism had tried to deny to his intellect only a year or so previously. The phrase "wood beyond the world" functions as an early equivalent for what Lewis later called Joy.

While the writings of Morris were not the only influences on Lewis's atheism and conversion, they nourished a sense of longing which had been with him since his early experience with Edith Nesbit's

---

[29] *The Voyage of the Dawn Treader* (New York: Macmillan, 1952). The phrase is used nine times between pages 174 and 208.
[30] *The Pilgrim's Regress*, 128.
[31] Lewis, "On Stories," *Of Other Worlds*, 18f.

(1858–1924) Bastable series of children's stories and Beatrix Potter's (1866–1943) stories of talking animals, but eventually his encounter with Morris's works led Lewis to realize that this longing pointed beyond this world to something else. Morris (with an assist from Yeats) was a precursor to Lewis's encounter with George MacDonald, who was to have great influence on him.

GEORGE MACDONALD (1824–1905)

Lewis tells us that he discovered George MacDonald at age 16, while studying with W. T. Kirkpatrick, and from then on always appreciated his writings, but for a long time ignored MacDonald's Christianity.[32] Later in life he paid MacDonald the ultimate compliment, describing MacDonald as his master and stating that he had not written a book in which he had not quoted MacDonald.[33] Lewis wrote, "George MacDonald had done more to me than any other writer; of course it was a pity he had that bee in his bonnet about Christianity. He was good *in spite of it*."[34] The more complete story of MacDonald's influence will be told in the next chapter.

G. K. CHESTERTON (1874–1936)

In *Surprised by Joy*, Lewis tells us that he first read Chesterton during World War I, and then a great deal thereafter. Lewis reports, "I liked him for his goodness."[35] He goes on to tell us, "I did not know what I was letting myself in for. A young man who wishes to remain a sound Atheist cannot be too careful of his reading."[36] He wrote that Chesterton had more sense than all other modern writers put together, except for his Christianity.[37]

---

[32] Lewis, "On the Reading of Old Books," *God in the Dock*, 203.
[33] C. S. Lewis, *George MacDonald: An Anthology* (New York: Simon & Schuster, 1947), xxxii. Both statements appear in the same sentence in this anthology.
[34] Lewis, *Surprised by Joy*, 213.
[35] Lewis, *Surprised by Joy*, 191.
[36] Lewis, *Surprised by Joy*, 191.
[37] Lewis, *Surprised by Joy*, 213.

The collection of essays Lewis read during the war apparently motivated him to read at least eight other Chestertonian works, including *Magic* (Chesterton's first play, published in 1913, read by Lewis in 1922), *Robert Browning* (dealing with the works of the poet Browning, published in 1903, which Lewis read in 1922), *Manalive* (published in 1912, read in 1923),[38] *St. Francis of Assisi* (published in 1923, read in 1924), and *The Club of Queer Trades* (a collection of stories on making a living through unusual means, published in 1905, read in 1926).[39] He also read *George Bernard Shaw* (published in 1909, read in 1926), *Eugenics and Other Evils: An Argument Against the Scientifically Organized State* (published in 1922, read in 1926), and *The Everlasting Man* (published in 1925, read in 1926).

George Herbert (1593–1633)

In his autobiography, Lewis writes with mild irony about God's traps for catching people: "There are traps everywhere—'Bibles laid open, millions of surprises,' as Herbert says, 'fine nets and stratagems.' God is, if I may say it, very unscrupulous."[40] The phrase "fine nets and stratagems" appears in Herbert's poem "Sinne" ("sin"), which Herbert included in his collection of poems, *The Temple*, published posthumously in 1633; the book later made Lewis's top ten list.[41] Those nets and stratagems, Herbert wrote, included afflictions and anguish, parents and schoolmasters, pulpits and Sundays, the sorrow that comes after sin, and Bibles laid open. Herbert writes of the many ways in which God catches our attention, some of them the positive

---

[38] *The Lewis Papers* 8:154. This part of *The Lewis Papers* contains an unpublished portion of Lewis's diary.

[39] As far as we know, Lewis did not read Chesterton's major apologetic work, *Orthodoxy*, during this period of his life.

[40] Lewis, *Surprised by Joy*, 191.

[41] Don W. King has described how the poems in Herbert's *The Temple* influenced the poems Lewis wrote for *The Pilgrim's Regress* ("George Herbert, *The Temple*," in David Werther and Susan Werther, eds., *C. S. Lewis's List: The Ten Books That Influenced Him Most* [New York: Bloomsbury Academic, 2015], 67–92).

messages from sermons and Bibles, others the pain of a guilty conscience and the afflictions that drive us to God,

> Pulpits and Sundays, sorrow dogging sin,
>   Afflictions sorted, anguish of all sizes,
>   Fine nets and stratagems to catch us in,
> Bibles laid open, millions of surprises,
>
> Blessings beforehand, ties of gratefulness,
>   The sound of glory ringing in our ears:
>   Without, our shame; within, our consciences;
> Angels and grace, eternal hopes and fears.[42]

Lewis claimed that Herbert was the most alarming[43] of all the writers he was reading as an undergraduate in the English School of Oxford University.[44]

What made George Herbert so alarming? Certainly the Christianity in all of his poetry was the major reason, but one specific reason may appear in the poem "The Flower." In this poem Herbert compares the spiritual life to the death of a flower in winter and its revival in spring. The poem's last word, *pride*, became what Lewis later considered to be his besetting sin. This is probably one reason why Lewis felt that Herbert understood the quality of life as it is lived from moment to moment, since Lewis mentioned this skill of Herbert in the same paragraph where he described Herbert as the most alarming. Reading Herbert, whose poetry T. S. Eliot called "the personal record of a man very conscious of weakness and failure, a man of intellect and sensibility who hungered and thirsted after righteousness,"[45] would have impressed Lewis. Herbert spoke both to the head and to the heart,

---

[42] F. E. Hutchinson, ed., *The Works of George Herbert* (London: Oxford University Press, 1941), 45f.; spelling modernized.

[43] Lewis, *Surprised by Joy*, 213f.; King, "George Herbert, *The Temple*," *C. S. Lewis's List*, 67–92.

[44] Lewis, *Surprised by Joy*, 214. This refers to the years 1922 and 1923.

[45] T. S. Eliot, *George Herbert* (London: Longmans, Green, 1962), 22f.

the need for honest self-reflection, awareness of personal flaws, and flower-like renewal in the spring.

George Herbert once described his poems as "a picture of the many spiritual conflicts that have passed betwixt God and my soul, before I could subject mine to the will of Jesus my Master."[46] The struggle in Herbert's soul, though that of a Christian wanting to become more like Christ, may well have spoken to Lewis about his struggles of a different kind during the 1920s, and this could explain one of the reasons why Herbert's poetry resonated with him. Lewis was certainly aware of the fundamental beliefs of the Christian faith; he just did not believe them.

SAMUEL JOHNSON (1709–84), EDMUND SPENSER (1552–99), AND JOHN MILTON (1608–74)

Samuel Johnson, the brilliant wit, writer, and creator of the first standard dictionary of the English language, was a prominent figure in eighteenth-century English history. In his entrance exam to Oxford University in 1916, Lewis wrote an essay based on a quotation by Johnson, which was a testimony to his importance. Lewis claimed, "Johnson was one of the few authors whom I felt I could trust utterly; curiously enough, he had the same kink. Spenser and Milton by a strange coincidence had it too."[47] That kink was his Christianity. That Lewis frequently read, quoted, and referred to Johnson for the remainder of his life is sufficient evidence for the importance of Samuel Johnson to Lewis. He considered James Boswell's *Life of Samuel Johnson*—a book many have called the greatest biography ever written in the English language—one of the ten most influential books he ever read on his vocational attitude and philosophy of life.[48]

---

[46] Margaret Drabble, ed. *The Oxford Companion to English Literature*, 5th edition (Oxford: Oxford University Press, 1995), 455.

[47] Lewis, *Surprised by Joy*, 213.

[48] *The Christian Century*, Vol. 79, No. 23 (June 6, 1962): 719.

Edmund Spenser's *The Faerie Queene* also had a big influence upon Lewis, especially for its character development,[49] becoming a model for the long poem that Lewis always wanted to write and exploring themes that spoke to his heart. The plot of this long, narrative poem tells of a journey that Arthur makes to Fairyland before he becomes King Arthur.[50] This, Doris Myers writes, fed young Lewis's hunger for fantasy.[51] Perhaps that is why Lewis enjoyed it first of all as a fairy tale,[52] but he became increasingly interested in the poem as moral allegory.[53] He later praised the experience of reading *The Faerie Queene* as a poem that trains our emotions and helps us adjust to living,[54] apparently influences that Spenser was having on Lewis in his early years. Later Lewis's Chronicles of Narnia, *The Abolition of Man*, and *That Hideous Strength* would owe much to Spenser's Fairyland.[55] Spenser's depictions of evil, both courtly and biblical, as well as his geographical descriptions, portrayal of monsters, parallel universe, and many other themes appear in Lewis's writings.

Lewis had first read John Milton's *Paradise Lost* at age 8. In 1916, he bought a copy of this epic poem and reread it twice in the next few months, and again in 1917.[56] He came to appreciate *Paradise Lost* so much that he later wrote *A Preface to Paradise Lost*, an influential work that challenged the then popular idea that Satan was Milton's hero, and defended the ritual diction of the poem as language that Milton

---

[49] Lewis, *All My Road Before Me*, 193. The date is February 9, 1923.

[50] Doris T. Myers, "Spenser," *Reading the Classics with C. S. Lewis*, ed. Thomas L. Martin (Grand Rapids: Baker, 2000), 88.

[51] Myers, "Spenser," *Reading the Classics with C. S. Lewis*, 92. Lewis read Spenser at least as early as February 1915, while living with the Kirkpatricks, although he may have read Spenser earlier. See "Chronologically Lewis" for Feb. 13, 1915.

[52] C. S. Lewis, *Studies in Medieval and Renaissance Literature* (Cambridge: Cambridge University Press, 1998), 133.

[53] Myers, "Spenser," *Reading the Classics with C. S. Lewis*, 93.

[54] C. S. Lewis, *The Allegory of Love: A Study in Medieval Tradition* (Oxford: Oxford University Press, 1936), 358. See also *English Literature in the Sixteenth Century Excluding Drama* (Oxford: Clarendon Press, 1936), 175, 393.

[55] Myers, "Spenser," *Reading the Classics with C. S. Lewis*, 98.

[56] *Collected Letters of C. S. Lewis*, I, 278.

had inherited from Homer.[57] The overwhelmingly Christian nature of *Paradise Lost*, as Lewis put it, could not help but have influenced him, even if only subtly at first.[58] He later described the poem as presenting "the great central tradition,"[59] an apparent reference to the core truths of the Christian faith.

From his early collection of poems, *Spirits in Bondage*, Lewis also saw some hope for the future described by John Milton. In his poem "Milton Read Again (In Surrey)," Lewis wrote of Milton, "Your Spirit, Master, has been close at hand."[60] He found in Milton "treasures rare" and "new pleasures."[61]

SIR THOMAS MALORY (1405–71)
AND W. B. YEATS (1865–1939)

On May 11, 1924, Lewis reread Sir Thomas Malory for the first time in a decade, remarking that he enjoyed it greatly, commenting especially on Balin. Reading about Balin might have caused the partial awakening of his own conscience, since Lewis wrote about Balin's superhuman guilt and his bad luck.[62] Sir Thomas Malory is, of course, the major writer who has bequeathed to us the medieval legend of King Arthur and the Knights of the Round Table. Lewis reread Malory's *Le Morte d'Arthur* multiple times during his lifetime, reading Malory at least as early as 1914. He also read various books related to the Arthurian legend, such as the anonymously written *Sir Gawain and the Green Knight*. Although Lewis recognized that Malory had not originated the Arthurian legend,[63] he praised him highly for his

---

[57] Charles A Huttar, "Milton," *Reading the Classics with C. S. Lewis*, 163.

[58] *A Preface to Paradise Lost* (New York: Oxford University Press, 1942), 92.

[59] Lewis, *A Preface to Paradise Lost*, 92.

[60] *Spirits in Bondage: A Cycle of Lyrics* (New York: Harcourt Brace & Company, 1984), 32.

[61] *Spirits in Bondage*, 32. Lewis once stated that Dante and St. Augustine were at least as influential as Milton (*Collected Letters of C. S. Lewis*, II, 630).

[62] Lewis, *All My Road Before Me*, 322.

[63] C. S. Lewis, *The Discarded Image: An Introduction to Medieval and Renaissance Literature* (Cambridge: Cambridge University Press, 1964), 210.

romantic prose style. He described Malory, alongside Bunyan and Trollope, as a master of perfect naturalness in imitating normal conversation.[64] He once wrote to Arthur Greeves (whom he addressed in many of his letters as Galahad in honor of Malory's famous knight) that though he did not consider Malory a great author, nor a model character,[65] he appreciated him for his writing ability.[66]

Lewis appreciated far more about Malory than his prose style. In a letter to Greeves, Lewis compared Malory with William Morris and George MacDonald;[67] in a later letter, he wrote about enjoying Malory's romantic charm,[68] particularly his ability to create another parallel world; and in a still later letter, he expressed his appreciation for the mystical parts of Malory, i.e., the parts about the Sangreal, the Holy Grail.[69] When in 1916 Lewis read George MacDonald's *Phantastes*, he claimed that he met there everything that he had enjoyed in Malory, Spenser, Morris, and Yeats, four powerfully imaginative writers.[70] Lewis especially liked Malory's ability to write about adventure, chivalry, and dragons, creating a world of his own that seemed so real that Malory could almost be considered a historian.[71] He liked the character development of Launcelot, Guinevere, and other characters,[72] and he also enjoyed the virtues that these characters

---

[64] "The Vision of John Bunyan," *Selected Literary Essays*, 146. See also Lewis, *English Literature in the Sixteenth Century Excluding Drama*, 297, where Lewis compares a sixteenth century author to Malory, able to write almost as good a sentence as Malory.

[65] Malory was apparently convicted of theft, extortion, robbery, attempted murder, and rape. Lewis does not think we need to assume that Malory was guilty of everything of which he was convicted (*Studies in Medieval and Renaissance Literature*, 104f.).

[66] *Collected Letters of C. S. Lewis*, I, 103.

[67] *Collected Letters of C. S. Lewis*, I, 169, March 7, 1916.

[68] *Collected Letters of C. S. Lewis*, I, 192, June 14, 1916.

[69] *Collected Letters of C. S. Lewis*, I, 227, October 4, 1916.

[70] Lewis, *Surprised by Joy*, 179.

[71] *Collected Letters of C. S. Lewis*, I, 245.

[72] C. S. Lewis, *Spenser's Images of Life*, ed. Alastair Fowler (Cambridge: Cambridge University Press, 1967), 115.

displayed. He later considered the reading of Malory, along with many other greats in English history, essential preparation for the university course in English literature, frequently mentioning him in company with Virgil, Shakespeare, Bunyan, Spenser, and many others.[73] Malory did not offer him support for his atheism, but further awakened in him both his love for the imaginative worlds of invention and his awareness of the problem of guilt. These two elements undermined his conviction that other worlds and personal guilt were purely figments of the imagination.

Fellow Irishman W. B. Yeats originally appealed to Lewis's early interest in occultism. In the same year that he discovered Yeats, Lewis wrote to Arthur Greeves, "W. B. Yeats ... writes plays and poems of rare spirit and beauty about our old Irish mythology. . . . His works have all got that strange, eerie feeling about them, of which we are both professed admirers."[74] Lewis's temporary interest in the occult seems to have been influenced by Yeats, whom Lewis visited twice in Oxford in March 1921 and whom Lewis especially read during his years with Kirkpatrick and later at Oxford University.

Yeats taught Lewis literary pleasure, that is, the pleasure of recognizing the expressed emotion of the author.[75] Yeats also taught Lewis about other worlds, especially a world of transcendent beauty and wonder, a world that truly existed and which Yeats truly believed in. It is not surprising that Lewis mentioned the discovery of Yeats at the same time that he mentioned the discovery of William Morris, since both authors spurred in him that sweet desire for another world, a longing that he would eventually call Joy.[76] Some of that transcendence pointed Lewis in the direction of the occult for a time, but he claims that he never actually practiced it.[77] Yeats caused Lewis to

---

[73] *Collected Letters of C. S. Lewis*, II, 644. See, for example, C. S. Lewis, "High Brows and Low Brows," *Rehabilitations*, 108.

[74] *Collected Letters of C. S. Lewis*, I, 59. The date is June 1914.

[75] Lewis, "Early Prose Joy," 19.

[76] Lewis, "Early Prose Joy," 18.

[77] Lewis, "Early Prose Joy," 20.

misread Plato by thinking of this other world as a psychical world (another world in our minds) rather than a parallel spiritual world (another world out there). In so doing, he taught Lewis about the art of magic[78] and the art of communicating with that other world.[79]

As Lewis read Yeats, he wondered if there actually were people who believed that another world of transcendent beauty and wonder existed behind the natural world. Then he thought that perhaps these stories were not entirely fiction and that something like the lands he desired really existed.[80] When Lewis met Yeats, he was frightened by that very possibility.

Summary

Lewis read many other authors during his younger years, and some of those authors will be described, along with their influence upon him, in chapters 3 through 6. The authors described in this chapter taught Lewis the power of the imagination, the allure of other worlds, the honest appraisal of the world we live in and the people with whom we come in contact, the value of honestly seeing ourselves with our flaws, and depth of thought and emotion. In comparison with the authors who lacked the religious outlook—people like Voltaire, Shaw, and Wells, people with whose views he was sympathetic—the Johnsons and Miltons of the world inspired and challenged him, while the Voltaires of the world appeared thin.[81]

---

[78] "Magic" refers to the work of spiritualists, not the stage magician who pulls a rabbit out of a hat.
[79] Lewis, "Early Prose Joy," 20.
[80] Lewis, "Early Prose Joy," 20.
[81] Lewis, *Surprised by Joy*, 213f.

CHAPTER 3

THE CHESS GAME BEGINS

"The gods hate me—and naturally enough considering my
usual attitude towards them."

—C. S. Lewis, *Collected Letters*

In *Surprised by Joy*, Lewis describes the major moves that God made
against him in three imaginative ways: as a fishing expedition, a fox
hunt, and a chess game. Each of these analogies, of course, implies that
God was active in searching for Lewis, chasing him, arguing with him,
cornering him, reeling him in, and eventually capturing him. In
Lewis's final and most elaborate comparison, the chess-game analogy,
God cornered Lewis primarily in four chess moves, but certainly with
many other moves. Since Lewis called the second move the equivalent
to the loss of one's remaining bishop,[1] the first move, by implication,
was the loss of the first bishop. This chapter will cover the years 1916
to 1922, the years leading up to those first two chess moves, including
his entrance to Oxford University, his service in World War I, and his
adoption of an essentially atheistic version of materialism.

1916: *PHANTASTES*

World War I began in June of 1914, and Lewis went to study with
Kirkpatrick on September 19, 1914. He decided to shield his thinking

---

[1] Lewis, *Surprised by Joy*, 221.

from thoughts of war, making what he called a treaty with reality. He would eventually enlist in the war effort, the war being the major reality, but until then he would be his own man.[2] One book changed these plans, challenging this treaty with reality by showing him another dimension of reality through the lens of fantasy.

Lewis's return to belief in God began with the discovery of George MacDonald's *Phantastes: A Faerie Romance*,[3] on a chilly Saturday afternoon, March 4, 1916, at the Leatherhead Train Station, a two-and-a-half-mile walk from Great Bookham. The book affected him so profoundly that he recalled the precise location where he purchased it, the crisp weather of that day, and the approximate time of day. In the summer, he had frequently walked to Leatherhead and taken the train back, chiefly because of the opportunity to go swimming at Leatherhead. In the colder months, however, he went to get his hair cut or to browse through the book selection. On this particular day in March, books were the attraction. After purchasing a used copy of *Phantastes*, he was so captivated by the book that he read much of it at Kirkpatrick's home that first night, finished the book three days later, and wrote to Arthur Greeves about it for the next three weeks and then again in June and July. This book, he stated, baptized his imagination,[4] starting him on an entirely new path. Baptism always means the end of one way of life and the start of a new one. As Lewis himself indicates, this baptism prevented his imagination from wandering into the evil forms of Romanticism, to which he was drawn by the occult writings of Yeats, even while his intellect remained closed to such ideas.[5]

Prior to this discovery, and for several years afterward, his imagination and his intellect stood opposite each other,[6] as though he had erected a wall in his mind between them, the former rich and fruitful, the latter insincere and unproductive. His intellect was the friend of

---

[2] Lewis, *Surprised by Joy*, 158.
[3] The Greek word *Phantastes* means fantasies.
[4] Lewis, *George MacDonald*, xxxiii.
[5] Lewis, *All My Road Before Me*, xxxvii. See also *Surprised by Joy*, 176.
[6] Lewis, *Surprised by Joy*, 170.

his atheism, but it had allowed him to take brief and tentative excursions into magic[7] in his search for something more. His imagination enjoyed *Phantastes* without allowing his intellect to be affected.[8] His intellect understood truth—factual, rational, logical, ordered statements—while his imagination understood love. He did not think that the things his imagination loved were actually true, but *Phantastes* began to change his mind.

Many years later, while writing about a hypothetical conversation with George MacDonald, Lewis put into words the impact that *Phantastes* had had on him:

> I tried, trembling, to tell this man all that his writings had done for me. I tried to tell how a certain frosty afternoon at Leatherhead Station when I first bought a copy of *Phantastes* . . . had been to me what the first sight of Beatrice had been to Dante: *Here begins the New Life*. I started to confess how long that Life had delayed in the region of imagination merely: how slowly and reluctantly I had come to admit that his Christendom had more than an accidental connection with it, how hard I had tried not to see that the true name of the quality which first met me in his books is Holiness.[9]

The delay between seeing a certain something in MacDonald's books and recognizing the true name of that certain something as Holiness was long, since Lewis came to believe in God more than fourteen years after his purchase of *Phantastes*.

Phantastes had what Lewis later called "cool, morning innocence" and holiness before which his unholiness stood in stark contrast. Later he called it goodness.[10] Although he initially perceived this goodness only dimly, and though he said he was entirely without religion and ethics at this time in his life, he also recognized the story as something

---

[7] Lewis, *Surprised by Joy*, 178; "Early Prose Joy," 22.
[8] Lewis, *George MacDonald*, xxxiii.
[9] C. S. Lewis, *The Great Divorce* (New York: Macmillan, 1946), 65. *The Great Divorce* was first published in 1945.
[10] Lewis, *George MacDonald*, xxxiv.

good in itself, portraying a world in which right and wrong clearly stood out. He also recognized that goodness was part of what he desired, something shocking in itself for a person living, as he wrote about himself, without ethics.[11]

In *Phantastes*, MacDonald clarified that longing which Yeats and Morris had aroused in Lewis two years earlier. That longing had been confused in Lewis's mind, sometimes seeming to be merely a type of daydreaming, while at other times appearing as a plain desire for another world.[12] The goodness of *Phantastes* began to shape Lewis's understanding of ordinary things, enabling him to see something remarkable in common things. Lewis stated that at this time in his life Joy had come and gone, here one moment and gone the next. Now, however, he saw Joy come out of the book and transform everything.[13] He had begun to see that Joy was active; Joy actually had a mind of its own.[14]

Lewis wrote several poems that Easter,[15] little more than a month after the discovery of *Phantastes*. These poems express Lewis's atheistic state of mind, but also the impact that *Phantastes* was having on him. The poem "Loneliness" reflects the solitude of someone who walks in the woods and valleys. A spirit whispers in his ear that there is no one to pity him, that there is no one to hear him if he prays. The poem confirms the fact that at the time, Lewis saw no connection between the story of *Phantastes* and anything ethical or religious. The poem "*Laus Mortis*," whose Latin title means "Praise of Death," may have been inspired by the reading of Dante's *Divine Comedy* and

---

[11] Lewis, "Early Prose Joy," 23. He does not, however, give us any further details.

[12] Lewis, "Early Prose Joy," 20f.

[13] Lewis, *Surprised by Joy*, 181.

[14] The argument from desire was developed by Lewis, and modern philosophers state that the argument from desire has "a high degree of probability since everything else man genuinely needs does in fact exist" (Phil Fernandes, "The Absurdity of Life without God," in *The Big Argument: Does God Exist?* eds. John Ashton and Michael Westacott [Green Forest, AK: Master Books, 2006], 385).

[15] Easter took place on April 23 in 1916.

Virgil's *Aeneid*,[16] both of which Lewis had been reading earlier that year. In *"Laus Mortis,"* Lewis wrote about the realm of Hades, where the inhabitants are not affected by the surge of negative or positive emotions. This pessimistic poem may have been inspired by the war. The last Easter poem was entitled "In His Own Image," in which Lewis spoke out against the wickedness of mankind. After the title of the poem, Lewis included a note about the great wickedness of the human race in the time of Noah, according to Genesis 6, and the pernicious race of the sons of men according to writer Jonathan Swift. That they were written at Easter is easily explained as a time when Lewis had time off from his studies, so no resurrection or Holy Week themes invaded these poems.

The Joy that Lewis sought was near at hand, and it simultaneously turned him away from the occultism that had once excited him.[17] Still, that experience with *Phantastes* was one that he deliberately suppressed. God is more dreadful than ghosts, he claimed, so he put this new knowledge out of his mind as best he could.[18]

From this time until about 1921, Lewis attempted to hold to naturalism, or materialism, i.e., the position that denies the existence of the supernatural. His appreciation of *Phantastes* certainly did not make him a theist, and his excursions into the occult were not excursions in the direction of God. He would relapse into occult or erotic fantasy and then realize that this was not what he desired. He would spend a few days thinking that there was more than the material world, and then he would return to the comfortable world of materialism.[19] He was ambivalent, sometimes thinking as a materialist and at other times almost thinking as a supernaturalist.

At this time, Lewis found atheism both unproductive and uninteresting. Writing about his love for the music of Wagner, the writings

---

[16] Don W. King, *C. S. Lewis, Poet: The Legacy of His Poetic Impulse* (Kent, OH: Kent State University Press, 2001), 47.

[17] Lewis, "Early Prose Joy," 22.

[18] Lewis, "Early Prose Joy," 23.

[19] Lewis, "Early Prose Joy," 23, 29f.

of Morris and Yeats, and his enjoyment of MacDonald and similar authors, he stated, "Nearly all that I loved I believed to be imaginary; nearly all that I believed to be real I thought grim and meaningless. The exceptions were certain people (whom I loved and believed to be real) and nature herself. . . . I chewed endlessly on the problem: 'How can it be so beautiful and also so cruel, wasteful and futile?' "[20] Nature sent opposite messages to Lewis, making him wonder about the source of such intricate beauty in nature while at the same time insisting on a purely materialistic universe.

Over the next half-dozen years Lewis gradually and reluctantly gave up his materialism, later calling it a philosophy for boys,[21] because he learned that the answers of materialism to the question of suffering were far more inadequate than were religious answers. The religious view offered both hope for the next life and a comforting presence in this life, whereas the materialistic view offered only fatalistic resignation. He wrote about *Phantastes*, "I met there all that had already charmed me in Malory, Spenser, Morris, and Yeats. But in another sense all was changed. I did not yet know . . . the name of the new quality, the bright shadow, that rested on the travels of Anodos.[22] I do now. It was Holiness."[23] Lewis stated that he heard in the story of Anodos (whose name means "Ascent") the voice of his mother or his nurse, or the voice from the world's end (another echo of William Morris).[24] He did not, however, set aside materialism as a result, because he managed to put this sense of holiness out of his mind.[25] Just seven months after discovering *Phantastes*, he wrote to Arthur Greeves, "I am not laying down as a certainty that there *is* nothing

---

[20] Lewis, *Surprised by Joy*, 170.

[21] Lewis, "De Futilitate," *Christian Reflections*, 71.

[22] Anodos is the major character in *Phantastes* who journeys through the woods and has out-of-this-world experiences.

[23] Lewis, *Surprised by Joy*, 179.

[24] Lewis, *Surprised by Joy*, 179f. See also William Morris, *The Well at the World's End*.

[25] Lewis, "Early Prose Joy," 23.

outside the material world."[26] He still held to a materialistic position, but he was no longer as certain as he had been.

This discovery of a little known book marks an unusual beginning to a very long journey, but the length of this journey has its advantages. During those fifteen years, Lewis looked into every explanation that was available to him, searching at times and resting comfortably at other times, convinced of his atheism at times and wanting to pursue the vision he experienced in *Phantastes* at other times, alternately doubting and sure of himself.[27] In fact, Lewis once said that he had been deceived by every one of the false answers available to him, but that he had thought through them sufficiently to discover their flaws.[28] We learn the most from his destination, but we also learn from the dead ends that he faced and the reasons why he found them to be dead ends.

Just two months after discovering *Phantastes*, Lewis began to write "The Quest of Bleheris."[29] He wrote this poem about a young man with plans to marry his sweetheart Alice, but lacking the excitement that should accompany these plans. Bleheris decides to go on a quest to prove that he is worthy of her love, so he sets out to search for Striver, a miracle-worker living beyond the mountains in the north. Bleheris visits the local priest before beginning his quest. The priest gives him a flask of holy water to aid him in his quest, and the narrator, Lewis, comments about the folly that believes that this man-made bauble could help him against the powers of evil. Arthur Greeves apparently reacted against this part of the story, and Lewis replied, probably not fully honestly, that he was sneering at religious superstition rather

---

[26] *Collected Letters of C. S. Lewis*, I, 231, October 12, 1916.

[27] In "Early Prose Joy," 23, Lewis wrote about oscillating between following the new revelation he saw in *Phantastes* and relapsing into erotic or occultist fancy.

[28] Lewis, *The Pilgrim's Regress*, 203.

[29] Katherine Harper, "C. S. Lewis's Short Fiction and Unpublished Works," in *C. S. Lewis: Life, Works, and Legacy*, Volume 2, ed. Bruce L. Edwards (Westport, CT: Praeger, 2007), 161f. The summary of the poem is adapted from Harper's summary. The original manuscript is kept in the Bodleian library, sixty-four pages in length.

than Christianity itself.[30] At the Hostel of the Crossways on the first night of his quest, Bleheris has to choose between three possible companions: Wan Jadis, Gerce the Desirous, and Hyperites. The first is a youth on his own quest to find Yesterday, the second is searching for Tomorrow, and the third is a middle-aged voice of reason and a servant of Striver, apparently someone living neither in the past nor in the future. Without being told of Bleheris's quest, Hyperites announces that Bleheris is searching for Striver, which evokes awe in Bleheris.

Although Bleheris should have chosen the voice of reason and experience, i.e., Hyperites, he chooses the youth Wan Jadis, preferring the voice of the past to the voice of the future or the voice of experience. When Bleheris chooses Wan Jadis, Gerce expresses his disappointment with that choice. In the figure of Gerce, David C. Downing sees the young Lewis rejecting the schemes of the dreamers, who use their vague ideology to search for a man-made future. Utopia usually needs a clearer vision and a better plan to reach it.[31]

Bleheris and Wan Jadis set out to look for the Land of Tomorrow, abandoning the quest to find Striver. They use a small boat to cross a marsh. The boat capsizes, Wan Jadis is drawn into the mud of the marsh, but Bleheris is saved from drowning by a rose bush that comes to life in the form of a naked young woman. Bleheris then returns to the Hostel of the Crossways. The three remaining men—Bleheris, Gerce, and Hyperites—then go to a distant city to pursue Alice. Lewis had planned to reveal the rose bush woman as Bleheris's true love, but the plot became bogged down. After Bleheris reaches the city of Ralholt, where a Christian cathedral and a temple of Odin stand side by side, the manuscript ends. Lewis seems to affirm that Christian myth and Norse myth can stand as equals, a position consistent with his view that Christianity was simply another one of the many mythologies, but he apparently did not know where to take his story next.

---

[30] *Collected Letters of C. S. Lewis*, I, 216. This letter is dated July 18, 1916.
[31] Downing, *The Most Reluctant Convert*, 72f.

David C. Downing's extensive summary and analysis of the poem make it clear that the poem reflects a writer whose future was uncertain and whose goals in life were unclear.[32] As Downing explains, *The Pilgrim's Regress* will later make the claim "that all human loves are mere copies of the more perfect divine love."[33] Perhaps even the love of Bleheris was such a human love, merely a copy of the divine love.

During the summer of 1916, Lewis wrote "Sonnet," a fourteen-line poem showing his true "religious" commitment—he had not bowed to any shrine except that of poetry. His "Sonnet—To Sir Philip Sidney" echoes the sentiments of "Sonnet," praising Sir Philip Sidney (1554–86) for his poetry. When Lewis commends Sidney for walking a nobler path than John Milton, he praises Sidney for not attempting to justify the ways of God, as Milton did. A deeply religious person, Sidney used poetry only to educate and inspire. At the end of 1916, Lewis wrote the poem "Decadence." In this poem with Arthurian overtones, Lewis describes the world as old and sad, but he longs for a world beyond this world. *Phantastes* had encouraged a longing within him, and he imagined it as fulfilled in the stories of King Arthur.

Two final poems were written at Christmastime, both of them expressing Lewis's longing for an afterlife. "Couplets" celebrates spring in the world of nature, friendship, and faery. In this poem Lewis also speculates about life after death, wondering whether he might be able to enjoy the hills of County Down in that afterlife. In "Hylas," Lewis puts words into the mouth of Hylas, a youth in Greek mythology who was abducted by water nymphs. Hylas is also the Greek word for matter, an appropriate name for someone committed to materialism at this point in life.[34] The poem reflects a lonely and cold existence in the afterlife as well as the pessimism of its author. The year ended with

---

[32] Downing, *The Most Reluctant Convert*, 67–80.

[33] Downing, *The Most Reluctant Convert*, 78.

[34] Furthermore, Hylas appears as a character in Edmund Spenser's *The Faerie Queene* and also in George Berkeley's *Three Dialogues between Hylas and Philonous*, both of which he may have read by this time.

yearning for another life, awakened by *Phantastes*, but without a clear destination for that yearning.

1917: MATERIALISM, YEATS, AND MAETERLINCK

The reading of *Phantastes* was one of the reasons that Lewis later wrote about the wavering of his materialistic faith near the end of his time with Kirkpatrick,[35] a period that concluded on April 25, 1917. These two-and-a-half years had prepared him for scholarship exams that he hoped would earn him a place at one of the Oxford colleges. And so they did.

However much Lewis enjoyed his time with Kirkpatrick, conflicts with his father continued and probably led him to write the poem "Ballade on a Certain Pious Gentleman" during Easter 1917.[36] This "pious gentleman" was undoubtedly his father Albert Lewis. The poem sarcastically describes a sanctimonious man who thinks he is wise and virtuous, whom Lewis describes as his enemy and a hoarder of money. The young Lewis states that he would rather be damned than to share the heavenly realms with this man. His father's religious behavior, including churchgoing, contrasts with the son's dependence on his father's financial support and independence from the church.

In 1917, after the end of the Great Bookham period with Kirkpatrick, Lewis began his studies at Oxford University, having won a scholarship in Classics[37] to University College. Shortly after arriving in Oxford, he signed up for the Officers' Training Corps, which prepared him for service in the war. He stayed at Keble College during his training and eventually arrived in France twelve days prior to his nineteenth birthday as a second lieutenant in the Third Battalion of the Somerset Light Infantry.

The poem "Exercise" was written in the very same month when Lewis arrived in Oxford to begin his university studies. In "Exercise," Lewis asks rhetorical questions about the disappearance of glory and

---

[35] Lewis, *Surprised by Joy*, 174.
[36] In 1917, Easter was on April 8.
[37] The study of the Greek and Latin languages as well as Greek and Latin literature.

faery. The young Lewis was inquiring about his future, which the First World War clearly brought into question.

In his personal correspondence, Lewis especially wrote about William Butler Yeats, who stood apart from all the other poets that he was reading at this time.[38] Yeats actually believed in another world, and he also believed that contact between that other world and the physical world was possible. While Yeats saw that contact happening through magic, that belief still challenged Lewis's confidence in the findings of some in the sciences.[39] Yeats was not a Christian, and yet he believed in a world beyond the senses, influencing Lewis away from materialism toward a belief in spiritual reality.

Lewis also read Maurice Maeterlinck (1862–1949), a 1911 winner of the Nobel Prize in Literature. He had read Maeterlinck's major work, *The Blue Bird*, in French already in 1916, but he read much more of Maeterlinck during the first half of 1917. In fact, in the previous year Lewis had written to Arthur Greeves that he had developed an interest in mystical philosophy,[40] something he owed in part to Maeterlinck. Maeterlinck introduced him to spiritualism, theosophy, and pantheism.[41] In one of Maeterlinck's works, *The Great Secret*, David C. Downing writes, Maeterlinck "flatly stated that Christianity was unsatisfactory as an answer to spiritual questions,"[42] but Maeterlinck's spiritualism also created doubts within Lewis about his materialistic creed. Perhaps Lewis was writing about this very period in his life, when, decades later, he stated, "Now that I am a Christian I do have moods in which the whole thing looks very improbable: but when I was an atheist I had moods in which Christianity looked terribly probable."[43] Since he had such moods (plural, not singular), he must have thought in this manner on multiple occasions—after meeting

---

[38] He had discovered Yeats in 1914 while at Malvern College. See, for example, his letter to his father on May 17, 1914 (*Collected Letters of C. S. Lewis*, I, 57).

[39] Lewis, *Surprised by Joy*, 174.

[40] *Collected Letters of C. S. Lewis*, I, 176f. The date is March 16, 1916.

[41] Lewis, *Surprised by Joy*, 175.

[42] Downing, *The Most Reluctant Convert*, 104.

[43] Lewis, *Mere Christianity*, 140f.

Coghill, after reading Chesterton and Herbert, after *Phantastes*, after reading Maeterlinck. and on other occasions.

During May and June, Lewis also read William Fletcher Barrett's *Psychical Research*, and then recommended it to Arthur Greeves. In 1882, Barrett had founded the Society for Psychical Research and two years later the American Society for Psychical Research. Lewis insisted to Arthur that psychical phenomena do not prove the existence of real spirits. Nevertheless he described the book as extraordinary, awakening an old interest of his.[44] Later this summer his reading of Frederic Myers's *Science and a Future Life*, a survey of the paranormal, and Sir Oliver Lodge's *Raymond, or Life and Death*, a book about communicating with the dead through spirit mediums, showed his continuing interest in the paranormal.[45]

Oddly enough, one topic that Lewis thought about frequently was God. Then again, it is not really so odd. One can hardly reject an idea without first having understood it, so the idea of theism, if truly rejected, must be seriously considered. Paradoxically, at the same time he was rejecting the idea of theism, it also began to appeal to him. For example, in May, Lewis had a conversation with another under-graduate on the improbability of God.[46] And then, in June 1918, he wrote, "I believe in no God, least of all one that would punish me for the 'lusts of the flesh': but I do believe that I have in me a spirit, a chip, shall we say, of universal spirit."[47] During the month of July, he was reading Bishop Berkeley's *Principles of Human Knowledge*, par-ticularly the part about proving the existence of God.[48] The topic of God's existence shows up frequently in his letters. But it also shows that though he read Berkeley, he did not at this time accept Berkeley's

---

[44] *Collected Letters of C. S. Lewis*, I, 313.
[45] David C. Downing, *Into the Region of Awe: Mysticism in C. S. Lewis* (Downers Grove, IL: InterVarsity Press, 2005), 149.
[46] *Collected Letters of C. S. Lewis*, I, 310. The date is May 27.
[47] *Collected Letters of C. S. Lewis*, I, 379.
[48] *Collected Letters of C. S. Lewis*, I, 330f.

conclusions.[49] One may assume that Lewis was here open to considering the arguments of the other side. George Berkeley (1685–1753) had been an Irish Anglican clergyman who was made Bishop of Cloyne in 1734, and a philosopher, one of the English Idealists. A few months later, Lewis wrote, "The gods hate me—and naturally enough considering my usual attitude towards them."[50] Clearly, God was not just frequently in Lewis's thoughts, but also his letters and conversations.

1918: OXFORD UNIVERSITY AND WORLD WAR I

Lewis had crossed to the front lines in France on November 17, 1917. While serving in the infantry, Lewis met an officer by the name of Laurence B. Johnson, the Commander of one of the army's companies. He stated that Johnson was moving toward theism, and that the two of them argued that topic and many others. The most important thing for Lewis, however, was that Johnson was a man of conscience, and he admired that. As a result, wrote Lewis, "It crossed my mind for the first time since my apostasy that the severer virtues might have some relevance to one's own life."[51]

By "the severer virtues" Lewis meant such things as truthfulness, chastity, self-control, and devotion to duty. At the same time, however, Lewis told his friend Leo Baker that, despite the fears he faced in France, he never sank so low as to pray.[52] He was impressed by Johnson's position, but certainly not convinced by it.

Besides challenging his views of life, Lewis's war experience also challenged his purely biological view of the common man. Seeing death and destruction all around him, he wrote about his reverence for

---

[49] Adam Barkman writes that Berkeley's ethics were "divine command ethics," the same ethics as those of the church in which Lewis grew up, which would explain one reason why he did not accept Berkeley (*C. S. Lewis & Philosophy as a Way of Life* [Allentown, PA: Zossima Press, 2009], 317).

[50] *Collected Letters of C. S. Lewis*, I, 358. The letter is dated February 21, 1918.

[51] Lewis, *Surprised by Joy*, 192.

[52] Baker, "Near the Beginning," *C. S. Lewis at the Breakfast Table*, 6.

the ordinary man, especially Sergeant Harry Ayres, the man who was killed by the same artillery shell that wounded him.[53] In facing the horrors of war, he developed a new appreciation for the ordinary person, just as he had earlier come to appreciate the ordinary in nature. Later, Lewis would write, "There are no ordinary people,"[54] and he forever after had an appreciation for the average person. Devin Brown calls this viewpoint Lewis's appreciation of "the sacramental ordinary,"[55] especially since the ordinary always has far more to it than meets the eye. Perhaps, he thought at this time, the ordinary is not so ordinary after all.

While serving on the front lines, Lewis continued his interest in literature. In February, while hospitalized in Le Tréport, France, with trench fever, he read the collection of essays that introduced him to Chesterton's writings. He does not name the exact collection of essays he read (there are ten different collections written by Chesterton and published before 1918, the year he read Chesterton), but he met Chesterton for the first time in these essays. An August 7 letter to Arthur Greeves found Lewis growing in his appreciation of poet William Wordsworth and expressing his enjoyment at having recently read George MacDonald's *The Princess and the Goblin*.[56] Although he had previously disliked Wordsworth, his opinion was changing.[57] These two authors fueled Lewis's imagination, perhaps aided by Chesterton, even though the ability of that imagination to convey truth was being suppressed during these materialistic days. A short time later he expressed similar thoughts about American essayist and poet, Ralph Waldo Emerson, enjoying the weighty character of his writings, perhaps especially Emerson's emphasis upon freedom and individuality.[58]

---

[53] Lewis, *Surprised by Joy*, 195f.

[54] Lewis, "The Weight of Glory," in *The Weight of Glory and Other Addresses*, 39.

[55] Devin Brown, *The Christian World of The Hobbit* (Nashville: Abingdon Press, 2012), 146–50.

[56] *Collected Letters of C. S. Lewis*, I, 393.

[57] *Collected Letters of C. S. Lewis*, I, 154, November 19, 1915.

[58] *Collected Letters of C. S. Lewis*, I, 398.

Two months later,[59] while recuperating from war wounds, Lewis wrote to Arthur Greeves for the first time from Perham Downs Camp in Salisbury Plain about his recent reading experiences. He stayed there until mid-November, and during that time he wrote several letters to Arthur and his father. Sometime during that six-week period in Salisbury Plain he read French philosopher Henri Bergson (1859–1941) and wrote about Bergson in *Surprised by Joy*.

> Intellectually [reading Henri Bergson] . . . had a revolutionary effect on my emotional outlook. Hitherto my whole bent had been toward things pale, remote, and evanescent; the water-color world of Morris, the leafy recesses of Malory, the twilight of Yeats. . . . Bergson . . . did not abolish my old loves, but he gave me a new one. . . . I became capable of appreciating artists who would, I believe, have meant nothing to me before; all the resonant, dogmatic, flaming, unanswerable people like Beethoven, Titian (in his mythological pictures), Goethe, Dunbar, Pindar, Christopher Wren, and the more exultant Psalms.[60]

One of Henri Bergson's major achievements was to elevate the role of intuition and experience above that of science and reason, an evaluation which Lewis learned from him, but Lewis also learned to appreciate the creativity of the above named composers, authors, and architects. All of this seems to have affected Lewis at a level much deeper than the rational, including the dismissal—or at least the blunting—of some of his pessimism. Lewis was beginning to doubt that life consisted exclusively of the material world.

1919: THE NEW LOOK

In January 1919, with the war now over and his convalescence complete, Lewis returned to Oxford University to prepare for Honour

---

[59] The date of the event related to Lewis's activities is not fully certain, but October 6 is close, if not precisely accurate. See *Collected Letters of C. S. Lewis*, I, 403.
[60] Lewis, *Surprised by Joy*, 198.

Moderations.[61] In spite of the influence of Maeterlinck and Bergson, he resolved at this time to be a consistent materialist, one who believed in "atoms and evolution and military service."[62] He had wavered between materialism and something more, and now he wanted to waver no longer. He was avoiding God, resisting the idea of God more than concluding that there was no God. In a passage describing the years 1919 to 1921, Lewis tells of adopting the New Look. He turned away from pessimism, self-pity, thoughts of the supernatural, and the romantic.[63] He was from now on definitely going to hold a firmly materialistic view of the universe and suppress anything that might suggest a world of spirits, the Spirit, or spiritualism.

However, this effort did not entirely work. Instead of coming through literature, as it had in the past, Joy came through his remembering of the past—especially his brother's toy garden of moss, flowers, and twigs that had aroused Joy—and his experience of nature.[64] Previously he had experienced Joy in Northern mythology and in the writings of Yeats and Morris; now he tried looking at the past. At this time, he probably felt as he would describe later in 1922, that what he desired was simply a state of mind rather than something objectively real outside himself.[65]

The causes of Lewis's retreat from romanticism to the New Look were multiple: the atheist Irish priest Frederick Macran, who helped Lewis to avoid thinking about immortality; two weeks spent with Dr. Askins, the brother of Mrs. Janie Moore[66] who was losing his sanity,

---

[61] The study of Greek and Latin texts.

[62] Lewis, *Surprised by Joy*, 174.

[63] Lewis, *Surprised by Joy*, 201. This turning away from romanticism apparently included such writers as William Morris. Lewis did not mention William Morris between June 1919 and March 1921.

[64] Lewis, "Early Prose Joy," 14, 24.

[65] See especially Lewis, *Surprised by Joy*, 168.

[66] Mrs. Moore was Lewis's surrogate mother whom he "adopted" when he returned from the war. He and Paddy, Mrs. Moore's son, had made a pact that if one of the two survived the war, the survivor would look after the deceased soldier's parent. Since Lewis's mother had died in 1908 and Paddy's father was separated from his mother, each of them effectively had only one parent.

thinking that he was being dragged down to Hell;[67] and the new psychology (i.e., Sigmund Freud) with its understanding of the subconscious, fantasy, and wishful thinking (and Lewis's banishment of the legendary island Avalon of the King Arthur story and the mythological figures in Greek mythology, the Hesperides, i.e., the banishing of his imagination[68]).

For Lewis the New Look, elsewhere called the Spirit of the Age, included "the belief that the only reality is the universe as revealed by the senses."[69] Nature, not God, kills and then puts aside the beauty that once was.[70] He called Joy merely "aesthetic experience,"[71] refusing to think of it as evidence for something out of this world. Instead, it was something inside him. Everything that might point to the supernatural he interpreted as purely natural. This New Look seems to have carried him at least through 1921, but probably also through 1922 and most of the first half of 1923.

Lewis wrote about his materialism,

The materialistic universe had one great, negative attraction to offer me . . . one had to look out on a meaningless dance of atoms (remember, I was reading Lucretius), to realize that all the apparent beauty was a subjective phosphorescence, and to relegate everything one valued to the world of mirage. That price I tried loyally to pay. For I had learned something from Kirk about the honor of the intellect and the shame of voluntary inconsistency. And, of course, I exulted with youthful and vulgar pride in what I thought my enlightenment. In argument with Arthur I was a very swashbuckler. Most of it, as I now see, was incredibly crude and silly. I was

---

[67] This happened between February 21 and March 12, 1923.

[68] Lewis, *Surprised by Joy*, 204.

[69] Devin Brown, *A Life Observed: A Spiritual Biography of C. S. Lewis* (Grand Rapids: Brazos Press, 2013), 119. The Spirit of the Age is one of the enemies John faced in *The Pilgrim's Regress*, 47.

[70] Lewis, *Spirits in Bondage*, 14.

[71] See, for example, Lewis, *The Pilgrim's Regress*, 77.

in that state of mind in which a boy thinks it extremely telling to call God *Jahveh* and Jesus *Yeshua*.[72]

His alleged enlightenment demonstrates the fierce independence and the personal autonomy that Lewis so highly prized at this time in his life. He ended 1919 steeped in full-blown materialism, and yet he had some doubts about materialism because of his dabbling in Barrett's *Psychical Research*, because of Bergson and Maeterlinck, and simply because of his inability to be a consistent materialist.

There was also another chink in Lewis's armor. On September 18, he wrote to Arthur Greeves that he was reading Wordsworth again, this time *The Prelude* and, something he thought funny, he was enjoying it.[73] Although he claimed to be a materialist, his materialism was weakening. One suspects that the man who told his undergraduate friend Leo Baker, "You can't start with God. I don't accept God!"[74] was protesting too much.

The year 1919 also brought significant changes in his circle of friends, since this is the year that Lewis met Owen Barfield,[75] whom he once called his antiself, and A. C. Harwood, the former a student at Oxford University and the latter from Michael Hall, Kidbrooke, a kindergarten through age 18 school in East Sussex whose curriculum was based on the works of Rudolf Steiner. Both Barfield and Harwood became lifelong friends of Lewis, sharing their homes with Lewis and visiting Lewis in his home, writing letters back and forth, discussing ideas both in person and through correspondence, and taking long walks together. But their friendship did not bring any major changes in Lewis's thinking until years later, with one exception. Part of the New Look that Lewis adopted was what he later called "chronological

---

[72] Lewis, *Surprised by Joy*, 172f. Lewis used *Yeshua* three times in his letters, once on October 12, 1916 and twice six days later on October 18, both times writing to Arthur.

[73] *Collected Letters of C. S. Lewis*, I, 466.

[74] Baker, "Near the Beginning," *C. S. Lewis at the Breakfast Table*, 4. Baker and Lewis met during the Michaelmas term of 1919.

[75] *Owen Barfield on C. S. Lewis*, 17, note a.

snobbery," the uncritical acceptance of the intellectual climate of the day, what he also called the Spirit of the Age. In 1919, Lewis assumed that later ideas were better ideas and that anything that had fallen out of date was discredited. Barfield challenged those assumptions and within a few years—by 1923 at least—convinced Lewis that a lot of old ideas were better ideas that had stood the test of time.

One other event that had a major impact on Lewis occurred in 1919: the publication of his first book. On March 20, 1919, William Heinemann published Lewis's collection of poems, *Spirits in Bondage: A Cycle of Lyrics*. Writing to his friend Arthur Greeves, Lewis explained the gist of these forty poems: "Mainly strung round the idea that . . . nature is wholly diabolical & malevolent and that God, if he exists, is outside of and in opposition to the cosmic arrangements."[76] The position summarized by Lewis here is agnosticism rather than atheism, doubt rather than denial, hesitance rather than hardheadedness. Not only that, but in these poems, Lewis contradicts himself, both describing God as diabolical and malevolent and claiming that God was outside of the universe, which he was supposed to have created. How can one blame God for creating an imperfect universe and then state that God had nothing to do with it? Concerned for the tone of his brother's poetry, Warren wrote to his father about his brother's cycle of poems, stating that "no useful purpose is served by endeavoring to advertise oneself as an Atheist."[77] In these poems, Lewis demonstrated his most strident opposition to the idea of God.

Don W. King wrote about this cycle of lyrics in *Spirits in Bondage*:

> Above all else it shows Lewis living as a frustrated dualist. On the one hand, in a number of *morose* poems he rails against man's inhumanity to man and against a God he denies yet blames for man's painful condition. . . . On the other hand, many *sanguine* poems . . . show his delight in Nature's beauty and mystery, while others expose his longing to know more

---

[76] *Collected Letters of C. S. Lewis*, I, 397. The letter is dated September 12, 1918.
[77] Lewis, *Spirits in Bondage*, xxxvii. See also *The Lewis Papers* 6:84.

intimately a reality that transcends the merely physical, often characterized by the world of "faery."[78]

And yet that beauty, Lewis contended at this time in his life, was only apparent beauty,[79] a position that his materialism forced him to take. If accepted in the conventional sense, beauty means that something exists above and beyond the atoms of materialism—something Lewis would not accept.

Parts of this cycle of poems, especially Part I, "The Prison House," speak words of protest "against a silent, uncaring heaven." His "Ode for New Year's Day," written while under fire during the war, "speaks of the final death of Theism."[80] His homeland, Northern Ireland, is merely a "dreary shroud" with "colorless skies," "blurred horizons," and "lonely desire" (the poem "Irish Nocturne").

The poem "French Nocturne" drew on Lewis's war experience, especially his work in the trenches. Lewis uses his base town in France—Monchy-le-Preux—as the sub-title of this poem. The town is described as "a sacked village, stark and grim."[81] Here Lewis does not have a vision of a better world to escape to. He describes himself as a wolf, one that, like his fellow men, has a throat that "can bark for slaughter"[82] but is unable to sing. The plane that appears to be flying to the moon reflects the dreams that Lewis once had, but has no longer. "Soldiers cannot dream, a distinguishing human quality," writes Don W. King, "since now they are vicious animals."[83]

Only in the realm of faerie did Lewis see some hope, perhaps only for escape from his dim surroundings, but hope nevertheless. This appears in "The Satyr." A satyr is a goat-like semi-human creature

---

[78] Don W. King, "Early Lyric Poetry: Spirits in Bondage (1919) and 'Joy' (1924)," in C. S. Lewis: Life, Works and Legacy 2:234.
[79] Lewis, Surprised by Joy, 172f.
[80] McGrath, "New Look," The Intellectual World of C. S. Lewis (Chichester, UK: Wiley-Blackwell, 2014), 34. The date is January 1918.
[81] Lewis, Spirits in Bondage, 4.
[82] Lewis, Spirits in Bondage, 4.
[83] King, "Early Lyric Poetry," 236.

often thought of as a personification of Nature. In this poem Lewis writes about "the power of faery to draw us out of this world and into one of beauty, mystery, and danger."[84] He observes, "All the faerie kin he rallies/Making music evermore."[85] Perhaps, as he states in his poem "Victory," his pessimism could be muted by "the yearning, high, rebellious spirit of man."[86] Unfortunately, those at work must strive with "red Nature and her ways,"[87] a phrase that echoes the English poet Tennyson's lyrics about nature, which is "red in tooth and claw." Even in "Hymn (For Boys' Voices)" he describes the beauty of nature and invites us to stand in awe. Likewise the poem "Our Daily Bread," a title that echoes a phrase from the Lord's Prayer, points to "a sight of lands beyond the wall . . . a strange god's face,"[88] showing once again Lewis's ambivalence toward God, but probably also his raising of nature to the level of reverence that, as a young boy, he had previously reserved for God. At the end of this same poem when Lewis writes "the beast become[s] a god,"[89] he foreshadows *Dymer*, his long narrative poem under construction at this time in his life, another work that deals with the theme of a beast becoming a god.

Lewis also saw some hope in literature, specifically in John Milton. In "Milton Read Again (In Surrey)," Lewis writes of Milton, "Your Spirit, Master, has been close at hand." And yet, for all the hope Lewis found in Milton, a sense of dread always seemed to linger nearby. As described in "Spooks," the end is merely death. Don W. King calls "Apology" Lewis's "most bitter and ironic war poem,"[90] using Despoina as the name for Persephone, Queen of Hades, whom he addresses in this poem. The poem contains despair and gloom, along with a pessimistic ending.[91]

---

[84] King, "Early Lyric Poetry," 246.
[85] Lewis, *Spirits in Bondage*, 5.
[86] Lewis, *Spirits in Bondage*, 7.
[87] Lewis, *Spirits in Bondage*, 7.
[88] Lewis, *Spirits in Bondage*, 60.
[89] Lewis, *Spirits in Bondage*, 8.
[90] King, "Early Lyric Poetry," 237.
[91] King, "Early Lyric Poetry," 238.

But Lewis did not merely protest the meaninglessness of life. He railed against a God he did not believe existed. In "Ode for New Year's Day," he complained that it is vain to pray since we are unable to resist the Power that slays. He has "lifted up [his] voice to God, thinking that he could hear/The curse wherewith I cursed Him because the Good was dead."[92] He writes that God does not care about our virtues, our hopes, or our fears. In "De Profundis,"[93] he writes that he would not bow down to God or love Him. Later in the same poem he proudly states, "Thou art not Lord while there are Men on earth."[94] The shocking nature of this particular poem is one of the reasons that Warren Lewis wrote to his father, stating that it would have been better if this cycle of poems had not been published.[95]

Lewis understood that there was evil in the world, and he chose to personify that evil in the recognizable image of Satan. In "Satan Speaks," Satan states that he was the Creator rather than God, indicating that Lewis was adopting the then popular interpretation of Milton—that Satan was the hero of *Paradise Lost*—a position he would later refute. In the same poem, Satan invites that other God to come if he actually exists. Satan complains of the silent God, whom many have called upon, but in vain, receiving no answer. God was not answering Lewis, at least not in the way that Lewis wished.

The answer to Lewis's complaint was simple—he complained because he hoped there was a God out there. When this God met him at the end, he asked in the poem "To Sleep" that God might lead him in a friendly manner, without wearing a frightful mask. Lewis wanted this God to rescue him from his prison. In the poem "In Prison," he wrote more about pain and the futility of life. While Lewis was still claiming atheism as his creed, and trying to live as a consistent materialist, he complained more about the inconsistencies between

---

[92] Lewis, *Spirits in Bondage*, 14.
[93] Latin for "out of the depths," reflecting Psalm 130.
[94] Lewis, *Spirits in Bondage*, 21.
[95] Warren Lewis, *The Lewis Papers, Letters and Papers: Memoirs of the Lewis Family* 6:84, cited in King, "Early Lyric Poetry," 239.

God's goodness and the pain in this world than about the lack of a divine presence.

In the first poem in Part III, a poem called "Song of the Pilgrims," Lewis expresses his yearning for something more, writing, "But, ah God! we know/That somewhere, somewhere past the Northern snow/Waiting for us the red-rose gardens blow."[96] There is a brighter future, some hope in God, a "country far away,"[97] in whose "gardens we shall sleep and play/Forever and forever and a day."[98] What a statement for an atheist to make!

"Tu Ne Quaesieris"[99] expresses the futility of Lewis's own attempts to heal his "torn desires," i.e., torn by being drawn both to God and to his own personal ambitions. Lewis writes, "When this live body that was I/Lies hidden from the cheerful sky,"[100] what is life if he must hope and yet fail? The fortieth and last poem, "Death in Battle," describes the speaker, lying on the battlefield and longing for the realm of the dead. Now that he is dead and alone, he asks for the gates to be opened for him. He desires "to be ever alone," but also dwelling "in the garden of God."

The ambivalence of Lewis is evident in *Spirits in Bondage*. He denied God's existence, and yet he complained about the way that God oversaw His universe. He saw pain and heartache in this world, and he called out to the God in whom he did not believe.

1920–21: Honour Moderations and Greats

During the first two months of 1920, Lewis was in the final stages of preparing for Honour Moderations exams, which took place in March at Oxford University. Honour Moderations was the study of Greek and Latin texts—the first half of his degree—while Greats was the study of ancient history and philosophy—the second half of the

---

[96] Lewis, *Spirits in Bondage*, 47.
[97] Lewis, *Spirits in Bondage*, 48.
[98] Lewis, *Spirits in Bondage*, 48.
[99] From a poem by Horace in Latin, meaning "Do not ask."
[100] Lewis, *Spirits in Bondage*, 68.

degree.[101] This was another year of atheistic materialism for C. S. Lewis, and his upcoming exams may have prevented him from focusing on anything but his studies. However, a few months later, Lewis was rereading Henri Bergson. In a letter to Arthur, he wrote that he was reading Bergson once again, finding much of it clear which just a year previously had been obscure to him.[102] While Lewis understood philosophy better by this time, Bergson had also challenged his materialism, particularly in Bergson's argument that reality seemed to have purpose. This coincides with a statement Lewis later makes in "Early Prose Joy," his original attempt at an autobiography that from his fourteenth year of age until his second year at Oxford University he adopted naturalism as his creed.[103]

Later in 1920, in a letter to his friend Leo Baker, Lewis complained that his imagination seemed to have died (clearly from self-inflicted wounds), and in the same letter he proposed some sort of an idea of God, but a God whom we could not know.[104] Lewis was ambivalent on the subject, unable to prove there is no God, but also drawn by many things, especially the beauty of the world around him, to think that God might exist.

Twice in March, 1921, Lewis accompanied fellow undergraduate William Force Stead to the home of William Butler Yeats, who had moved to Oxford just a few years earlier. Lewis had previously idolized the poetry of Yeats, so he looked forward to meeting the great one in person. He thought these meetings would make him appreciate Yeats all the more, but they had the opposite effect. This was the approximate time when Lewis was taking brief jaunts into the occult,

---

[101] Also known as *Literae Humaniores.*

[102] *Collected Letters of C. S. Lewis*, I, 494. The date of the letter is June 19, 1920.

[103] Lewis, "Early Prose Joy," 29. He had returned to Oxford University in January 1919, which makes 1920 his second year at the university.

[104] *Collected Letters of C. S. Lewis*, I, 507, September 25, 1920. This sounds like the position of F. H. Bradley, who claimed that God could not be known. Lewis read Bradley in 1922.

getting excited about the experience, then becoming frightened enough to scurry back into his materialism.[105]

As he entered the Yeats home on Broad Street for the first time, he walked past two etchings by William Blake, later describing them as "rather wicked."[106] The most famous etching from *The Book of Job*, as described by David C. Downing, shows "a gray-bearded man lying on a coffinlike box and looking down with wide, fearful eyes at claw-handed creatures below him who are clutching at his body and trying to wrap him in a chain. Drawing on Milton's epic poem, *Paradise Lost*, Blake created images of towering flames, fanged serpents and dog-headed dragons."[107] These etchings, along with the visits with Yeats, motivated Lewis to steer clear of the occult in the years ahead. A. C. Harwood later wrote that Lewis "had a natural horror of the occult,"[108] a horror that probably originated in these visits.

A few months later, Lewis commented in a letter to his brother Warren, "The trouble about God is that he is like a person who never acknowledges your letters and so in time you come to the conclusion either that he does not exist or that you have got his address wrong."[109] In the same letter, Lewis wrote about winning the undergraduate writing contest for his essay on Optimism, which included, among other points, the argument that the existence of God makes no difference whatsoever. One wonders about the influence of family members, however, when one learns about his ten-day trip through the small villages of southwest England with his father, Uncle Gussie, and Aunt Annie. During a walk one evening, Uncle Gussie expressed his view that the universe worked and gave evidence of an intelligent mind behind it.[110] Although Lewis dismissed those ideas in his letter

---

[105] Lewis, "Early Prose Joy," 30.

[106] *Collected Letters of C. S. Lewis*, I, 530.

[107] Downing, *The Most Reluctant Convert*, 113.

[108] A. C. Harwood, "About Anthroposophy," in Como, *C. S. Lewis at the Breakfast Table*, 25.

[109] *Collected Letters of C. S. Lewis*, I, 555. The date is July 1, 1921.

[110] *Collected Letters of C. S. Lewis*, I, 572f. The date is July 24, 1921.

to Warren, the conversation was important enough to be noted in his diary.

However, Lewis elsewhere indicates that Berkeley once swept away his materialism in about half an hour, moving him temporarily into Idealism, even though he returned to materialism a week later.[111] While we have no record of Lewis reading Berkeley during these two years, he was reading philosophy as part of Greats, which began in April or May of 1920 and concluded in June 1922. He must have read Berkeley during this time, and his comments in "Early Prose Joy" suggest that he did so during his first year reading philosophy.[112] At this time his materialism was apparently still strong enough to dismiss Berkeley's God as simply another interfering self who threatened his autonomy.

But little movement happened for Lewis in either of these years, leaving the four chess moves and events surrounding them still in his future. The early 1920s appear to be the time that Lewis wrote the poem entitled "The Carpet Rises in the Draught." This poem describes the Lewis home, Little Lea, as an empty house with empty rooms and empty beds. It is a gloomy place, lacking beauty, especially after the death of Lewis's mother, Flora, in 1908, but now also in light of the conflict Lewis often had with his father while home in Belfast, leading him to prefer the company of Mrs. Moore—the mother of one of his friends—to that of his father. Lewis found sunless light and cold at Little Lea, reminding the reader of the loneliness and friendlessness of Lewis's youth.

1922: Greats and the Retreat from Realism

On April 1, 1922, as twenty-three-year-old Lewis neared the completion of his first undergraduate degree, he began once again to keep a rather regular diary. As a next step, he was contemplating another degree in English, or, perhaps, a doctorate in philosophy. He was very clear that Christianity was not going to be part of that future.

---

[111] Lewis, "Early Prose Joy," 30.
[112] Lewis, "Early Prose Joy," 30f.

Later that month, Lewis wrote that he had been persuaded somehow to attend Highfield Church with Mrs. Moore's daughter Maureen because it was Easter Sunday.[113] His reaction to the priest, the Rev. Alfred George Clarke, mixed both positive and negative comments. He was not pleased to attend a worship service, but Maureen had enough influence with him to convince him to attend worship on one of the high holy days of the Christian church.[114]

However, the implications of his position were causing him some anxiety. One month after he started his diary, Lewis wrote that Owen Barfield was feeling miserable and explained that Barfield did not believe in life after death and therefore was living with the finality of his existence.[115] Lewis was feeling the hopelessness of a purely materialistic position, which has no expectation for life beyond the grave, but he at least felt comfortable writing about it. The honesty and openness of his positions cannot be doubted, for a more secretive man would have kept such pessimism inside himself.

Shortly thereafter, Lewis read Bernard Bosanquet's *The Philosophical Theory of the State*, undoubtedly in preparation for his exams in June. Bosanquet (1848–1923) was a follower of the German Idealist philosopher George W. F. Hegel. Bosanquet's views on religion were focused on this world, and he had wondered whether the Bible could be trusted to say anything meaningful or to relay accurate portrayals of actual events. While he saw the value of religion, he minimized the supernatural. At the same time, Bosanquet did not consider himself an

---

[113] Lewis, *All My Road Before Me*, 21, on April 16. The church, named All Saints' Church, is located on Lime Walk, less than a mile to the west of Holy Trinity, which later became the home church of the Lewis brothers.

[114] On January 13, 1923, less than a year later, Maureen entered the picture once again. Lewis described in his diary Maureen's coming first communion as "the uncomfortable sacrament" (*All My Road Before Me*, 179). He also compared it to being forced to see a pig killed (*The Lewis Papers* 7:300). The church and its teachings were not part of his plans at this point in his life.

[115] Lewis, *All My Road Before Me*, 40, on May 24.

atheist or an agnostic. He thought of religion as reasonable, something that any rational person would adopt.[116]

In *The Philosophical Theory of the State*, Bosanquet also draws on his teacher T. H. Green, another a British Idealist, who asked how to maintain the common good, but he viewed the individual as mere cells in the society with the State having paramount importance. He held that universal ideas are not merely the result of our experiences. Everything is pervaded by mind. Bosanquet's book describes the relationship between society and the state, both of which should aim at the well-being of all their citizens while limiting their interference with those same citizens.[117] Bosanquet seems to have influenced Lewis in his understanding of relationships among people and between people and society as a whole. Lewis mentioned Bosanquet later in his book *The Four Loves*, which describes the characteristics of four Greek words for love.[118]

On June 3, while in the Oxford Union, Lewis read a copy of Sigmund Freud's *Introductory Lectures*. Freud was an important part of the New Look in Oxford in the 1920s, especially his idea that wishful thinking, which for him included religious thinking, should be discarded by all serious-minded people, and Lewis needed to know about Freud's ideas for his exams. He mentioned Freud in his early letters only once, in a neutral sense, in a letter to his brother Warren.[119] In his diary, Lewis mentioned Freud only three times, all in the same year: May 26, June 3, and June 4, 1922. This suggests that he rejected many of Freud's theories rather soon after reading about them, especially in view of the fact that his conversation with Doc Askins and Mrs. Stevenson on May 26 included a condemnation of Freud.[120] If

---

[116] The date was May 26, 1922. On Bosanquet, see plato.stanford.edu/entries/bosanquet, "Bernard Bosanquet," 3.3 Religion.

[117] www.brlsi.org/events-proceedings/proceedings/25060.

[118] Lewis mentioned Bosanquet in the chapter on affection, the first of the four loves (*The Four Loves* [New York: Harcourt Brace & Company, 1988], 52).

[119] The date is July 9, 1927 (*Collected Letters of C. S. Lewis*, I, 707).

[120] Lewis did not reject everything that Freud taught. In fact, he wrote that we are indebted to the Freudians for teaching us about the cowardly evasion of useful

Lewis ever adopted the Freudian part of the New Look, he set it aside shortly thereafter. Strangely, the atheist Freud seems to have influenced Lewis very little either with his atheism or with his psychological theories, except for his understanding of the unconscious.[121]

On June 8–14, Lewis sat for six days of Exams in Greats, excluding Sunday, writing six hours each day for these exams in philosophy and ancient history.[122] Just a few months later he began his study of English literature. During the next twelve to eighteen months, he began to see some of the flaws in the philosophy of Realism. Today formal Realism commonly refers to the view that a reality exists independent of the mind, which is a view that even most theists hold, but Lewis used it to refer to materialism, that is, a reality that consists only of physical material and which excludes non-physical substances such as souls, angels, and God.

In *Surprised by Joy* Lewis talks about finishing Greats in 1922, but he does so *after* describing a retreat from Realism toward Idealism.[123] While the chronology is uncertain, i.e., whether the retreat from

---

self-knowledge (*Letters to Malcolm: Chiefly on Prayer* [London: HarperCollins, 1977], 34).

[121] Barkman, *C. S. Lewis & Philosophy as a Way of Life*, 278, n. 47, which cites *Letters to Malcolm*, 79. See *A Grief Observed* (New York: HarperSanFrancisco, 1961), 76. However, see *Mere Christianity*, 88f., where Lewis is comfortable with Freud when Freud is writing about his specialty, i.e., psychoanalysis.

[122] *Collected Letters of C. S. Lewis*, I, 593.

[123] Lewis, *Surprised by Joy*, 212. In *C. S. Lewis & Philosophy as a Way of Life*, Barkman goes into more detail than Lewis himself does, describing Lewis as holding Lucretian Materialism between 1912 (or even earlier) and 1917 (23ff.), then Pseudo-Manichean Dualism between 1917 and 1919 (30ff.), then Stoical Materialism from 1919 to 1924 (35), Absolute Idealism from 1924 to 1925 (42), Subjective Idealism between 1925 and 1926 (47), then back to Absolute Idealism in 1926 until 1928 (47), and finally Subjective Idealism again from 1928 until his conversion to theism in 1930 (49). Although a generalization, Lewis's materialist phase lasted from 1912 until 1924 and fits more consistently with his atheism. His Idealist phase, then, ran from 1924 until his adoption of theism in 1930 and is more akin to agnosticism than atheism. The reader who wishes to pursue the nature and extent of those stages is referred to *C. S. Lewis & Philosophy as a Way of Life*.

Realism began before or after Greats, Lewis's growing attraction to Idealism is certain. Idealism, which states that matter is in some sense unreal, that everything we know is in the mind of the knower and, therefore, mental, was a prominent philosophy held by many in the teens and 1920s.[124]

On June 11, during the time he was taking exams for Greats, Lewis rose late that Sunday morning, took a bike ride into Oxford, then walked through Christ Church and to the top of a hill where he sat down in the woods to enjoy the beauty of nature. He viewed the landscape in the direction of Wytham, i.e., north from Christ Church, calling it almost a polished brightness. He later stated in his diary that he got "a whiff of the real joy," but it was only momentary.[125] At this time he was still attempting to live as a consistent materialist. The Joy that had been planted and nurtured years earlier made a sudden and unexpected appearance,[126] possibly while he was reading something in one of the exams or while reading William James. That same day, after reading the classic psychological study of conversion,[127] William James's *Varieties of Religious Experience*, for most of the afternoon, Lewis wrote about Doc Askins, the brother of Mrs. Moore: "The more I read the more I see that the sayings of the Doc and his like are simply taken from a tradition which is as much a ready-made orthodoxy to them as the Bible and Prayer Book are to old-fashioned people."[128] He later described William James's chapter on mysticism as the most interesting,[129] and it caused him to look within himself for what he

---

[124] C. E. M. Joad, *Great Philosophies of the World* (London: Thomas Nelson, 1937), 75f. called Idealism "perhaps the most important movement in the history of philosophy."

[125] Lewis, *All My Road Before Me*, 48.

[126] This may be the event that Lewis wrote about in "Early Prose Joy," 26, when, apparently in 1922, the old longing came back on him in full force.

[127] So states Lewis R. Rambo, *Understanding Religious Conversion* (New Haven: Yale University Press, 1993), 9.

[128] Lewis, *All My Road Before Me*, 48.

[129] Lewis, *All My Road Before Me*, 50.

desired.[130] Mysticism later helped him move to belief in God, and this whiff of real joy was to some extent a mystical experience.[131] Lewis may have appreciated James's understanding of mysticism as something that "defies expression, that no adequate report of its contents can be given in words."[132] Reason alone cannot create faith. Whatever it was, this whiff encouraged his move away from Realism toward a less materialistic creed.

In "Early Prose Joy," Lewis describes William James's book as one that encouraged him to think that he was looking for an internal state of mind, an imaginative thrill,[133] rather than something outside himself. But as he was thinking about what he was then experiencing, the experience of Joy disappeared. He couldn't understand why the feeling disappeared.

Just one week after his exams in Greats, Lewis woke up in a state of depression, something he had been experiencing with regularity this year. He found himself in a quandary, his search for Joy seemingly fruitless and his materialism ending in nothingness. Later that morning, he read David Hume's *Enquiry Concerning the Principles of Morals*, which, he wrote, contained nearly all of Lewis's own fallacies in ethics,[134] itself a rather depressing thought. He found it easier to see his own mistakes in the writings of someone else. One of those fallacies was to derive morals from feelings and, on the other hand, to derive facts from reason and intellect. Facts have the same meaning for all, Hume thought, while feelings are private and individual. Facts, therefore, have strong validity, while feelings are merely personal and arbitrary, two faulty positions still held by many people today. The truth is that people sometimes make up their own facts and some emotions are completely valid and universal.

---

[130] Lewis, "Early Prose Joy," 25.
[131] So writes Alan Griffiths, "The Adventure of Faith," in Como, *C. S. Lewis at the Breakfast Table*, 22.
[132] William James, *The Varieties of Religious Experience* (Cambridge, MA: Harvard University Press), 301f.
[133] Lewis, *Surprised by Joy*, 168.
[134] Lewis, *All My Road Before Me*, 51, June 18.

Another point with which Lewis may have disagreed is Hume's contention that all knowledge is derived from experience. Correspondingly, Hume denied the possibility of knowledge beyond the senses, which would include the denial of the possibility of knowing God. His philosophy advocated that which promotes the general welfare for the entire community, although Hume recognized that welfare involves more than happiness.

After his exams in Greats and while attending a meeting of the literary society known as the Martlets, Lewis heard that an examiner had said that Lewis always disagreed with Plato.[135] Lewis seems to have opposed the ideas of Plato at this time,[136] though it was probably only a rejection of a more simplified version of Idealism. Plato believed in the existence of universal ideas, which must exist before we actually experience them, a position opposite that held by Hume. Plato also believed people have an innate desire for the Good, the True, and the Beautiful, but they mistake copies of these ideas for the real thing.[137] This sounded too much like a position that allowed for God, so Lewis rejected it. He later wrote that Christianity came from the genius of the Hebrew prophets and that it had met Neo-Platonism at the right time. If Neo-Platonism is part of the origin of Christianity, Lewis probably thought at this time, then it must be wrong.[138]

Later that summer, Lewis read part of British philosopher F. H. Bradley's *Appearance and Reality*, in which Bradley argued that reality lies behind the appearance of things, and the appearance of things is

---

[135] *Collected Letters of C. S. Lewis*, I, 594.

[136] Lewis, *All My Road Before Me*, 53. According to Adam Barkman, Lewis was a Kantian at this time (*C. S. Lewis & Philosophy as a Way of Life*, 327).

[137] Adam Barkman, "Rudolf Otto, *The Idea of the Holy*," in *C. S. Lewis's List: The Ten Books That Influenced Him Most*, 116f. The ten books: Chesterton's *The Everlasting Man*, Rudolf Otto's *The Idea of the Holy*, Arthur Balfour's *Theism and Humanism*, George MacDonald's *Phantastes*, James Boswell's *Life of Samuel Johnson*, Boethius's *The Consolation of Philosophy*, William Wordsworth's *The Prelude*, George Herbert's *The Temple*, Virgil's *The Aeneid*, and Charles Williams's *Descent into Hell*.

[138] Lewis, "Early Prose Joy," 35.

only appearance. Behind appearance also lies the Absolute, but our minds cannot fully comprehend the Absolute. If the Absolute is another name for God, that means that God is not accessible. Then, a few weeks later, Lewis read more of Bradley. Bradley's book *Logic*, he wrote, gave the death blow to Realism, moving Lewis even closer to Idealism.[139] Lewis was reading Bradley and other philosophers while he was preparing to take the course in English. He probably still thought that his future would lie in philosophy, but that English was another viable option. As Lewis states in his autobiography, "Realism had been abandoned; the New Look was somewhat damaged; and chronological snobbery was seriously shaken."[140]

On September 3, Lewis read two tales of Leo Tolstoy, "Where God Is, There Is Love"[141] and "The Godson."[142] He was—at the time—

---

[139] He states that he eventually became "a transcendental idealist of the orthodox 'absolutist' school" ("Early Prose Joy," 31). Lewis read Bradley on July 23 and then again August 9, 1922. By the "absolutist" school, or "Absolute idealism," Hegel distinguished his theory both from the "subjective" idealism of Berkeley and Hume and the "transcendental" idealism of Kant. Like Kant, and against the subjective idealists, Hegel insisted that individual human selves are also just an "appearance," no more real than the material world. Against Kant, Hegel insisted that we can know there is a Universal Self behind the appearances of scientific data.

[140] Lewis, *Surprised by Joy*, 216.

[141] A delightful story about a shoemaker who wants to meet Christ and does so in the form of a man shoveling snow, a woman with a child, and a woman selling apples, all of whom he befriends, a Russian version of the story in Matthew 25:35, 40.

[142] A story based on Matthew 5:38–39, "An eye for an eye," and Romans 12:19, "Vengeance is mine, I will repay." The story is about a peasant who has a son and seeks a godfather and a godmother for his child. A stranger volunteered to be the godfather and sent the peasant to the next village to find a godmother. Both attended the child's baptism. At age 10, the boy gave his godmother Easter greetings, but the family had not seen the godfather since the boy's baptism, so he set out to find his godfather. He found his godfather and gave him Easter greetings. His godfather invited him to his home the next day on the other side of a forest where he lived in a palace with a golden roof. He lived there for thirty years, forbidden to open the door to a sealed room. One day he opened the door and saw a throne and sat on it. He caused much trouble and was sent to atone for

impressed by neither of them. Tolstoy was a Christian, albeit of a very heterodox type, so this reaction suggests that Lewis was far from the Christian faith at this time. At the same time, he was not averse to reading works by great authors whose worldview he rejected. On October 2, we find more evidence of the same non-Christian perspective. Lewis wrote in his diary that a modern poem about the Ultimate should not be about good and evil, as in *Paradise Lost*, but should have what Hegel calls dialectic, i.e., give and take; statement and compromise.[143] This explains Lewis's favorable impression of Bosanquet, who was a follower of Hegel, and his dismissal of basic biblical themes in *Paradise Lost*, such as sin, grace, and redemption.

Four days later in his correspondence, Lewis stated that a person gets very little definite teaching in the Gospels. This comment reflects a higher critical, or liberal, stance, similar to what Bosanquet held, and doubts about the historical reliability of the Gospels, including both the teachings of Jesus and the accounts of his death and resurrection. If you do not have to take the Gospels in their normal and natural meaning, then you do not have to take them seriously. Those views are summed up in the person of Mr. Enlightenment, whom John meets in *The Pilgrim's Regress* and who represents the scientific viewpoint,[144] and in the views of Mr. Broad, who represents a liberal church perspective.[145] That liberal stance had been expressed a few years earlier, when Lewis wrote to his father about all of the additions that the followers of Jesus had allegedly added to the Gospels since the first century.[146] This was undoubtedly one of the obstacles he had to face

---

his evil. He then went about doing good, eventually atoning for his sins with good and sharing what he had learned with others.

[143] Or what Hegel called thesis, antithesis, and synthesis.

[144] Lewis, *The Pilgrim's Regress*, 20.

[145] Lewis, *The Pilgrim's Regress*, 112f.

[146] *Collected Letters of C. S. Lewis*, I, 242. The letter is dated October 27, 1916. In 1922, therefore, Lewis seems to have held the position that he later rejected in his essay "Fern-seed and Elephants." In that essay, Lewis argued that (1) Biblical critics lack literary judgment (they read between the lines of ancient texts, not understanding extra-biblical literary genres, e.g., reading John's Gospel as a

during the next few years, namely the attitude that the Bible cannot be relied upon to convey accurate historical truth. Without a historically reliable Bible, the events it recounts cannot have happened in the way described, and we have little or nothing to believe.

Besides the depression Lewis was experiencing, his negative outlook on life appeared in a variety of ways during these days. Just as the Michaelmas term was beginning, his friend Jenkin commented that natural beauty affected him as the suggested background of a happiness that was not there, probably an idea consistent with the conversation he was having with Lewis at the time. Jenkin's idea also expressed the position that Lewis would later adopt, namely that nature was a pointer to something outside our experience.[147]

In October, Lewis began his course of studies in English language and literature. At some point during the fall term, he read Boethius, most probably his *Consolation of Philosophy*.[148] He learned from Boethius one of the classic expositions of the teaching that the miseries we face in this world are compatible with its creation and guidance by some sort of a completely good Being,[149] that nothing in this world can truly satisfy, and that all of these experiences, even the negative ones, point us to the Eternal.[150] Boethius included the best of the pagan

---

romance); (2) Some claim that the real teaching of Christ came rapidly to be misunderstood and has been recovered only by modern scholars; (3) Some claim that miracles do not occur; and (4) Attempts to recover the genesis of a text often err (as on Plato or Shakespeare).

[147] See, for example, C. S. Lewis, *Reflections on the Psalms* (New York: Harcourt Brace Jovanovich, 1958), 81. On nature and art as pointers, see *Collected Letters of C. S. Lewis: Volume III, Narnia, Cambridge, and Joy 1950–1963*, edited by Walter Hooper (London: HarperCollins, 2006), 583f.

[148] Lewis states that as he began his English studies, which started in 1922, he read Boethius and others because of their influence on English literature. See Lewis, "On the Reading of Old Books," *God in the Dock*, 203. His first reference to Boethius occurs in his diary on November 9, 1922.

[149] Lewis, "God and Evil," *God in the Dock*, 22.

[150] C. S. Lewis, "Helen M. Barrett, *Boethius: Some Aspects of his Times and Work*," in *Image and Imagination* (Cambridge: Cambridge University Press, 2013), 206.

philosophers in his writings, especially Plato and Aristotle,[151] something that must have influenced Lewis to consider setting aside his anti-Plato thinking. Since Lewis later listed Boethius's *Consolation* as one of the ten most influential books on his vocational attitude and philosophy of life, he must have absorbed these ideas from Boethius, whether consciously or subconsciously.

He probably did so subconsciously, since the first page of *The Pilgrim's Regress* contains quotations from Boethius and Plato, stating that the road home is not always clear, that the object of desire is not always evident, the source of truth not always certain.[152]

For Lewis, the best of the pagan teachers and myth-makers provided a glimpse of the cosmic story, i.e., incarnation, death, and rebirth.[153] In them could be found the magic that was built into the universe before the beginning of time.[154] Lewis's treatment of the pagan philosophers—especially Plato and Aristotle—on their own merits led him to find value in those ideas that foreshadowed, or anticipated, themes that were more fully developed in biblical theology, much as Boethius did.[155]

Then, on November 11, his pessimism reappeared when Lewis talked with Doc Askins about death and the other horrors hanging over a person. A few days later, Lewis wrote in his diary that he had been suffering from the fear of death and that Jenkin felt the same way, which explains the reason for his conversation with the Doc. That afternoon he and Jenkin explored a dark church, a black stream, a graveyard, a half-rotten tree, and a dark wood with dead leaves, all of these images echoing the deathly fear he had at this time.[156] Later in the month he discussed the existence of God with a friend of the

---

[151] Chris Armstrong, "Boethius, *The Consolation of Philosophy*," *C. S. Lewis's List*, 135.

[152] Lewis, *The Pilgrim's Regress*, 1.

[153] Lewis, "Is Theology Poetry?" *The Weight of Glory and Other Addresses*, 98.

[154] C. S. Lewis, *The Lion, the Witch and the Wardrobe* (New York: Macmillan, 1950), 159f.

[155] Armstrong, "Boethius, *The Consolation of Philosophy*," 144.

[156] Lewis, *All My Road Before Me*, 141.

family.[157] These three conversations—with Jenkin, Doc Askins, and a friend—indicate the uneasiness that Lewis was feeling at this time about death and what might lie beyond. In fact, Lewis had several conversations with Jenkin on similar topics during the autumn.[158]

Some six weeks later, this uneasiness seems to have been expressed in another way. On Christmas Day, at home in Belfast with his father and brother, after morning communion and an unpleasant early Christmas dinner, while reading Matthew Arnold's *Empedocles on Etna, and Other Poems* that evening, Lewis recognized Empedocles's first lyric speech to Pausanias as an expression of what he could call his own philosophy of uncertainty, probably in these words of Empedocles: "The Gods laugh in their sleeve/To watch man doubt and fear,/Who knows not what to believe/Since he sees nothing clear,/And dares stamp nothing false where he finds nothing sure."[159] Lewis's materialism had brought relief from the interference of God, but it also brought hopelessness and confusion along with it, his mind crumbling into a flabby, sensual, and unambitious state.[160] The relief had arrived instantly, but despair came along shortly thereafter.

Lewis also had other matters to consider. He had started his course of English study on October 12, meeting with his English tutor, F. P. Wilson, whom he described as fat and youngish, on October 13, for the first time. Because of his previous wide reading in English literature, he was able to complete in nine months a program that normally takes three years. He took his English literature exams on June 14–19, 1923, earning First Class Honors for the third time in his undergraduate career. English literature became his life's work in the decades ahead.

---

[157] The friend is Mrs. Stevenson, and the date is November 30, 1922. See *The Lewis Papers* 7:286.

[158] See also the entries for November 21 and December 4, 1922, as well as those for December 4 and 5 with George Fasnacht in Joel D. Heck, "Chronologically Lewis."

[159] Lewis, *All My Road Before Me*, 159.

[160] Lewis, *All My Road Before Me*, 159.

For Lewis the year 1922 had been a year of struggling with his atheism, beginning to set aside Realism and being drawn toward Idealism. Two other events in November and December probably prepared Lewis for an even more unsettling year in 1923, and that was the reading of two of Dean William Inge's essays and later one of his books, *Outspoken Essays*, the latter during his Christmas holiday at Little Lea in Belfast. Inge (1860–1954) was an Anglican priest, graduate of King's College, Cambridge, who became Dean of St. Paul's Cathedral in London.

The first essay, which dealt with eugenics, impressed him a great deal, probably leading him to try more of Inge. Inge was in favor of eugenics, particularly in regard to the breeding of offspring, a position he later found countered by Chesterton. Later that month he read Inge's essay "Confessio Fidei,"[161] which argued that our consciousness of time suggests something non-temporal in people. This article caused him to think of the implications of this idea, namely that people are designed to live even after death. The entire collection of essays especially focused on two topics: social science and the state of religion. Inge was a student of Christian mysticism, author of two books—*Christian Mysticism*, and *Outspoken Essays*. The chapter in *Christian Mysticism* on mysticism concluded that "the aberrations or exaggerations of institutionalism have been, and are, more dangerous, and further removed from the spirit of Christianity than those of mysticism, and that we must look to the latter type, rather than to the former, to give life to the next religious revival."[162] Lewis's negative experiences with the institutional church, he no doubt concluded, were largely aberrations that should not rule out the validity of all religious experience. Having read William James's *Varieties of Religious Experience*, especially its description of a mystical experience, earlier this year, Lewis seems to have opened the door to more

---

[161] He read the first essay November 25, 1922, and the second one on the 28th.
[162] Dean William Inge, "Institutionalism and Mysticism," *Outspoken Essays* (London: Longmans, Green, and Co., 1919), online edition, citing the last line of this chapter.

of the same in Inge. He was coming to the awareness that religious experience was more than the sum total of creedal statements and doctrinal formulations.

CHAPTER 4

TWO BISHOPS

"All the books were beginning to turn against me."

—C. S. Lewis, *Surprised by Joy*

As the year 1923 began, Lewis fought to maintain his materialistic position. The tide began to turn even more so when some of his friends made him think again, and some of his readings—Bergson, Euripides, Samuel Alexander, Balfour, Bosanquet, Nietzsche—surfaced other concerns that he had previously suppressed. This chapter focuses on 1923 and 1924, including the loss of Lewis's two bishops in 1924, along with some of the other events leading up to and following those two moves.

In chess, bishops are often considered the most important pieces apart from the King and Queen, largely for their ability to move diagonally the entire length of the board. To lose both bishops is to experience a serious setback in the game, and Lewis described such losses in "Checkmate," the fourteenth and penultimate chapter of *Surprised by Joy*.

1923: SOMETHING ELSE

In early January, Lewis returned to James Frazer's *The Golden Bough* in the new abridged edition, apparently with a good deal of sympathy.[1] He had previously read Frazer during his years with Kirkpatrick, finding Frazer's explanation of Christianity as one of many mythologies convincing. Exactly one week after reading Frazer, Lewis began to reread George MacDonald's *Phantastes* at tea, returning to the book that had started him on his spiritual journey. He stated that the book tuned him to a higher pitch.[2] He did not return to it because of MacDonald's Christianity, since that creed is not apparent in the book. He returned to it because it stirred Joy within him, that is, because of its fantasy and its imaginative power.

Late in the month, Lewis wrote that he walked Owen Barfield back to Wadham College and that Barfield "said that when one had accepted the materialist's universe one went on and on to a point and suddenly exclaimed 'Why should *my* facts be the only facts that don't count?': then came the revulsion and you took a more spiritual view till that too worked itself to its reaction and flung you back to materialism."[3] That Barfield stated this and Lewis wrote it is an indication that it reflects Lewis's point of view at this time, i.e., *both* his materialism *and* his uncertainty about his materialism. It also reflects the change that took place in Barfield's own thinking during early 1923, since this is the period when he left materialism behind and adopted Anthroposophy, an essentially spiritual outlook on life.

As Barfield influenced Lewis on the philosophical side, another new friend influenced him on the literary side. Lewis first met Nevill Coghill, a fellow undergraduate also studying English, on February 2, 1923, in George Gordon's English literature discussion class, and they instantly became friends. Coghill was "a Christian and a thoroughgoing supernaturalist," and a very intelligent and well read one.[4] Lewis invited Coghill to dinner the very next week. At the discussion class where they met, Coghill, an undergraduate from Exeter College, presented a paper on Realism, presumably a paper that challenged the

---

[1] Lewis, *All My Road Before Me*, 170. On January 4.
[2] Lewis, *All My Road Before Me*, 177.
[3] Lewis, *All My Road Before Me*, 186. On January 26.
[4] Lewis, *Surprised by Joy*, 212.

materialism of the Realist position of the day since Lewis opposed Coghill's conclusions.[5] Most Christian theists are Realists today, and Coghill probably held that there is a real world that exists independent of us and that this is a truth held by all Christians.[6] Coghill's supernaturalism surprised Lewis, because he did not expect Christians to be intelligent and well read. But this meeting motivated him to take another look at both Coghill's Christianity and his own atheism. Coghill had taught him that Christians could be both intelligent and Christian at the same time. Shortly after telling the story of meeting Coghill, Lewis wrote, "All the books were beginning to turn against me."[7] For Lewis, the "rock-bottom reality"[8] of the senses was his Realist position. Though he saw flaws in Realism, he had not yet abandoned it. At the same time, he realized that Realism provided no basis for considering aesthetics and moral values to be objectively true.[9] If they are private opinions, why should my opinions be more valid than anyone else's? And if they are universally true, then what is the source of such universal truth?

The very next day, a beautiful spring morning, while taking a walk up Shotover and into Wheatley, Lewis wrote in his diary that he experienced the real joy again.[10] His use of the word *again* in the diary implies that this had been happening to him with some regularity, which means that nature, not the recent conversation with Coghill, caused the experience of joy. He had been having similar experiences of the beauty of nature in recent weeks. A very similar occurrence took

---

[5] Lewis, *All My Road Before Me*, 189.
[6] I am indebted to Angus J. L. Menuge, who read parts of this manuscript and made suggestions, for this insight.
[7] Lewis, *Surprised by Joy*, 213.
[8] Lewis, *Surprised by Joy*, 208.
[9] McGrath, *The Intellectual World of C. S. Lewis*, 8.
[10] *The Lewis Papers* 8:51. His entry for February 3, 1923 appears in *The Lewis Papers*, but not in *All My Road Before Me*.

place four months later,[11] and again two days after this experience, suggesting that these stabs of joy continued to happen.[12]

During three weeks in late February and early March,[13] the brother of Mrs. Moore, Dr. John H. Askins, who had developed an intense interest in the occult, experienced a breakdown and thought that he was going mad. Dr. Askins was visiting his sister in Oxford, and he had panic attacks at different times of the day and night, causing Lewis to lose a great deal of sleep, making it nearly impossible to continue his studies, and resulting in the frequent restraining and sedation of Askins. On April 6, Doc Askins died of heart failure, an event that profoundly demonstrated the frail and faulty universe in which he lived. Years later Lewis cited the Doc's madness as one reason for "a retreat, almost a panic-stricken flight, from all that sort of romanticism which had hitherto been the chief concern of my life."[14] This created a dilemma for Lewis, since such an experience motivated him to move away from the spiritual while his reading was moving him away from materialism and toward the spiritual.

Books were beginning to turn against him because this is the year that Lewis was reading Chesterton, MacDonald, Johnson, Spenser, Malory, and Milton, and he was finding that their views made great sense to him, except for their Christianity.[15] He was learning that, like Coghill, these authors were both intelligent and Christian. He was also reading the anonymous Christian poem The Dream of the Rood, William Langland, John Donne, Thomas Browne, and George Herbert.[16] The authors whom he should have liked for their atheism— George Bernard Shaw, H. G. Wells, John Stuart Mill, and Edward

---

[11] The date is June 22, 1923. See The Lewis Papers 8:128.
[12] The date is Sunday, June 24, 1923. See The Lewis Papers 8:129.
[13] February 21–March 12, 1923.
[14] Lewis, Surprised by Joy, 201.
[15] Lewis, Surprised by Joy, 213.
[16] See also Collected Letters of C. S. Lewis, III, 978, a letter dated October 13, 1958, for mention of various Christian authors who influenced Lewis during the years before he became a Christian. He states that Christianity reached him at first almost entirely through the great works of these authors.

Gibbon—he thought thin. This did not motivate him to look more closely at Christianity, at least not at this time, but it did lead him to question the philosophy of Realism.[17] The following two paragraphs explain some of the reasons why.

In early April, Lewis and his brother Warren visited Salisbury and had supper there. After supper, Lewis was struck by the remarkable simplicity and consistent Gothic architecture of Salisbury Cathedral in the moonlight.[18] Approximately five days later, Lewis wrote to his father about "all these mysterious leaks through of Something Else into our experience." And yet he also wrote in the same paragraph, "Whatever else the human race was made for, it at least was not made to know."[19] He thought there was Something Else but that we could not know that Something Else. This probably reflects the influence of Bosanquet, Hegel, and other writers, but it certainly reflects the Idealism of F. H. Bradley, namely his view that the Absolute cannot be comprehended.

In the years 1922 and 1923, Lewis gradually became uncertain of his own materialism. One of the many reasons was that his close friends Owen Barfield and A. C. Harwood moved from materialism to Anthroposophy in mid-1923,[20] a philosophy that held to spiritual realities beyond the senses. Anthroposophy was developed primarily by Rudolf Steiner (1861–1925) at the end of the 19th and the beginning of the 20th century. Steiner—an Austrian philosopher who founded the Anthroposophical Society in 1913—believed that his "spiritual science" could give a person knowledge of "supersensible

---

[17] Lewis, *Surprised by Joy*, 215.

[18] *Collected Letters of C. S. Lewis*, I, I, 639.

[19] *Collected Letters of C. S. Lewis*, I, I, 640.

[20] The July 7, 1923, entry in Lewis's diary says Harwood had spoken of "his new philosopher, Rudolf Steiner," who had made the burden roll off his back and given a promise of immortality. Obviously, then, Harwood's adoption of Anthroposophy had just recently occurred. In an email on December 24, 2014, Walter Hooper told me that Barfield adopted Anthroposophy weeks or months before Harwood did. Therefore, Harwood probably adopted Anthroposophy shortly before July 7, 1923, and Barfield prior to that. See *All My Road Before Me*, 254.

realities," i.e., truth about real and factual things that exist outside of our physical experience, truth that was "reproducible, reliable, and useful."[21] Anthroposophy attempts to answer deep spiritual questions and holds to a spiritual world that is directly accessible to experience through the development of imagination and intuition.[22] Lewis thought that if his two close friends saw meaning in the spiritual realm, then perhaps there was something to it.

As stated earlier, Harwood probably adopted Anthroposophy shortly before July 7, 1923, and Barfield a few weeks or months prior to that. While not Christians, both Barfield[23] and Harwood now believed in a supernatural world. Because of this new position, Barfield offered Lewis an understanding of knowledge that was much closer to Idealism than Realism, and it is no coincidence that the first half of 1923 found Lewis continuing to move slowly away from Realism, vacillating between Realism and Idealism.[24] He had earlier described the reading of Bradley's *The Principles of Logic* as dealing a death blow to Realism, probably during the second half of 1922.[25] Early 1923, then, is probably the time about which Lewis stated that he was compelled to give up Realism.[26] Realism had satisfied an emotional need for nature to be self-existent and independent, i.e., independent of God, leaving him with the ability to maintain his own independence, and it had provided a foundation for the materialism he had adopted earlier.[27] But now he began to see that his ideas about the validity of thinking were not characteristic of Realism, which offered an explanation of life through chance, natural selection, and vast amounts of time, unable to explain how a valid idea could come from mere biology. One also can't derive "what ought to be" from "what is."

---

[21] Thorson, *Joy and Poetic Imagination*, 3.
[22] www.waldorfanswers.org/Anthroposophy.htm
[23] However, Barfield was later baptized in 1949.
[24] See McGrath, *Intellectual World*, 38f.; Lewis, *Surprised by Joy*, 208.
[25] Lewis, "Early Prose Joy," 31.
[26] Lewis, *Surprised by Joy*, 209.
[27] Lewis, *Surprised by Joy*, 209.

In fact, at this time many of his ideas were characteristic of both theism and Idealism, even though he did not admit it.

This year also marked the beginning of the "Great War" between Lewis and Barfield, a war of words in which each side would score several victories, with the bulk of them going to Barfield.[28] Barfield later described the Great War as a disagreement over "whether imagination is a vehicle for truth or whether it is simply a highly desirable and pleasurable experience of the human soul."[29]

During the recent attempts to help Doc Askins, Lewis, Mrs. Moore, and her other brother Rob Askins had tried to find him medical help at a hospital in Henley. In his attempts to talk sense with Doc Askins, who was convinced he was going to hell, Lewis had recently denied the existence of hell,[30] and now Barfield and Harwood were giving him reason to think that there might be such a place, as well as a heaven, a God, and all sorts of other spiritual realities. But he resisted their arguments. In July, Lewis and Harwood went for a morning swim at Parson's Pleasure where they lay on the grass between swims and talked about Harwood's new allegiance to Rudolf Steiner. Lewis recorded in his diary a conversation with Harwood about Steiner's Anthroposophy, thinking that immortality was the bait that Harwood had swallowed, the empty promise that attracted him. In reply to Harwood, Lewis argued that the spiritual forces which Rudolf Steiner, the founder of Anthroposophy, found were either mythological *people* or else no-one-knows-what.[31]

Shortly thereafter, a two-week visit from Arthur Greeves resulted in still more debate. In July, Arthur came to see Lewis in Oxford. During that visit Lewis argued with Arthur about immortality.[32] Lewis denied immortality and Arthur affirmed it. Lewis was also in regular

---

[28] Lewis, *Surprised by Joy*, 207. The first clear reference to the Great War is a conversation between Lewis and Barfield on January 26, 1923.

[29] *Owen Barfield on C. S. Lewis*, 138.

[30] On March 10, 1923, Lewis told Doc Askins, the brother of Mrs. Moore, that "there was no such place as Hell" (Lewis, *All My Road Before Me*, 217).

[31] Lewis, *All My Road Before Me*, 254, July 7, 1923.

[32] Lewis, *All My Road Before Me*, 258.

conversation at this time with the atheist priest Macran, the man who wanted to be immortal but avoided whatever might help him to realize immortality. These arguments with Barfield, Harwood, and Greeves, and probably also Coghill, show this to be a very contentious period in Lewis's life, a time when his atheistic point of view was being challenged and he was fighting back.

While some forces seemed to be moving Lewis away from materialism, other forces seemed to draw him toward romance, which was for him an other-worldly experience. For example, one day that summer Lewis awakened with a headache and tired, tried to write some of *Dymer* and failed, then tried in vain to read Wordsworth, but was able to read some German romance, specifically, the next story in *Rübezahl*. He liked the language of fairy tales, thinking that it smelled good.[33] Although he still believed this world was all there is, he was strongly drawn to stories about other worlds.

According to Lewis himself, Barfield destroyed Lewis's chronological snobbery and, as a result, he forever understood that later is not always better, that newer is not always truer, that more recent is not necessarily more decent, that one must decide the truth of a matter on the basis of its merits rather than on the basis of fashion or as a consequence of the passage of time or an idea going out of style. Old books, and many of their assumptions, ought not to be dismissed without good reasons. Sometimes that which is earlier is better, because it is true.

As already indicated, after Barfield's conversion to Anthroposophy, what Lewis called the Great War (undoubtedly an intentional echo of the term commonly used for World War I) between Lewis and Barfield began, but it escalated in 1927 and 1928.[34] Lewis wrote of that

---

[33] The exact date is July 3 (Lewis, *All My Road Before Me*, 251). The *Rübezahl* is a playful mountain spirit in German and Czech folklore; he is the Lord of Weather in the mountains.

[34] What Lewis called "the Great War" was his philosophical battle with Barfield, extended over most of a decade, about the nature of truth. The first known reference to the "Great War" is from January 26, 1923, but it may have started earlier than this date since the conversation seems to be continued from previous

Great War that it never became a quarrel. It could have if Barfield had returned Lewis's rather violent language with the same force. Nevertheless, Lewis described it as an unceasing disputation and a turning point in his life.[35] As Lewis grew and matured, he increasingly found his own ideas under attack, not only from writers, but also from his friends, whether Barfield and Harwood or from Coghill and others.

Again, that fall, Lewis began rereading Bergson's *L'Evolution Créatrice*,[36] a book, George Santayana claimed, that pointed to life as simply miraculous. In a book that Lewis read a few months later, Santayana called Bergson's views "myth or fable."[37] Bergson saw some sort of a power behind nature. He also saw naturalism as inadequate to explain nature, holding instead to vitalism, a position designed to explain the energy and obvious purpose in the universe, and Lewis saw strength in that argument.

In September 1923, even while he was considering the purpose Bergson saw in the universe, Lewis was allowing his imagination to open himself up to other ways of thinking. Lewis was considering rewriting the Cupid and Psyche myth in poetic verse, and the poem "On Cupid and Psyche" was the result.[38] In the poem he blamed not Venus's envy, but man's desperation, for the sacrifice of Psyche. Human sacrifice had to be made in order to bring the needed rains to the king's lands, and so Psyche was offered as that sacrifice. But Psyche was rescued by a god. Psyche's twin brother, the prince Jardis, and the much older Caspian figure appear in the rest of this poem. What

---

conversations. Lewis met Barfield in 1919. Lewis himself, however, dates the Great War from Barfield's conversion to Anthroposophy in 1923 (Lewis, *Surprised by Joy*, 207).

[35] Lewis, *Surprised by Joy*, 207.

[36] French: "Creative Evolution."

[37] Lewis read Bergson on September 17. The book that called Bergson's views "myth or fable" is George Santayana, *Winds of Doctrine: Studies in Contemporary Opinion*, 2006 ebook, produced by R. Cedron, Sankar Viswanathan, and the Online Distributed Proofreading Team at www.pgdp.net, 74.

[38] Later in life, Lewis returned to the Cupid and Psyche myth in his book *Till We Have Faces*.

would have followed we cannot know, since Lewis never finished this poem, but it shows his growing appreciation of myth. He had already grown to appreciate Spenser's *The Fairie Queene* and the King Arthur legends of Sir Thomas Malory, but in those cases he simply received and enjoyed the myth; here he was creating myth.

A month later, Lewis began to read Owen Barfield's suggestive fairy tale *The Silver Trumpet* in its pre-publication form.[39] Like his thoughts about the Cupid and Psyche myth, this was undoubtedly a small part of Lewis's turn away from rejecting myth to embracing it, in part because he respected Barfield. Lewis was favorably impressed with the delightful story, which included the king of Mountainy Castle, twin sisters, a wicked queen, a dwarf, a magical trumpet, and two deaths and resurrections. Probably during the month of November, Barfield stayed with Lewis for one night, and Lewis noted that Barfield had completely given up on materialism.[40] That stay must have affected Lewis, since Barfield's change of mind was important enough for Lewis to mention in his diary.

If Lewis's poem "The Nameless Isle" was in fact written in 1930, just two months after Lewis's adoption of theism, that poem may have drawn on this story by Barfield, using a magic flute, instead of a magic trumpet, to transform the characters of the story. Both the flute and the trumpet, then, would represent the power of the Divine to change people's lives. Both of them are wind instruments, so that one's breath creates the sound.[41]

---

[39] Lewis, *All My Road Before Me*, 275. *The Silver Trumpet* was later published by Faber and Gwyer, Ltd. in 1925.

[40] Lewis, *All My Road Before Me*, 278.

[41] The Hebrew and Greek words for breath also mean "wind" or "Spirit," suggesting the activity of the Spirit of God.

1924: EURIPIDES'S *HIPPOLYTUS*

As the year 1924 began, Lewis was studying the writings of Henry More, a seventeenth-century theologian and Cambridge Platonist.[42] He read More's *An Antidote against Atheism*, and he continued reading More for the next month and a half. He also read other works of More, since he was considering writing a dissertation on him. This very consideration of More, coupled with his reading of Bertrand Russell soon thereafter, indicates an openness to reading views on both sides of a topic, since More held that "this Truth of the Existence of God [is] as clearly demonstrable as any Theorem in Mathematicks."[43] Russell held the opposite view.

Two days later, Lewis commented on Bertrand Russell's essay, an atheist manifesto, "The Free Man's Worship." Lewis called it an accurate statement of what he had believed a few years previously, but he also repeated his argument about the validity of reason, stating that the real difficulty is that if our ideals are purely natural products of evolution, no better or worse than other facts, they, too, fail to have any firm validity.[44] Bertrand Russell, a Realist, held a position that contained the same fatal flaw that the popular scientific picture faced, i.e., an inability to explain the development of valid reason from a purely naturalistic and godless worldview. If Lewis held these beliefs some years previously, then he was currently hovering close to Idealism, having rejected Realism, and far more an agnostic than an atheist at this time in his life.

Also at this time, Lewis visited the Oxford Union and brought home Harvard philosophy professor George Santayana's book *Winds of Doctrine: Studies in Contemporary Opinion*. He may have checked out this book because it contains a lengthy response to some of

---

[42] The date is January 2, 1924 (Lewis, *All My Road Before Me*, 280f.). Cited in Alister McGrath, "The 'New Look': Lewis's Philosophical Context at Oxford in the 1920s," Chapter 2 in *The Intellectual World of C. S. Lewis*, 39.

[43] Henry More, *An Antidote against Atheism*, Note to Anne, Viscountess Conway and Kilulta, 1662.

[44] McGrath, "The 'New Look,' " 46.

Bertrand Russell's writings, which he had read earlier, e.g., *A.B.C. of Atoms*, *Philosophical Essays*, and "The Free Man's Worship." Lewis apparently wanted to see what Santayana said about Russell.[45]

Lewis read Santayana's skeptical appraisal of both human reason and the anti-supernatural view of Christianity, especially as found in some forms of Roman Catholic theology. The anti-supernatural view of Christianity is one that strips the Bible of its miracles under the assumption that miracles don't happen. Santayana challenged modernism for failing to understand the Christian church and the power of its frank supernaturalism. While Lewis disagreed with Santayana's conclusions,[46] Santayana helped him see that his combative self-serving plan for his narrative poem *Dymer* was flawed.[47] Santayana included a chapter on the philosophy of Bergson, a philosophy that rejected the evolutionary doctrine that later things are better. Santayana disagreed with Bergson's entire system of philosophy, which seemed to hold to some sort of Absolute mind behind the universe and the possibility of immortality.[48] Lewis probably also disagreed with Santayana's conviction that the universe gave no evidence of a plan or an intention, siding instead with Bergson.[49] One thing is clear. In Lewis's *Summa*, a philosophical work written years later against Barfield's Anthroposophy,[50] Lewis seems to have agreed with

---

[45] On January 5, 1924. Shortly after this date, Lewis also read W. R. Sorley, *Moral Values and the Idea of God: The Gifford Lectures delivered in the University of Aberdeen in 1914 and 1915* (University Press, 1921).

[46] One can imagine Lewis disagreeing with this statement: "As Mr. Bertrand Russell has observed, one reason why philosophers often fail to reach the truth is that often they do not desire to reach it. . . . But professional philosophers are usually only apologists: that is, they are absorbed in defending some vested illusion or some eloquent idea" (*Winds of Doctrine*, 198).

[47] In rejection of an Idealism that turns into solipsism, Santayana wrote in Chapter 1, "You cannot well have the idea of a world in which nothing appears but the idea of yourself" (*Winds of Doctrine*, 191).

[48] Santayana, *Winds of Doctrine*, 151.

[49] Santayana, *Winds of Doctrine*, 214.

[50] The *Summa* was written in the summer of 1928 during the Great War with Barfield.

Santayana that the Spirit first disenchants and then re-enchants the world.[51] That is, the Spirit destroys our ideas that there is nothing above and beyond this world, and then the Spirit draws us to himself. But Lewis would have preferred replacing the word *Spirit* with *imagination* at the time of writing the *Summa*.

On January 12, Lewis borrowed two of Arthur James Balfour's books, *Theism and Humanism* and *Theism and Thought*, from the Oxford Union. Although we don't know who or what had commended these books to Lewis, Arthur James Balfour was an influential writer and thinker, very much in the public eye, who had been Prime Minister of the United Kingdom from 1902 to 1905. Balfour delivered the Gifford Lectures at the University of Glasgow in 1914. During World War I he replaced Winston Churchill as the First Lord of the Admiralty, he held many other important offices in England throughout his career, and he authored the Balfour Declaration that eventually led to the creation of the State of Israel in 1948.

That evening Lewis began reading *Theism and Thought*. Balfour helped Lewis to see that materialism was self-refuting, because it denied the possibility of truly valid knowledge.[52] If materialism is confident that valid knowledge is impossible, Balfour argued, how can that very conclusion of materialism itself be valid?[53] Or how can a materialist be confident that knowledge is impossible, since that very statement, "knowledge is impossible," is a piece of knowledge? Balfour also argued that aesthetic values (art, music, literature) cannot be

---

[51] *CLIVI HAMILTONIS SUMMAE METAPHYSICAS CONTRA ANTHROPOSO-PHOS LIBRI II* B:MS.Fascs.b91 (fols. 1–37). See also Norbert Feinendegen and Arend Smilde, eds., *The "Great War" of Owen Barfield and C. S. Lewis: Philosophical Writings, 1927–1930*, Inklings Studies Supplements No. 1 (Oxford, England, 2015).

[52] Colin Duriez, *Tolkien and C. S. Lewis: The Gift of Friendship* (Mahwah, NJ: HiddenSpring, 2003), 30; Arthur Balfour, *Theism and Humanism: The Book that Influenced C. S. Lewis* (Inkling Books, 2000), 135.

[53] This book, *Theism and Humanism*, also later appeared on Lewis's list of the ten most influential books he ever read on his vocational attitude and philosophy of life. See *The Christian Century*, Vol. 79, No. 23 (June 6, 1962): 719.

explained on a purely materialistic basis nor can a purely naturalistic ethical choice prefer one loyalty to another or move one from what one does to what one ought to do.[54] Lewis had learned this distinction from David Hume (1711–76), whom Lewis first read in 1918 while recovering from war wounds in a London hospital. Hume's Realism was of the type with which Lewis agreed, i.e., the view that holds to "the existence of real, spatiotemporal objects that exist separately of people's knowledge of them."[55] Lewis's attraction to Hume had prepared him for the arguments of Balfour, even though Lewis rejected much of Balfour's position at first glance.

Having read Balfour, Lewis may well have concluded that pure naturalism could not account for the validity of reason. Just a year-and-a-half later, on August 14, 1925, Lewis wrote to his father, stating that he took comfort in knowing that neither the materialist nor the scientist had the last word.[56] In 1944, he wrote about this inquiry,

> Long before I believed Theology to be true I had already decided that the popular scientific picture ... was false. One absolutely central inconsistency ruins it. . . . The whole picture professes to depend on inferences from observed facts. Unless inference is valid, the whole picture disappears. Unless we can be sure that reality in the remotest nebula or the remotest part obeys the thought laws of the human scientist here and now in his laboratory—in other words, unless Reason is an absolute—all is in ruins. Yet those who ask me to believe this world picture also ask me to believe that Reason is simply the unforeseen and unintended byproduct of mindless matter at one stage of its endless and aimless becoming. Here is flat contradiction. They ask me at the same moment to accept a conclusion and to discredit the only testimony on which that conclusion can be based. The difficulty is to me a fatal one; and the fact that when you put it to many scientists, far from

---

[54] Balfour, *Theism and Humanism*, 60, 102f.
[55] Barkman, *C. S. Lewis & Philosophy as a Way of Life*, 22.
[56] *Collected Letters of C. S. Lewis*, I, 649.

having an answer, they seem not even to understand what the difficulty is, assures me that I have not found a mare's nest but detected a radical disease in their whole mode of thought from the very beginning.[57]

This quotation, while referring back to a time in his life of an uncertain date, suggests that he was thinking about this matter in 1924.

Later that month, Lewis continued his reading of philosopher Henry More. Intrigued by the previous September's reading of Bergson, who saw some energy and purpose in nature, he also read H. Wildon Carr's translation of Bergson's *Energie Spirituelle*. In late January Lewis wrote that he had never seen the beauty of the religious parts of *The Fairie Queene*.[58] More and more he was seeing purpose in the world around him, as nature and religion were coming together in his mind.

The month of February found Lewis still working on Henry More's writings, this time More's *Defense of the Cabbala*, a Jewish mystical work. Two days after he read *Defense of the Cabbala*, he noted in his diary that for his friend Pasley religion was out of the question.[59] The mere fact that Lewis made this statement about Pasley, however, suggests that Lewis was seriously considering the question of religion.

THE FIRST CHESS MOVE

God's first chess move—the capture of Lewis's first bishop—took place when Lewis read the ancient Greek playwright Euripides's *Hippolytus*. He had first encountered Euripides, perhaps even the *Hippolytus*, at Gastons, the home of W. T. Kirkpatrick.[60] Since in late 1918, he had stated his dislike for Euripides in a letter to Arthur Greeves,[61] this reading in 1924 is undoubtedly the reading of the *Hippolytus* that affected him so deeply. He described the *Hippolytus* as

---

[57] Lewis, "Is Theology Poetry?" 135.
[58] Lewis, *All My Road Before Me*, 286.
[59] The date is February 24, 1924. See Lewis, *All My Road Before Me*, 290.
[60] Lewis, *Surprised by Joy*, 144.
[61] *Collected Letters of C. S. Lewis*, I, 408, October 15, 1918.

"splendid stuff."[62] The *Hippolytus* brought about the return of Joy to his life. This first chess move, then, took place between March 3 and 7, 1924.[63]

Lewis was in the midst of his course of studies in English. He was reading all the English masters, but recently he had begun reading Euripides's *Heracleidae*. On March 3, he read the first act of the *Hippolytus*. On March 4 he finished the *Heracleidae* and continued Euripides's *Hippolytus*. The next two days he also read Chesterton and wondered what impact Christianity had made on the pagans. After presenting a paper on moral values to a philosophical society (which received high marks) on March 7, he concluded his reading of the *Hippolytus*, including a read-through of Gilbert Murray's book *The Rise of the Greek Epic*. Lewis's diary for March 6 gives us the exact date of the first of the four chess moves.

He writes, "There was a transitional moment of delicious uneasiness, and then—instantaneously—the long inhibition was over, the dry desert lay behind, I was off once more into the land of longing, my heart at once broken and exalted as it had never been since the old days at Bookham."[64] This marked both the return of Joy and the end of a purely rational mindset, the materialistic New Look that characterized much of Oxford University, which probably also means the end of Lewis's commitment to Realism, and, hence, materialism (although it had probably already occurred), a turn away from atheism, and the adoption of Idealism.[65] Santayana's criticism of rationalism probably helped. In his diary for March 6, Lewis wrote that he came out of the dark library at four o'clock in the afternoon with the air "wonderfully

---

[62] Lewis, *All My Road Before Me*, 296.

[63] Joel D. Heck, "Chronologically Lewis." The first of these dates, i.e., 1918, is shortly after his time studying with Kirkpatrick. See *The Lewis Papers* 8:190. See also Lewis, *Surprised by Joy*, 217, where Lewis describes the first move coming as a result of reading the *Hippolytus*.

[64] Lewis, *Surprised by Joy*, 217.

[65] During this year Lewis writes about Idealist Bishop Berkeley, "We are rid of many atheistical arguments." "The Moral Good—Its Place Among the Values," 35. Cited in Barkman, *C. S. Lewis & Philosophy as a Way of Life*, 254.

bright and soft in color. It was like a summer evening at six o'clock. The stone seemed softer everywhere, the birds were singing, the air was deliciously cold and rare. I got a sort of eerie unrest and dropped into the real joy. Never have I seen Oxford look better."[66] Although he still thought he wanted the emotional experience of Joy, he had lost his first bishop in the chess match with God. As the capture of a bishop limits the strength and mobility of a chess player, Lewis's materialism had been cut off from its dominant position in his thinking.

Lewis wrote that the return of Joy occurred as the result of reading a chorus about the world's end.[67] Devin Brown has stated that the section from the *Hippolytus* that brought him Joy, especially in view of the fact that Lewis had previously banished Avalon and Hesperides from his thinking, was the following passage[68]:

> Oh God, bring me to the end of the seas
> To the Hesperides, sisters of evening, . . .
> Let me escape to the rim of the world
> Where the tremendous firmament meets
> The earth, and Atlas holds the universe
> In his palms.[69]

In fact, Lewis himself states that this was the passage that he was reading.[70] In the midst of his reading of the *Hippolytus*, Lewis wrote in

---

[66] Lewis, *All My Road Before Me*, 297f.

[67] Lewis, *Surprised by Joy*, 217.

[68] Lewis, *Surprised by Joy*, 204.

[69] *A Life Observed*, 128. Brown uses the translation from Euripides: *Four Plays in Modern Translations*, trans. Simon Goldfield and Kenneth Cavander (New York: Dell, 1965). This is another translation of the speech by the Chorus, slightly more than halfway through the play after a speech by Phaedra, that Gilbert Murray translates, "Yea, beyond that Pillar of the End/That Atlas guardeth, would I wend" (*The Hippolytus of Euripides* [London: George Allen & Unwin Ltd., 1922], 39). See also the Loeb Classical Library, *Euripides II*, LCL 484, 196f.: "To the apple-bearing shore of the melodious Hesperides would I go my way, there where the lord of the sea forbids sailors further passage in the deep-blue mere, fixing the sacred boundary of the skies, the pillar held up by Atlas."

[70] *The Lewis Papers* 8:191.

his diary that he also read some of G. K. Chesterton's *Life of St. Francis*,[71] particularly the chapter about naturalism.[72] He was probably referring to chapter 9, "Miracles and Death," in which Chesterton quoted Matthew Arnold. Chesterton challenged Arnold, who had stated that "miracles do not happen," and he challenged the inconsistency of historians who accept most of the historical narrative in the Bible, but rule out the supernatural. Chesterton argues, "There is only one intelligent reason why a man does not believe in miracles and that is that he does believe in materialism." Chesterton operated with the assumption that Ernst Renan and Matthew Arnold had wrongly understood the New Testament when they rejected the miracles of Jesus and when Renan saw Jesus as merely a man.[73] Lewis had purchased and read Renan during his undergraduate years at Oxford. Chesterton read the New Testament in a straightforward way, and, though not convinced, Lewis must have kept Chesterton's perspective in the back of his mind. Likewise, Chesterton's distaste for Schopenhauer, Nietzsche, and atheism probably also influenced Lewis.[74]

But what was it about the passage in the *Hippolytus* that so attracted Lewis? The passage that so impressed Lewis echoes earlier evocations of Joy, such as those from William Morris's *The Well at the World's End*. The end of the seas and the rim of the world, with their boundaries, suggest a realm beyond them, and such imagery must have helped him imagine something beyond materialism. An Atlas that can hold the universe in his palms likewise suggests some power greater than anything this world can offer.

---

[71] Originally published by George H. Doran Company, New York, in 1924.

[72] Lewis, *All My Road Before Me*, 297, March 5.

[73] Chesterton, *Life of St. Francis*, Chapter I, "Problem of St. Francis." For a reflection of Renan's position in Lewis, see, for example, the letter of October 27, 1916, where Lewis wrote to his father about the additions that Christ's followers had allegedly been adding on for twenty centuries (*Collected Letters of C. S. Lewis*, I, 242).

[74] See, for example, the opening paragraph of Chapter VI, "The Poor Little Man," *Life of St. Francis*.

THE SECOND CHESS MOVE

On March 8, God made his second chess move. Lewis took Samuel Alexander's *Space, Time and Deity* out of the Union and went to Wadham College, where he walked in the garden reading the introduction. In his autobiography, Lewis wrote "The next Move was intellectual, and consolidated the first Move."[75] He read Samuel Alexander's *Space, Time and Deity* about the difference between "Enjoyment" and "Contemplation," i.e., the difference between experiencing something (Enjoyment) and analyzing it (Contemplation), which included the idea that one cannot both enjoy something and contemplate it at the same time. He read more of Alexander two days later. This followed exactly on the heels of the first chess move and the reading of *Hippolytus*, and, as Lewis wrote, consolidated the first move.[76] This consolidation confirms the fact that the two moves happened close to each other. In fact, Lewis borrowed Alexander's book from the Oxford Union the day after he had finished reading the *Hippolytus*.

That second move involved Alexander's distinction between enjoyment and contemplation. Up until this time, he thought that he had been looking for the experience of Joy itself instead of the thing to which Joy was pointing, such as the difference between talking about some gourmet dish and actually eating it or the difference between reading a doctrinal creed and an experience of the living God. In his autobiography, Lewis wrote that when he analyzed, or contemplated, the sensation of Joy, or longing, it disappeared.[77] In *The Pilgrim's Regress*, he described it as imagining a picture in his mind and then trying to look in another part of his mind to see if the feeling of Joy were beginning.[78] He now realized that his enjoyment of Joy was the footprint of something other than Joy. He should be looking for

---

[75] Lewis, *Surprised by Joy*, 217.
[76] Lewis, *Surprised by Joy*, 217.
[77] Lewis, *Surprised by Joy*, 169.
[78] Lewis, *The Pilgrim's Regress*, 13.

something "Other and Outer"[79] rather than an internal experience. His experience of this longing, this sense of eternity, was not the Joy itself, but only its track. This brought him into what he called the "region of awe."[80] He had circumstantial evidence of the supernatural.

The second move, Lewis wrote, was the equivalent of losing one's last remaining bishop. Just as the loss of the second bishop limits the chess player's ability both to defend and to attack, so also Alexander's insight removed the possibility that Lewis was only looking for an emotional experience within him. He was forced to look elsewhere, outside of himself. He had learned that when he experienced Joy and looked inside himself, the Joy immediately disappeared.[81] He had been trying to analyze, or contemplate, the Joy while reading poetry, listening to music, or going for a walk, but he destroyed the Joy by trying to look at it. This led him to conclude that the Joy only came *through* poetry, music, and nature, but actually pointed elsewhere.

In the poem "Joy," Lewis attempts to describe Joy, the concept he elsewhere defined as a longing, or a desire, for something beyond this world. Although the poem was written in May 1922, its publication by *The Beacon* (where Owen Barfield worked) two years later coincided with Lewis's newfound insight that Joy was "out there" rather than "in here." The poem expresses the longing he had previously suppressed in an attempt to live a consistently materialistic life. Lewis describes the mood that beauty brings, and yet beauty could not provide answers to his questions. Beauty is fleeting, and yet it creates a longing for something.

On April 12, Lewis began reading Friedrich Nietzsche's *Beyond Good and Evil*.[82] Perhaps because of his new insight into Joy, he did not find that this atheist's writing resonated with him. He described Nietzsche's ideas as things the ordinary egoist believes and lives by.

---

[79] Lewis, *The Pilgrim's Regress*, 124.
[80] Lewis, *Surprised by Joy*, 221.
[81] See Lewis, *Surprised by Joy*, 169, where Lewis states that by looking inside himself he destroyed Joy instantly. See also *The Pilgrim's Regress*, 124.
[82] Lewis, *All My Road Before Me*, 314.

Though he did not set aside atheism at this time, he had probably already set Realism, i.e., materialism, to the side in late 1922. And he was now open to a consideration of theism, as his diary from the next month indicates. Exactly one month later, Lewis went to undergraduate friend Alfred Ewing's[83] place on Iffley Road in southeast Oxford to take a walk with Ewing. Lewis returned to Ewing's place for tea and, not coincidentally, they had a long talk about theism—a topic that was of great interest to Lewis.[84]

At the same time that Lewis was more open to theism, he was allowing Samuel Alexander's insight to affect him. Two months after reading Alexander, Lewis reread Malory for the first time since 1914, and he enjoyed Malory a great deal, especially the part about Balin's superhuman guilt and bad luck.[85] In Malory's story, Balin caused the Grail to be lost by defending himself with the Spear that had wounded Christ's side, striking the "dolorous blow" that wounded the Fisher King and that caused a wasteland to fall over all the land. This new appreciation confirms the conclusion that the rediscovery of Joy occurred when Lewis read the *Hippolytus* in March of this year. In addition, two months later, while walking the family dog Pat, Lewis writes that, because of the beauty of nature, Joy "came just within sight ... but didn't arrive," suggesting once again that his reading of the *Hippolytus* had only recently occurred and that he was now seeing Joy as triggered by something outside himself.[86]

---

[83] Alfred Cecil Ewing (1899–1973) took a First in Greats from Oxford University in 1920 and earned the D.Phil. in 1923. He later became Lecturer in Moral Science, Cambridge University (1931–54) and Reader in Philosophy, Cambridge (1954–66).

[84] Lewis, *All My Road Before Me*, 322.

[85] Lewis, *All My Road Before Me*, 322. The date was May 11, 1924.

[86] Lewis, *All My Road Before Me*, 328. The date was June 5, 1924.

FULL-TIME EMPLOYMENT

Lewis's life was about to change, bringing him to the verge of a full-time teaching position at Oxford University. On May 5, the Master of University College, Michael Sadler, offered Lewis a one-year teaching position in philosophy, filling in for E. F. Carritt (1876–1964), for the next school year. Carritt would be taking a leave of absence to teach at the University of Michigan for that year, so University College—Lewis's alma mater—needed a replacement.[87]

A week and a half later, in order to begin preparations to teach philosophy, Lewis sat for a long time in the Oxford Union reading Bosanquet's *Some Suggestions in Ethics*. He would have to read Bosanquet in order to teach philosophy, since Bosanquet was one of the leading philosophers of the day. Lewis especially liked the passage in chapter 4 about the Absolute eating out of your hand.[88] The most poetic description of the Absolute was the one he most appreciated. In that passage Bosanquet describes the relationship between human beings and the lower animals. People feel enlarged by having a dog or horse or bird as a friend, and friendship with an animal carries an anticipation of the Absolute. The quiet trust of a friendly animal is attractive, and that experience is "as if the Absolute came to eat out of your hand."[89] Since in Idealism the Absolute is an expression of some intelligent mind, Lewis was clearly open to what Idealism was offering and had probably adopted Idealism as his current position. He also thought Bosanquet's point of view right on most topics, including this one.[90]

---

[87] Carritt would be replacing philosopher Robert D. H. Parker in Michigan.

[88] Lewis, *All My Road Before Me*, 323. This took place the morning of May 15.

[89] Bernard Bosanquet, *Some Suggestions in Ethics* (London: Macmillan, 1918), Chapter 4, "Unvisited Tombs," 80.

[90] Lewis, *All My Road Before Me*, 323. Lewis's writing about the fourth chess move, then reading *The Everlasting Man*, may be further evidence that he had become an Idealist in 1924.

In June, Lewis picked up the writings of George Berkeley again, this time, as with Bosanquet, to prepare to teach undergraduates.[91] In rereading Berkeley, Lewis saw him in a new way which led him to reject the Italian school of Idealism. He was probably referring to the ideas of Giovanni Gentile, a school of thought that could not allow for something to exist beyond experience, i.e., something spiritual or supernatural.[92] At the same time he withdrew some of his old criticisms of Berkeley, particularly Berkeley's doctrine of Notions, largely because he had recently learned Samuel Alexander's distinction between enjoyment and contemplation. Notions, Lewis now felt, could be looked *through* (enjoyed), but not *at* (contemplated). They could be experienced but not analyzed from a distance; they could be enjoyed but not contemplated. Berkeley's "notion" was a name for the enjoyed, Lewis thought. If Lewis was an Idealist at this point, that explains his favorable impressions of both Bosanquet and Berkeley. If Alexander was correct in the distinction between enjoyment and contemplation, or between experience and analysis, then Berkeley could be correct in his doctrine of "notions." He also began to think that there might be a God, whose Spirit was related to Lewis's spirit and whose Spirit might be the ultimate Spirit, the ultimate self.

His reading of the English Idealists probably cemented his rejection of Realism. On June 9, Lewis received more information about the teaching position, which explains why he picked up Berkeley again three days later. On June 14, he finished Berkeley's major work, *A Treatise Concerning the Principles of Human Knowledge*, and then he started reading philosopher David Hume. The next February he would review his notes on Berkeley and Hume, since both philosophers were part of his tutorials. Likewise, he was reading Immanuel Kant, also an

---

[91] Lewis, "Early Prose Joy," 34. Lewis stated that he returned to Berkeley purely for reasons of preparing to teach philosophy for Carritt, but he was surprised by his new insights into Berkeley. The date is June 12, 1924.

[92] Lewis, "Early Prose Joy," 31f.

Idealist, during this year, learning more about Idealism from several sources.[93]

Had Lewis really adopted Idealism? Most likely he had. As stated earlier, he had probably rejected Realism in late 1922, and Idealism was the major alternative. He also seems to have turned away from atheism without adopting theism by becoming an Idealist, which allows one all the comforts of theism without having to believe in God. The Absolute, Lewis wrote, was as different from God as a book is different from a friend, always available but making no demands.[94] And he had written during this year about the Idealist Bishop Berkeley, "We are rid of many atheistical arguments."[95] He much more highly regarded the Idealist philosophers.

On the same day that Lewis finished Berkeley's *Treatise*, he reread Book I of Wordsworth's *The Prelude*. In a letter to Arthur Greeves, he commented that *The Prelude* was beginning to replace *Paradise Lost* as his "literary metropolis"—suggesting that this 14-book autobiographical poem (or series of poems) was serving as a major source for his own understanding of poetry.[96] Mary Ritter argues that Lewis's understanding of imagination, romanticism, and Joy were drawn from *The Prelude*.[97] Just three months after the first two chess moves, and during the same year in which Joy returned, Lewis was beginning to appreciate Wordsworth, whom he had met first in 1915, and disliked. Not only did Lewis in years to come return again and again to *The Prelude*, but he also came to consider it one of the ten most influential books on vocational attitude and philosophy of life he had ever read.[98] The *Hippolytus* had opened him to Joy, or longing, and *The Prelude*

---

[93] Barkman is convinced that Lewis was "almost certainly an Idealist at the time" that he wrote a 1924 essay, "The Whole" (*C. S. Lewis & Philosophy as a Way of Life*, 237). Coincidentally, F. H. Bradley died in Oxford on September 18.

[94] Lewis, "Early Prose Joy," 31.

[95] C. S. Lewis, "The Moral Good—Its Place Among the Values," 35. Cited in Barkman, *C. S. Lewis & Philosophy as a Way of Life*, 254.

[96] Lewis, *All My Road Before Me*, 333, June 14, 1924.

[97] Mary Ritter, "William Wordsworth *The Prelude*," *C. S. Lewis's List*, 95f., 103.

[98] *The Christian Century*, Vol. 79, No. 23 (June 6, 1962): 719.

confirmed this understanding. Wordsworth's insight into Nature, his "spots of time" in which he sensed something divine, and even Wordsworth's poem "Surprised by Joy" guided Lewis's understanding of poetry, desire, and the divine.

SUMMARY

Most of the changes inside Lewis happened during the first half of 1924, especially when he lost both of his bishops. The first move, the loss of his first bishop, took place on March 6 when Lewis was reading Euripides's *Hippolytus*. It marked a retreat from materialism, which was already shaky by that time, and the return of Joy (longing). The second move, the loss of his second bishop, took place on March 8 when Lewis read Samuel Alexander's *Space, Time and Deity*. Alexander's book distinguished between "enjoyment" and "contemplation." Lewis learned that one cannot both enjoy and contemplate at the same time, and he then concluded that Joy pointed to something outside himself rather than something inside his own mind.

With the onset of his first year of full-time teaching, Lewis found himself devoting much of his time to preparation for lectures and tutorials. Then he taught philosophy for E. F. Carritt during the Michaelmas term, the Hilary term, and the Trinity term of the following school year. Such focus on philosophy caused Lewis to reexamine his own approach to life, especially as he read the writings of important philosophers, agreeing with some of their ideas and rejecting others. Having completely set aside the materialistic philosophy of Realism, he had probably become an Idealist.

CHAPTER 5

THE CHESS GAME CONTINUES

"All my ideas are in a crumbling state at present."

—C. S. Lewis, *All My Road Before Me*

The chess game continued. Lewis had not adopted Christianity, or any other religion, but he seems to have become an Idealist in the tradition of Bradley, Bosanquet, and Berkeley. He was also studying Idealism because it was the dominant philosophy held in Oxford at this time, and because he actually had to tutor students about Idealism.[1]

1925: C. S. LEWIS, IDEALIST

During 1924, because of the first two chess moves and his second look at the writings of George Berkeley, Bernard Bosanquet, T. H. Green, and others, Lewis had adopted Idealism.[2] This change of position actually brought him nearer to Christianity. He began to see that F. H. Bradley's use of the metaphor of the Absolute, which he described elusively, made Bradley something of a mystic, drawing on his own imaginative and spiritual experience to enable him to escape from complete skepticism, but still unable to say what the Absolute actually was.[3] Bradley insisted on the existence of the Absolute, but he

---

[1] Lewis, *Surprised by Joy*, 222.
[2] Lewis, "Early Prose Joy," 34.
[3] Lewis, "Early Prose Joy," 34.

could not actually describe it clearly. This led Lewis to think that if metaphor were useful, the Christian story of God becoming man, or even the ideas of death and resurrection, was as good a metaphor as any other metaphor, certainly far easier to understand and to describe. And how is it, Lewis asked himself, that the Christian metaphor, which he liked the least, shaped the entire course of European history if it were only a metaphor?[4]

We read little else from Lewis's writings about his spiritual journey during this year for two primary reasons, which caused him to stop writing in his diary for five-and-a-half months. First, he was deeply involved in reading philosophy as E. F. Carritt's replacement during the 1924–25 school year. Second, he was also very busy applying for faculty positions. One of those applications proved to be successful.

Trinity term at Oxford University began on April 15, Lewis's last term teaching as Carritt's temporary replacement. On May 20, Lewis received a phone call from Magdalen College Master Sir Thomas Herbert Warren, informing him that he had been elected a Fellow of Magdalen College to teach English and philosophy. Later that day Lewis sent a telegram to his father, telling his father the good news. Shortly thereafter, he wrote to his father with a grateful heart, expressing his appreciation for his father's financial support and generosity over the past six years.

Lewis's Magdalen Fellowship officially began on June 15. His first year of teaching was very, very busy, as it is for all first-year teachers. He had to prepare for both lectures and tutorials that would occur during the coming year, and his duties would include some tutoring in philosophy as well as English, and to that we now turn.

That summer, Lewis wrote to his father, indicating that he took comfort in knowing that neither the materialist nor the scientist had the last word and that he had set aside the evolutionism of Charles Darwin and Herbert Spencer as based "on a foundation of sand; of

---

[4] Lewis, "Early Prose Joy," 35.

gigantic and irreconcilable contradictions an inch below the surface."[5] His reading of Arthur Balfour's *Theism and Humanism* was undoubtedly one of the reasons for this statement, since Balfour argued that because science does not provide an adequate basis to explain reason, ethics, and aesthetics, it "saws off the branch on which it is supported. It kicks down the ladder by which it has climbed."[6] A couple of years later, he wrote to his father about needing more faith to believe some things in science than in theology.[7] Having taught the philosophy of both Realists and Idealists, he understood both of them far better. Realism had supported Darwinism, while Idealism had challenged it.

Another implication is that nature was somehow connected to his longing, but at this point he did not clearly see this connection, writing in his diary about the beauty of nature. As he sat and enjoyed nature, he came very close to the real joy, but not quite.[8] Nature pointed to the source of his longing, but that source was not nature itself. The beauty of nature whispered to Lewis, as John Piper has written: "This beauty will not satisfy your soul; it beckons you toward something you do not yet know."[9]

1926: HARRY WELDON

In the evening of April 27, 1926, Lewis was settling down in his larger sitting room at Magdalen to read Walter W. Skeat's introduction[10] when Thomas D. ("Harry") Weldon, Magdalen College Fellow and Tutor in Philosophy, arrived. Lewis and Weldon had to work together, since Lewis was teaching some of the philosophy students

---

[5] *Collected Letters of C. S. Lewis*, I, 649. The date of the letter is August 14.

[6] Balfour, *Theism and Humanism*, 165.

[7] *Collected Letters*, I, 680. The date of the letter is March 30, 1927.

[8] Lewis, *All My Road Before Me*, 375, September 4, 1925.

[9] John Piper, "What God Made is Good—and Must be Sanctified," in *The Romantic Rationalist: God, Life, and Imagination in the Work of C. S. Lewis*, edited by John Piper and David Mathis (Wheaton, IL: Crossway, 2014), 138.

[10] See Lewis, *All My Road Before Me*, 379. Probably Walter William Skeat, *An Etymological Dictionary of the English Language*, revised and enlarged (Courier Dover Publications, 1910).

that Weldon could not accommodate. His arrival led to their drinking whiskey and talking late into the evening in front of a burning fire. Among other topics, they discussed the historical truth of the Gospels, and Weldon and Lewis agreed that there was a lot that could not be explained away. Weldon then made what would, for Lewis, be a pivotal comment about death and resurrection: "Rum thing," Weldon noted. "It almost looks as if it had really happened once."[11] Whether the whiskey had caused him to lower his defenses or he was just speaking the sober truth, Weldon was referring to the death and resurrection of Jesus, as recorded in the four New Testament Gospels. The effect upon Lewis was devastating. If Weldon, the hard-boiled atheistic philosopher, was not safe, then who was? Following this, Lewis began to take a closer look at the New Testament, eventually concluding that the events described there were far more historical than he had previously thought. The event was so significant that Lewis took up his pen to continue his diary after several months of silence, probably so that he could record this encounter.

Weldon was a friend and colleague in the field of philosophy, but Lewis met many other Fellows in many other academic disciplines as well. Since Lewis's primary field was English, friendships in the English faculty became especially important. When Lewis began teaching for the English Faculty, he made two very important friends in that discipline: H. V. D. "Hugo" Dyson, then of Reading University,[12] and, on May 11, at a meeting of the English Fellows of Oxford University, J. R. R. Tolkien.[13] Both men were devoted Christians and both remained close friends for the rest of his life, providing an influence that is impossible to overestimate.

In May and June of this year, both the negative and the positive sides of Lewis's spiritual life showed themselves. First, while taking their dog Pat for a walk over the fields to Stowe Woods, Lewis came to

---

[11] Lewis, *Surprised by Joy*, 223.
[12] Dyson (1896–1975) joined the Oxford University English faculty in 1945 at Merton College. Lewis met Dyson no later than July 28, 1930.
[13] Lewis, *Surprised by Joy*, 216.

the realization that he was becoming a prig by showing righteous indignation against certain modern pretensions, and he realized that he did not know how to solve this priggishness.[14] While he did not name those modern pretensions, he had the wisdom to be able to look at himself and dislike what he saw. Perhaps because of this, over the next month he attended Magdalen College chapel at least three times. On May 9, he attended Chapel and read Deuteronomy 8 as one of the readers of the day. Whether that was because of a growing sense of his spiritual need or because he was assigned that task, or both, we do not know. Two weeks later, Lewis again attended chapel and read the first lesson. Then, two weeks after this, he left home at about 5:30 a.m. in order to attend chapel. These three chapel incidents probably reflect his recent conversation with Weldon and Lewis's interest in looking more closely at the New Testament Gospels and the Christian faith, but they may also show Lewis attempting to understand his priggishness. Chapel attendance would give him greater contact with the Gospels and put him in touch with people he could speak with about his concern. His adoption of theism was still four years away, but most people do not make major life decisions overnight, especially those that involve a reappraisal of one's entire orientation to life. And if Lewis was anything, he was a careful and thoughtful scholar.

About a month after the "Rum thing" conversation, after contemplating daisies, buttercups, and hawthorn, Lewis wrote in his diary, "All my ideas are in a crumbling state at present."[15] Clearly he was shaken. That same night, he walked with Harry Weldon, both of them returning to Lewis's rooms to drink whiskey and talk about the ideal state, eugenics, and the witch hunts of the seventeenth century, topics that appear in G. K. Chesterton's *Eugenics and Other Evils*.[16] Weldon must have recommended the book, because Lewis started reading it about two weeks later. With the crumbling of his ideas, it is no wonder that *Dymer*, which was to be published by J. M. Dent four months later,

---

[14] Lewis, *All My Road Before Me*, 383, May 1.
[15] Lewis, *All My Road Before Me*, 401, May 26, 1926.
[16] Lewis, *All My Road Before Me*, 401, May 26.

shows the ambivalence of an author who both denies God's existence and yet seems to affirm it.

A few days later, Colin Hardie[17] took Lewis to Hertford College to hear Samuel Alexander speak to the Philosophical Society. Lewis probably wanted to meet, or at least see, the man whose book had taught him the distinction between enjoyment and contemplation. They met the Welsh philosopher H. H. Price in Hertford quad and remained there chatting until Alexander appeared. Alexander read a paper on artistic creation, attacking Italian philosopher Benedetto Croce in the process. The second part of the paper dealt with cosmic creation, which, Lewis stated, was beyond him.

On June 2, Lewis took undergraduates William Hetherington and Robert Hamilton for a tutorial on philosophy at noon, with Hetherington talking intelligently about modern Idealism. As stated above, in his early years as a tutor, Lewis took students in both philosophy and English. That he would cover one of the current trends in philosophy is not surprising, but it must also have been a topic of interest for Lewis since Idealism gave him some hope that he might discover the source of the longing he felt when reading Morris or Yeats or Wordsworth. Two days later, the weather suggested autumn to Lewis and gave him a brief sense of what he used to call "the real joy," telling us that this topic was still prominent in his thinking. Perhaps he sensed a relationship between his experiences of Joy and the Absolute Mind of Idealism. Two weeks later, Lewis conducted a tutorial on the British Idealist George Berkeley, which confirms the fact that he was reading and teaching Idealism, especially its leading proponent Berkeley, during his early years as a tutor.

At the same time, Lewis was reading widely—theology, philosophy, and English, some of them imaginative books that he enjoyed, such as those of George MacDonald and William Morris. Weldon's comment had also sent him back to the Gospels to check out their

---

[17] The date is May 30. It is unclear which of two brothers this was—William (Frank) or Colin Hardie, but it was probably Colin. Colin was later one of the Inklings; Frank was not.

record of the death and resurrection of Christ, and he continued to read Chesterton. He also read Richard Hooker's *Of the Laws of Ecclesiastical Polity*, noting that the law of human nature, or reason, is a copy of the eternal law, which is God's very nature.[18] Hooker helped him to see that God is good, not the cause of evil, and that natural law is a reflection of God Himself.

Then, in June, Lewis began reading G. K. Chesterton's *Eugenics and Other Evils*,[19] the book he and Weldon had discussed less than a month earlier. Lewis did not comment on his reading of the book, but this reading shows his continued respect for Chesterton's work. Lewis's resistance to the unrestricted power of the State and to the use of science in that tyranny—expressed in *Dymer* during this year[20]— may have taken some cues from *Eugenics and Other Evils*.[21] Chesterton wrote, "Eugenics . . . evidently means the control of the few over the marriage and unmarriage of others; and probably means the control of the few over the marriage and unmarriage of the many." In *The Abolition of Man*, Lewis later wrote, "The final stage is come when Man by eugenics, by pre-natal conditioning, and by an education and propaganda based on a perfect applied psychology, has obtained full control over himself."[22] He also wrote, "Man's conquest of himself means simply the rule of the Conditioners over the conditioned human material."[23] In *Eugenics and Other Evils*, Chesterton opposed the practice of eugenics, i.e., disallowing certain people to marry and have children. He opposed eugenics for several reasons, one of which

---

[18] C. S. Lewis, marginalia in his edition of *Of the Laws of Ecclesiastical Polity*, cited in Barkman, *C. S. Lewis & Philosophy as a Way of Life*, 347, n. 151.

[19] Originally published in 1922 by Cassell, London. See *All My Road Before Me*, 411f., June 12.

[20] *Dymer* was accepted for publication on June 1, and Lewis was correcting proofs for much of that month.

[21] G. K. Chesterton, *Eugenics and Other Evils*, online edition, 82.

[22] *The Abolition of Man or Reflections on Education with Special Reference to the Teaching of English in the Upper Forms of Schools* (New York: Simon & Schuster, 1996), 69.

[23] Lewis, *The Abolition of Man*, 82.

was the arbitrary selection of a group of people to decide who could have children and who couldn't. Chesterton also began and ended with a criticism of Friedrich Nietzsche, whom Kirkpatrick had quoted favorably during the years Lewis studied with him and whom Lewis himself had rejected as an egoist just a couple of years earlier. In addition, Chesterton's criticism of atheism in two parts of the book probably cemented Lewis's rejection of that conviction.[24] Lewis was undoubtedly an agnostic at this point in his life, no longer holding to atheism.

All during the 1920s, Lewis wrote misleading letters to his father. Albert was under the impression that his son was a practicing Christian. In his June letter, for example, Lewis wrote about the importance of Christianity in Sir Walter Raleigh's letters.[25] He was writing in such a way as to mislead his father into thinking that he still held to the Christian faith, but without clearly committing himself one way or the other. However, by this time, he was more seriously looking at some of the Christian elements in the books he was reading and could honestly reflect that reading in his letters.

On June 13, Lewis reread some of Maurice Hewlett's autobiographical fairy story, *Lore of Proserpine*, which caused him to think of Christina dreams[26] and melting, as if he were a man of snow. Less than two weeks after reading Hewlett, Lewis began to reread George MacDonald's *Lilith*, one of his darker stories, but also an imaginative

---

[24] In Part I, Chapter V, Chesterton speaks of "an atheistic literary style" that chooses words that suggest that things are dead, refuses to attribute human motive to the outbreak of war, and prefers to speak of "solidarity" rather than sympathy with the poor of France and Germany during the First World War. In Part II, Chapter I, Chesterton writes about "the horrid man who is an atheist and wants to destroy the home." For fairly complete notes on *Eugenics and Other Evils*, go to www.joelheck.com/downloads-links.php.

[25] *Collected Letters of C. S. Lewis*, I, 666, June 5, 1926.

[26] "Christina dreams" are wishful thinking and the idea that dreams of love can make one incapable of loving, that dreams of other sorts hurt rather than hinder. The idea is named after Christina Pontifex in Samuel Butler's novel, *The Way of All Flesh*. The story reflects rather poorly on the Church of England.

story about life, death, and salvation.[27] Lewis had long enjoyed MacDonald and returned to him again and again. MacDonald's books did not merely initiate Lewis's return to theism; they guided it. Lewis later began to reread William Morris's *The Well at the World's End* and found that the old Morris spell still worked. Lewis wrote in his diary, "I was a good deal bothered by the ease with which my old romantic world had resumed its sway. I shall know another time not to try to establish my conceit by patronizing Wm. Morris!"[28] Sometime later, Lewis was probably writing about this period in his life when he wrote that the imagination, sensing a world beyond the world's end, perceived things that were in some sense real.[29] Also at this time, while correcting the proofs of *Dymer*, he expressed discontent with this book, which would be published less than three months later.[30] At the same time, as Lewis had just stated in his diary in May, random books and experiences were causing him to become unsettled and were probably the cause of his concern over his priggishness.

THE CHESS GAMES SWINGS BACK

The third chess move linked Lewis's experience of Joy, or longing, with Idealism, which confirmed his inclination to think that there was a lot more to life than what is experienced by the five senses. It occurred sometime later than 1926, probably several years later. In June, Lewis reread John Masefield's poem *Dauber*, which supported what he called his "growing Idealism" in metaphysics, but somehow it also gave him a good realistic shock to counterbalance that Idealism.[31] The poem deals with the eternal struggle of the visionary person against materialism and ignorance and must have strengthened his adoption of Idealism. But the struggle was not only with philosophy.

---

[27] Lewis, *All My Road Before Me*, 418. June 25, 1926.
[28] Lewis, *All My Road Before Me*, 422.
[29] Lewis, *The Pilgrim's Regress*, 128. Here Wisdom is speaking to John, who is nearing the end of his journey.
[30] Lewis, *All My Road Before Me*, 422.
[31] Lewis, *All My Road Before Me*, 419. June 29, 1926.

In early September, Lewis wrote to Jenkin that he was growing daily more doubtful in all areas.[32] While holding somewhat hesitantly to Idealism,[33] he was ambivalent in nearly every direction.

Then, two days later, in the midst of such doubt, Lewis read Chesterton's *George Bernard Shaw*.[34] Shaw was an atheist, and Chesterton challenged some of Shaw's positions in this book. Lewis read these provocative Chestertonian words: "we can only really understand all myths when we know that one of them is true."[35] Four years later that idea helped Lewis to reconcile the mythical nature of the story of Christ with the general concept of myth. At the same time, Chesterton's disdain for the suggestion that later ideas are better ideas may also have affected Lewis and helped convince him of Barfield's similar position on this issue.[36] But probably the most important

---

[32] On September 8, 1926. See *Collected Letters of C. S. Lewis*, I, 669.

[33] This is the time that Lewis was wavering between subjective Idealism and absolute Idealism.

[34] A witty, light-hearted, yet serious portrayal of the brilliant atheist George Bernard Shaw (first published in New York in 1909 by John Lange Company) whom Chesterton considered a friend but opposed on many issues, and whom he simultaneously admired and respected. In this book he described Shaw as an Irishman, Puritan, progressive, critic, dramatist, and philosopher. For example, Chesterton writes of Shaw on page fifty-six, "He belonged to that Irish group which, according to Catholicism, has hardened its heart, which, according to Protestantism has hardened its head, but which, as I fancy, has chiefly hardened its hide, lost its sensibility to the contact of the things around it."

[35] Chesterton, *George Bernard Shaw*, 176.

[36] See, for example, this passage: "More than once he seemed to argue, in comparing the dramatists of the sixteenth with those of the nineteenth century, that the latter had a definite advantage merely because they were of the nineteenth century and not of the sixteenth. When accused of impertinence towards the greatest of the Elizabethans, Bernard Shaw had said, 'Shakespeare is a much taller man than I, but I stand on his shoulders'—an epigram which sums up this doctrine with characteristic neatness. But Shaw fell off Shakespeare's shoulders with a crash. This chronological theory that Shaw stood on Shakespeare's shoulders logically involved the supposition that Shakespeare stood on Plato's shoulders. And Bernard Shaw found Plato from his point of view so much more advanced than Shakespeare that he decided in desperation that all three were equal" (Chesterton, *George Bernard Shaw*, 201f.).

things Lewis gleaned from *George Bernard Shaw* were Chesterton's honest appraisal of Shaw, mixed with wit, jab, and his fundamentally Christian perspective. And probably early in this year, certainly prior to his second conversation with Weldon,[37] Lewis read *The Everlasting Man*, also by Chesterton, a book that helped him see a Christian outline of history that made sense for the first time in his life. Chesterton's *The Everlasting Man*, first published in September 1925, was a rebuttal of H. G. Wells's *Outline of History*, an extremely influential book that sold over two million copies. Whereas the atheist Wells saw human history as a series of blind endeavors, Chesterton saw history as full of purpose. To use Wells's words, *The Everlasting Man* provided Lewis with his first clear "outline of history."

If Lewis read *The Everlasting Man* in 1926, this was a year in which Lewis read a great deal of Chesterton—first *Eugenics and Other Evils*, then *George Bernard Shaw*, and probably thereafter *The Everlasting Man*. The conversation Lewis had with Weldon about the historical nature of the Gospels may well have impressed him because he had recently read *The Everlasting Man* in order to understand Chesterton's perspective on history. In that book Chesterton operated with the same sense of history that Lewis had encountered in *Life of St. Francis*. Lewis had begun to reconsider his dismissal of the Gospels as unreliable history.

As stated earlier, this is the year that *Dymer* was published. That lengthy narrative poem was released on September 18. The book, begun in 1922, is relevant because it serves as evidence that Lewis had not made peace with God by the autumn of 1926, even though it does not precisely identify Lewis's position on Christianity, Realism, or Idealism.

Begun as a prose story in December 1916 while Lewis was studying with Kirkpatrick, the early version of the story of *Dymer* did not succeed. He set it aside, and then, in April 1922, he began the poetic

---

[37] The two conversations are dated April 27 and May 26, 1926. See Lewis, *Surprised by Joy*, 223, where Lewis clearly indicates that he read *The Everlasting Man* before his April 27 conversation with Weldon.

version that was eventually published in nine Cantos by J. M. Dent. When it was republished in 1950, Lewis wrote a Preface that lamented the disturbing of its repose in its grave; he was aware of its shortcomings.

In *Dymer*, Lewis attacked the totalitarian state, his experiences in the public schools, the army, wishful thinking, the occult, and Christianity, portraying belief in Christ as an illusion that must be destroyed.[38] He railed against God while expressing hope for the future. He criticized civilization both for not being good enough and for being better than he. He described Dymer as one who rejected wishful thinking, or thoughtful wishing. Sigmund Freud had written persuasively about people believing things that they wished to be true. In the writings of Euripides, Edmund Spenser, Sir Thomas Malory, John Milton, William Morris, and the early W. B. Yeats, Lewis had come to long for the worlds that these writers described, but Freud and other writers had argued that he needed to escape from such illusions. Like Lewis, Dymer would have to resist the temptation to relapse into such worlds of fantasy.

Dymer was a reflection of Lewis himself; when he began to write *Dymer* in 1922, he was a twenty-three-year-old rebel (Dymer was nineteen in the poem). By the time the poem was published, i.e., 1926, Lewis was twenty-seven, but he was far less the rebel by then. Dymer murders his teacher (Canto I, stanza 10) and escapes into the world of nature (I, 21). He removes his clothes and then wanders lawlessly (III, 10) in search of desire. Finding a castle, he enters the castle, clothes himself in rich clothing, eats at a banquet table, and then has a sexual experience with an unnamed girl. His wanderings inspire others but fail to satisfy him, and, bizarrely, his lust with the unnamed girl begets a monster that later kills him. He is a man escaping from illusion, but he is also looking for Joy (V, 10). He begins, thinking the universe to be his friend. Trying to recapture his earlier joy, he finds that his rebellion against the City leads only to despair. Others had also

---

[38] Colin Duriez, *Tolkien and C. S. Lewis: The Gift of Friendship* (Mahwah, NJ: HiddenSpring, 2003), 42.

suffered by rebelling against the City in imitation of his rebellion, so he feels responsible for their suffering.

Dymer's ambivalence toward God shows itself in Canto V, stanza 15, where Dymer tells God to take back His world. He will have none of that world except for death. Dymer sees the Earth as a sinking ship, unable to be fixed (VI, 35). He begins to accept reality, and then he chooses to face his destiny. Dymer feels guilty for the example he has set and the misery he has caused, both by his rebellion and by his sexual indiscretion (IX, 13), feeling that somehow he must make amends (IX, 11). He comes against the monster which he had begotten and is killed by it (IX, 29–30). Upon his death, the sun rises, the birds sing, and the flowers bloom.

A month after the publication of *Dymer*, Lewis wrote to his friend Cecil Harwood that he was convinced that reason alone could not account for the richness and spirituality of the real world.[39] The man who was supremely confident about reason when he wrote to Arthur Greeves in 1916 had come to a far less confident appraisal of reason ten years later. Charles Darwin's foundation of sand was unable to explain the origin of reason. To achieve more knowledge, Lewis suggested, he would have to turn to the mystics. The Christian and pagan mystics saw something that orthodox Idealism did not, that God could come into the midst of people just as Shakespeare's character was in some sense present in Hamlet, Othello, and Iago.[40]

1927: UNHOLY MUDDLE

As far as the written records show, during the three-year period from 1927 to 1929, there were, with one major exception, few changes in Lewis's position. The end date for Lewis's on-again-off-again diary is March 2, 1927. As far as we know, his first letter of 1927 was sent to his father on March 30. The years 1927 and 1928 were the main years for the Great War letters between Lewis and Barfield, when Lewis resisted with great energy Barfield's belief in some spiritual world

---

[39] On October 28. See *Collected Letters of C. S. Lewis*, I, 670.
[40] Lewis, "Early Prose Joy," 36.

beyond the five senses. He probably threw most of his remaining energies into learning to teach, since he still was a young teacher, which explains the relatively few letters. But there is more to this story.

That war eventually convinced Lewis that he ought not to discard old books and ancient documents simply because of their age, and this assisted him in a reappraisal of the validity of the New Testament Gospels as historically accurate documents and a new understanding of the value of imagination, a reappraisal that had begun the previous year.

Lewis wrote,

> Here [i.e., in Anthroposophy] were gods, spirits, afterlife and preexistence, initiates, occult knowledge, meditation. "Why . . . it's *medieval*," I exclaimed; for I still had all the chronological snobbery of my period and used the names of earlier periods as terms of abuse. Here was everything which the New Look had been designed to exclude; everything that might lead one off the main road into those dark places where men wallow on the floor and scream that they are being dragged down into Hell. Of course it was all arrant nonsense. There was no danger of *my* being taken in. But then, the loneliness, the sense of being deserted.[41]

Once again Lewis experienced unease over ultimate realities and a sense of loneliness, both of them heightened by the change of thinking in his good friends Barfield and Harwood, the death of Mrs. Moore's brother, Doc Askins, and the continued disagreement with Barfield over Anthroposophy.

Although many of the Great War letters by both Lewis and Barfield are not precisely dated, some of those letters may be dated to the first two months of 1927. Lewis's references to the *Theaetetus*, one of Plato's dialogues on the nature of knowledge, in February 1927 may be the context for the Great War letter in which he mentions the

[41] Lewis, *Surprised by Joy*, 206.

Theaetetus to Barfield.[42] That would place his poem "The Lord Is a Jealous God—A Careful Shepherd" in January 1927. This four-line poem Lewis described to Owen Barfield in one of his Great War letters as pessimistic, since it portrays the Lord as a careful shepherd, but also one who wields the sacrificial knife to cut the throat of the sheep for sacrifice. At a time when he was not a theist, he compared a shepherd to an evil god.[43] Lewis's thoughts about God were clearly not favorable.

On March 30, Lewis wrote to his father about his busy academic term, i.e., the Hilary term, which was about to end.[44] Two months later, he wrote to his father that his summer term was always his busiest one.[45] Later, during Michaelmas term 1927 (the autumn term), he wrote in his diary about being busy every Monday night with play reading, Tuesday night with the Mermaid Club,[46] and every Wednesday night with students who read Anglo-Saxon, plus other biweekly meetings with the Kolbitár or Icelandic Society and with a philosophical meeting and supper.[47] In that same letter he wrote that he had very little free time that was available for anything he chose.[48] He had only five free evenings every two weeks,[49] so his limited free time may explain his limited writing about his atheism or agnosticism or about

---

[42] The Great War letter known in *Collected Letters of C. S. Lewis*, III, as Series I, Letter 3, has been tentatively dated to July 1927 by Walter Hooper. The poem is cited in Series I, Letter 6, and the reference to the *Theaetetus* is Series I, Letter 7. Lewis began reading the *Theaetetus* on February 7, 1927, and is not known to have read it at any other time. See also Feinendegen and Smilde, *The "Great War" of Owen Barfield and C. S. Lewis*, 38, who date it in early 1927, probably February.

[43] *Collected Letters of C. S. Lewis*, III, 1623f. Hilary term ended on April 8, 1927.

[44] *Collected Letters of C. S. Lewis*, I, 678.

[45] *Collected Letters of C. S. Lewis*, I, 697. The date is May 28.

[46] The Mermaid Club was an undergraduate society that read Elizabethan and post-Elizabethan drama. Lewis was the president of the Mermaid Club during that school year, 1927–28.

[47] Lewis, *All My Road Before Me*, 445, n. 3; *Collected Letters of C. S. Lewis*, I, 732, 735f.

[48] *Collected Letters of C. S. Lewis*, I, 733.

[49] *Collected Letters of C. S. Lewis*, I, 736.

anything else. Some of that free time was undoubtedly devoted to the incessant domestic duties that Mrs. Moore imposed on him.

Later that fall, his father wrote to him, indicating that he had not heard from his son and hoping that it was merely due to the amount of work.[50] The young Oxford Fellow was learning the extent to which he could afford to busy himself with a myriad of activities. A letter to his father a few months later, on February 25, 1928, confirms this assessment.[51] Furthermore, since Lewis's last diary entry was March 2, 1927, he must have spent his available time in preparing for tutorials and responding to Barfield in the Great War.

Because he was now teaching English, Lewis needed to know more about the writings of John Milton than what he found in *Paradise Lost* and *Paradise Regained*. So in January, Lewis began reading Milton's prose tract *Reformation in England*, and later he read both *Prelaticall Episcopacy* and the first book of *The Reason of Church Government*. He liked the last one, because it was very Platonic, an indication that he had set aside his anti-Platonism and come to a more consistent Idealism.[52] While reading Milton, Lewis was also becoming more familiar with Milton's biblical worldview.

In addition to reading Milton, however, in January Lewis was also enjoying Samuel Butler's (1835–1902) *Erewhon Revisited*, which he had last read in 1924.[53] This imaginative story, published with the help of atheist George Bernard Shaw, was set in a country from which the protagonist Mr. Higgs had escaped. Returning sometime later, Higgs discovers that his departure has been viewed as an ascension, he has come to be worshipped as "the Sunchild," and some have established a church of Sunchildism. This book reflects the attitude Lewis had had earlier, that Christ as much as Loki, is the creation of people who want

---

[50] On November 23, 1927. See *The Lewis Papers* 9:306.

[51] *Collected Letters of C. S. Lewis*, I, 745ff.

[52] January 13; on January 17 he notes that he has finished *Prelaticall Episcopacy* and read the first book of *Reason of Church Govt.* See *All My Road Before Me*, 429, 431.

[53] Lewis, *All My Road Before Me*, 315.

someone to worship. This time, however, he thought the book poor, a possible indication that he found the condescending attitude toward Christianity distasteful.[54]

A very important January 18 diary entry shows the confusion in Lewis's mind that still existed in early 1927. One day after reading a good deal of Milton, he wrote in his diary,

> Was thinking about imagination and intellect and the unholy muddle I am in about them at present: undigested scraps of anthroposophy and psychoanalysis jostling with orthodox idealism over a background of good old Kirkian rationalism. Lord what a mess! And all the time (with me) there's the danger of falling back into most childish superstitions, or of running into dogmatic materialism to escape them.[55]

If, in September of 1926, Lewis had been growing daily more doubtful about nearly everything, he was no less doubtful in January of 1927. But he was an Idealist, holding to "orthodox idealism"; it was other ideas that were creating the unholy muddle. He later wrote that during this time in his life, he did not dare to speak of the various difficulties and objections he was feeling,[56] especially the difficulty in talking about the Absolute, or the mind behind the universe, without describing it as God. His objections to Idealism, including its similarity to theism, were among the reasons why he had wavered between two versions of Idealism.[57] At the same time, his March 30 letter to his father asked who wrote the statement that science required more faith than theology, indicating that he was questioning some of the conclusions of some scientists.[58]

The childish superstitions which he mentioned were probably belief in God and accompanying convictions, a belief that he had as a

---

[54] Lewis, *All My Road Before Me*, 426.
[55] Lewis, *All My Road Before Me*, 431f. The date is January 18, 1927.
[56] Lewis, "Modern Theology and Biblical Criticism," *Christian Reflections*, 162f.
[57] That is, the Absolute Idealism of Immanuel Kant and the Subjective Idealism of George Berkeley.
[58] *Collected Letters of C. S. Lewis*, I, 680.

child but now thought of as superstition,[59] so this quotation indicates that the third chess move—Check—had not yet happened. Five days later, he wrote in his diary about taking a long walk to try to get rid of the oppression he felt.[60] While he did not specify the type of oppression, it was probably spiritual oppression, which was the only kind of oppression he voiced in his letters and diary from time to time, or "the steady, unrelenting approach" of Him whom he did not want to meet.[61]

On the same day that he and Barfield discussed death and the supernatural, Lewis wrote in his diary, "Pulled up my blind to see the stars, thought suddenly of Bergson: then of how I have been playing the devil with my nerves by letting things I really don't believe in and vague possibilities haunt my imagination. I had a strong conviction of having turned a corner and soon getting all the 'nurse and grandam[62] from my soul.' "[63] He no longer wanted to flirt with the supernatural and its "childish superstitions."

On February 22, ten months after the "Rum thing" comment from Harry Weldon, Lewis again drank whiskey with Weldon, and the two of them talked until after midnight. After his conversion to Christianity, Lewis became unhappy with the maneuverings of Weldon, especially in Magdalen College politics.[64] That they were talking with each other at length in February 1927 suggests that Lewis was still far from becoming a Christian and that he enjoyed the company of Weldon.

---

[59] Brown, A Life Observed, 133.
[60] Lewis, All My Road Before Me, 435, January 23, 1927.
[61] Lewis, Surprised by Joy, 228.
[62] An archaic word for "old woman."
[63] Lewis, All My Road Before Me, 439f., January 26, 1927.
[64] On July 7, 1929, Lewis wrote to his father about Weldon's "sinister presence" (Collected Letters of C. S. Lewis, I, 801).

But Lewis's mind was struggling with the implications of ideas in MacDonald,[65] Coleridge,[66] the poet de la Mare,[67] and Plato.

Alan Griffiths wrote that when he first met Lewis, apparently during Michaelmas term in the autumn of 1927, Lewis had moved beyond atheism to belief in a Universal Spirit, i.e., an Idealist position. Nevertheless, Lewis would not at this time have regarded this Universal Spirit as God.[68] As previously stated, by this time Lewis was no longer an atheist, but he was also not a theist.

As indicated above, Lewis's teaching schedule, meeting schedule, and interaction in his "Great War" with Owen Barfield consumed much of his energies, but his "unholy muddle" was probably far more likely to be the cause of his lack of movement in his spiritual journey.

1928: *POETIC DICTION* AND THE GREAT WAR

The Great War letters between Lewis and Barfield continued. Lewis wrote his major work against Barfield's Anthroposophy, which he called his *Summa*,[69] in the summer and finished it in November. Alan Griffiths stated that Lewis lent this *Summa* to him, a work that convinced Griffiths to become an Idealist.[70] The *Summa*, wrote Griffiths, outlined Lewis's idea of the Universal Spirit behind all

---

[65] On February 28, Lewis was pleased to learn that Hetherington, a student of Lewis's whom Lewis has been tutoring at least since April 1926, was an admirer of George MacDonald's *Phantastes* (*All My Road Before Me*, 456).

[66] On April 18, Lewis was reading Coleridge's *Biographia Literaria*. See *Collected Letters of C. S. Lewis*, I, 685.

[67] On June 26, Lewis wrote to Arthur Greeves, rating de la Mare above all other moderns, including Yeats, and describing him as "nearer than anyone else to the essential truth of life" (*Collected Letters of C. S. Lewis*, I, 700).

[68] Griffiths, "The Adventure of Faith," *C. S. Lewis at the Breakfast Table*, 16.

[69] *Summa* is Latin for "highest." The full title is *Clivi Hamiltonis Summae Metaphysices contra Anthroposophos Libri II*, that is, in English "The Highest Books of the Metaphysics of Clive Hamilton against the Anthroposophists." For a full description of the Great War between Lewis and Barfield, see Thorson, *Joy and Poetic Imagination*.

[70] Griffiths, "The Adventure of Faith," *C. S. Lewis at the Breakfast Table*, 13.

phenomena, a position that the German philosopher G. W. F. Hegel had held and one that was essentially pantheistic.[71]

One other major event took place early this year: the publication of Owen Barfield's book *Poetic Diction*.[72] Among other things, Barfield distinguished between myth and allegory, a distinction that helped both Lewis and Tolkien. He also argued that all language is metaphorical, that imagination creates meaning with metaphor, and that all words had an original concrete meaning. This book profoundly influenced Lewis, who later recommended the book to many people. Several years earlier, Lewis had learned from Bradley that the Christian story, or metaphor, was at least as compelling as any other explanation of the universe.[73] Barfield confirmed this idea, even though Barfield was an Anthroposophist, not a Christian.

Very possibly after Barfield's book was published, Lewis wrote "He Whom I Bow To," the first of sixteen poems that appeared in *The Pilgrim's Regress* when it was published in 1933. While the book was written in 1932, some of the poems undoubtedly pre-date the book or at least reflect a time prior to his conversion to theism. Their precise dates, however, are uncertain, and this one seems as well suited for 1928 as for 1929, the former date following upon Barfield's book and the latter date occurring at the time when Lewis wrote another poem on the subject, entitled "Prayer." Since *The Pilgrim's Regress* presents an allegorical defense for Christianity, reason, and romanticism, all of these poems say something about Lewis's spiritual journey, or regression, back to the faith of his youth.

The poem "Prayer" invites the Lord to translate the speaker's feeble attempts at prayer into the meaning that he intended. It is spoken

---

[71] Griffiths, "The Adventure of Faith," *C. S. Lewis at the Breakfast Table*, 13. This is the absolute Idealism of Hegel rather than the subjective Idealism of Berkeley and Hume.

[72] By May 27, 1928, Lewis had purchased Barfield's *Poetic Diction*. See "Chronologically Lewis" at www.joelheck.com for that date.

[73] Lewis, "Early Prose Joy," 34f. The concepts in *Poetic Diction* had undoubtedly been expressed by Barfield in conversation with Lewis long before they were published in book form.

by John, the main character of the *Regress*, after he had separated from Vertue and was continuing his journey alone. He holds to the Absolute or the eternal Spirit or universal mind, which does not help him. Then he realizes that he has been praying, but he wonders if that had only been a metaphor. Or perhaps it was more than a metaphor.[74] In the prayer he invites the Lord to translate the metaphor of his prayer into something meaningful. He is resisting the idea of a personal God, preferring to think of God as a metaphor (Absolute, Spirit, mind), but he is still praying. In "He Whom I Bow To," Lewis likewise struggles with the idea of prayer, stating that all prayers make people idolaters, all people are self-deceived, and all prayers need God to translate our prayers into meaningful communication.

On May 27, Lewis told Barfield in a letter that he had spent much time during the last vacation in the Bodleian Library starting a book on the Romance of the Rose and its school, i.e., medieval love poetry.[75] This book eventually became *The Allegory of Love*, and it explains another major reason for the slow pace of change in Lewis's thinking between 1927 and 1929. Lewis indicated the same in a July 10 letter to his father, which suggests that research for the book consumed much of his time during this year.[76] At the same time, Lewis continued his heavy schedule of tutoring philosophy and English students, indicating such in a letter to his father.[77] He even wrote to Warren about his inability to write letters during term, confirming the heaviness of his teaching and research schedule. The continuation of the Great War between Lewis and Barfield, with Barfield's challenge of Lewis's ideas about metaphor and myth, added to Lewis's "unholy muddle." The year 1928 also contained a heavy work schedule and thorough research on his first book on literature, but little documented development in Lewis's thinking apart from his *Summa* against Barfield's Anthroposophism. However, that "little" was

---

[74] Lewis, *The Pilgrim's Regress*, Book Eight, Chapter IV, 138f.
[75] *Collected Letters of C. S. Lewis*, I, 764.
[76] *Collected Letters of C. S. Lewis*, I, 766.
[77] *Collected Letters of C. S. Lewis*, I, 777. The letter is dated November 3.

indicative of major changes taking place in Lewis's mind, since the *Summa* described Lewis's pantheistic and Idealist position.

1929: THE DEATH OF ALBERT LEWIS

Late in 1929, the death of his father profoundly affected C. S. Lewis as well as his brother Warren, but the months leading up to that event showed the same busy pattern of the previous several years, which added to the guilt he felt. Not only had he avoided spending time with his father in recent years; he remembered well the resentment he felt and the mockery he had made of the Pudaitabird in letters to his brother. Years later he wrote that no sin in his life seemed as serious as the abominable way in which he had treated his father.[78] In a March letter to Arthur Greeves, Lewis blamed his heavy schedule for his inability to make a purchase for Arthur,[79] and several months later he wrote about the many hours he was spending in the Bodleian Library, continuing his study of medieval love poetry for what would become his first great book of literary criticism, *The Allegory of Love*.[80]

While Lewis stated in *Surprised by Joy* that he became a theist in 1929, Lewis's conversion to theism—as recent scholarship has shown, and as will be evidenced in the next several pages—undoubtedly took place in Trinity term 1930 rather than 1929.[81] In a May letter to his father, Lewis showed his disdain for worship by calling it a mistake to attend a weekday Evensong in Salisbury, although his reasons were not religious.[82] However, it is likely that there were other reasons for avoiding worship, since his criticism appears motivated by more than mere externals.

---

[78] *Collected Letters of C. S. Lewis*, III, 445. The letter was written to Rhona Bodle on March 24, 1954.

[79] *Collected Letters of C. S. Lewis*, I, 785.

[80] *Collected Letters of C. S. Lewis*, I, 800.

[81] Trinity term in 1929 was from April 3 to July 6. See Alister McGrath, *C. S. Lewis: A Life, Eccentric Genius, Reluctant Prophet* (Carol Stream, IL: Tyndale House, 2013), 139–41; Lazo, "Correcting the Chronology: Some Implications of 'Early Prose Joy,'" 51–62.

[82] *Collected Letters of C. S. Lewis*, I, 795.

In July, Lewis read Andrew Lang's *Myth, Ritual and Religion*, including the story of the flood, which appears in nearly every culture in one form or another.[83] In this book, written from a Christian perspective, Lang criticizes the evolutionary views of religion held by Herbert Spencer and James Frazer, insisting that even among savages, pure religious beliefs existed at the beginning and degeneration followed rather than preceded such beliefs. He clearly distinguishes belief from myth and considers such belief to have something sacred about it. Although myth crept into such early religions, there was an early belief in a Creator in many of the world's religions as well as numerous flood stories and creation stories.

Tolkien had probably recommended that Lewis read Andrew Lang. Lang saw myth and religion as ideas in conflict with each other, but Tolkien, with whom Lewis was in regular conversation at this time, saw Christianity as mythical in the sense that the Christian story carried the same pattern of events as that which appears in pagan religions.

For Lang, religion in the distant past was rational, but myth contained both rational and non-rational elements. Occasionally, myth was an exaggeration and a distortion of fact, and its roots were to be found in the mental condition of the savage, which puts all forms of life on the same level. For Tolkien, however, myth also contained a gleam of divine truth, and the origin of myth is much earlier and more obscure than for Lang. One of the most important features of myth, Lang contended, was its totemism, which found kinship between human beings and the world of plants and animals, a feature that Lewis probably liked. His reading of *Myth, Ritual and Religion* at this time, however, very likely came as a reassessment of the value of myth, and he may well have been impressed with this statement in Lang's book: "the belief in one God is entire and universal among them."[84] He

---

[83] *Collected Letters of C. S. Lewis*, I, 800. This publication was originally published in two volumes in 1887 and then republished with a new Preface in 1901. Lewis probably read the 1901 edition.
[84] Andrew Lang, *Myth, Ritual, and Religion*, Chapter IV, 87.

was probably also impressed with the atonement myths, fertility myths, initiation myths, beginning of life myths, end of life myths, and many other practices that Lang described.

In August, when Lewis learned from x-rays that his father was seriously ill, he wrote to Albert about his own helplessness, stating that one could only give a handshake and a good wish. He did not state that he was praying for Albert, which he might have, had he already become a theist.[85] Nor did Lewis's letter to Owen Barfield in the following month show any sense of remorse over his role in the rift between father and sons or any effort to resolve that breach. That letter described many painful memories from the past, but no remorse. The same is true of a similar letter, written in the same month, to his brother Warren.[86] It is likely, however, that these memories remained vivid for him and that he came to see his own failings in the months ahead.[87] In spite of those painful memories, when it appeared that he was going to lose his father, Lewis made every effort to help his father, to spend time with his father, and to get his father the kind of medical attention he needed, almost as though he were attempting to pay a debt before it was too late. After completing a week of examinations in Cambridge, he left for Belfast and spent five-and-a-half weeks caring for Albert between August 13 and September 21.

Lewis left Belfast on Saturday, September 21, and later learned that his father died the following Wednesday afternoon, September 25, 1929. When he received the news, Lewis left Oxford that very same day to return to Belfast, arriving just a day after his father died. In spite of the almost endless conflict between father and sons, the loss of their father had a profound impact on both Lewis brothers. Lewis's former student, friend, and biographer George Sayer wrote that Lewis was

---

[85] *Collected Letters of C. S. Lewis*, I, 806. The date of the letter is August 5, 1929, well after the end of Trinity term, 1929, when Lewis writes in *Surprised by Joy* that his conversion to theism took place. Trinity term, 1929, ended on July 6.

[86] *Collected Letters of C. S. Lewis*, I, 819–821, 827.

[87] *Collected Letters of C. S. Lewis*, I, 820f. This connection became clearer to me because of the insight of my former student Danielle Valenzuela.

"bitterly ashamed of the way he had deceived and denigrated his father in the past, and . . . he had a strong feeling that Albert was somehow still alive and helping him."[88] Years later, Lewis wrote similarly to Vera Mathews about her father's death, suggesting that his father's death had had a major impact on him. He told her that in the weeks and months after a death, some good comes to the living from those who have died. He thought that his own father had helped him and had seemed to be near him.[89] A few years after he wrote to Mathews, he also wrote to Rhona Bodle, whose father had just died, "Oh how you touch my conscience! I treated my own father abominably and no sin in my whole life now seems to be so serious."[90] We also learn not only about Lewis's regret, but also his sense that his father had helped him in the weeks after Albert's death.

Nearly a year later, on June 7, 1930, we have another indication of the impact of his father's death. Lewis wrote to Arthur Greeves about a visit he made with Frederick Lawson to Lawson's father. Lawson was Fellow and Tutor in Law at Oxford University, and he had recently set up his widowed father in a little red cottage in the neighboring village of Holton. Lewis admired how the younger Lawson listened to his father and how much care he had taken to set his father up in this community, even bringing some of his own possessions from Merton College to furnish the cottage. When he saw how kindly Lawson treated his father, he recalled how abominably he had treated his own father.[91] These glimpses suggest that his conscience was awakened to his guilt, that the death of his father had a profound impact on Lewis's spiritual journey, and that his adoption of theism took place after the loss of his father, rather than before.

---

[88] Sayer, *Jack*, 224.
[89] *Collected Letters of C. S. Lewis*, III, 104, March 27, 1951.
[90] *Collected Letters of C. S. Lewis*, III, 445, March 24, 1954.
[91] *Collected Letters of C. S. Lewis*, I, 902f. See also *Collected Letters of C. S. Lewis*, III, 445.

This is also the year, it is suggested, Lewis wrote "When Lilith Means to Draw Me."[92] Lilith refers to sexual temptation in this poem, a temptation that draws one in, promising, but not delivering, satisfaction. What the pilgrim John truly longs for is God, so this substitute of sexual temptation does not fully satisfy, and he sings this song in order to resist. If the poem is in any sense autobiographical, Lewis may have seen the problem of longing for God in his own life in the story he related in *The Pilgrim's Regress*, especially at a time when the emotional impact of his father's death weighed heavily upon him.

During the last three months of 1929, two themes especially appear—the busy schedule he kept and the internal struggles with his spiritual life (Owen Barfield described him as an agnostic in religion at this time),[93] the latter probably heightened by the necessity of reading letters of condolence and arranging the disposition of his father's estate. For example, in October, Lewis wrote to Arthur Greeves about George Herbert's poem, "The Flower," which compares the spiritual life to the death of the flower in winter and its revival in spring.[94] As the autumn leaves began to fall, plants began to die, and he saw winter draw near, he realized that one must die to self before coming to life again. The poem ends with the word *pride*, which Lewis considered his besetting sin. When Lewis wrote that letter in 1929, shortly after his father's death, he was becoming more aware of his own shortcomings. That same day he had a conversation with Owen Barfield in which Barfield insisted that longing was an essential part of human nature. Then, on the very next day, Lewis had glimpses of "It," i.e., longing, and he wondered whether "the death of the natural always mean[s] the birth of the spiritual."[95] Not only does this indicate that he was struggling in his spiritual life, especially its connection to his father's death; it also means that the third chess move had not yet occurred. If it had, he would not have been wondering about that longing.

---

[92] *The Pilgrim's Regress*, Book Ten, Chapter VII, 189.
[93] *Owen Barfield on C. S. Lewis*, 129.
[94] *Collected Letters of C. S. Lewis*, I, 830. The date is October 3, 1929.
[95] *Collected Letters of C. S. Lewis*, I, 832. The date is October 4, 1929.

One week later, Lewis wrote to Arthur favorably about reading George MacDonald's *Diary of an Old Soul*, a semi-devotional book of daily poetic readings, admitting that he once would have scorned this book but now appreciated it.[96] That collection of seven-line poems spoke to his heart, spoke about Christ, and spoke to Lewis about his own self-centeredness, and it undoubtedly encouraged him to think outside of himself, moving him finally to do something about it. He also compared George Herbert to George MacDonald, showing both his preference for MacDonald because of his homespun flavor and the growing influence of both authors on his thinking. On October 16, he walked with Alan Griffiths, something that makes sense, given their relationship during this period when both men were seriously exploring the Christian faith. Then the next morning he walked with Griffiths again.[97] Since they were both considering a spiritual outlook on life at this time, they undoubtedly talked about the spiritual insights that each one was receiving from his readings.

A few weeks later, Lewis talked with Barfield about the spiritual world as home, drawing on both MacDonald and Chesterton for that homely imagery. The very next day, Lewis described himself as entangled with the world and not where he wanted to be, apparently on an emotional and intellectual plane, but perhaps also spiritually.[98] In early December near the end of term, he wrote to Arthur Greeves that he had too many irons in the fire, affirming his earlier statements about his heavy schedule and stating that this was not good. He wrote to Arthur that all these meetings and appointments were both difficult to maintain and bad for him spiritually.[99] This is the first clear indication that he was thinking about his spiritual life. He was thinking about clearing the decks so that he could deal with these spiritual matters.

---

[96] *Collected Letters of C. S. Lewis*, I, 834. The date is October 10, 1929.

[97] *Collected Letters of C. S. Lewis*, I, 834.

[98] *Collected Letters of C. S. Lewis*, I, 837. A diary-like entry dated November 6, 1929.

[99] *Collected Letters of C. S. Lewis*, I, 838. The diary entry is dated December 3, 1929.

In that same letter, he indicated that he had recently listened to Tolkien talk about the gods and giants of Asgard for hours.[100] This conversation indicates a continuation of Lewis's interest in the power of the human imagination. Then, a few days later, Lewis wrote to Tolkien about *The Lay of Leithian*, "I can quite honestly say that it is ages since I have had an evening of such delight. . . . The two things that came out clearly are the sense of reality in the background and the mythical value: the essence of myth being that it should have no taint of allegory to the maker and yet should *suggest* incipient allegories to the reader."[101] Those two ideas—the sense of reality and the nature of myth—were a necessary foundation for later seeing the connection between myths and the Christian "myth" as a conveyor of truth.

In late December, after the end of term and as his heavy schedule was easing up, Lewis wrote to Warren, then serving with the RASC in China, that he had had "no normal life or leisure—for ages."[102] The very next day, after reading John Bunyan's *Grace Abounding to the Chief of Sinners*, Bunyan's spiritual autobiography, Lewis wrote to Arthur Greeves, asking him what he thought of the darker side of religion. He was beginning to think that the old beliefs had much truth in them, writing, "Now that I have found, and am finding more and more, the element of truth in the old beliefs, I feel I cannot dismiss even their dreadful side so cavalierly. There must be something in it: only what?"[103] This letter demonstrates a reappraisal of the prospect of God's judgment against sin. Truth always has hard edges, and Lewis knew that the darker side of religion did not mean it wasn't true. It also confirms the 1930 date for Lewis's conversion to theism. He could not have been a theist prior to writing this letter on December 22, since he would not have expressed such confusion had he been a theist.

---

[100] *Collected Letters of C. S. Lewis*, I, 838. He probably did this one evening in late November.

[101] Tolkien, *The Lays of Beleriand*, 151, cited in Colin Duriez, *Tolkien and C. S. Lewis*, 48. The date of the letter is December 7, 1929, but it does not appear in *Collected Letters of C. S. Lewis*, I.

[102] *Collected Letters of C. S. Lewis*, I, 838.

[103] *Collected Letters of C. S. Lewis*, I, 850.

On Christmas Eve, after a day of Christmas festivities, including attendance at a Christmas Eve celebration where he heard the singing of part of Handel's *Messiah*, Lewis wrote that he felt "a blessed sense of charity."[104] Two days later, on Boxing Day, while out on a walk with Magdalen College historian Bruce McFarlane, Lewis and McFarlane walked through the beautiful village of Cumnor, enjoying the solitary calm and the pale blue sky, and then they came into the village of Stanton Harcourt and saw the towered manor house and the church. At that exact moment they heard the ringers at the church practicing, and he had a sense of "absolute peace and safety," enjoying the homeliness of the entire experience as well as its Englishness and its Christendom.[105] Then, in a letter to Arthur Greeves, Lewis wrote about the Absolute as though the Absolute were a person, and about the spiritual nature of the universe, even claiming that the vast, inhuman, and alarming aspects of the universe were exactly as they needed to be.[106] The year 1929 ended with Lewis thinking a great deal about spiritual matters.

---

[104] *Collected Letters of C. S. Lewis*, I, 852.
[105] *Collected Letters of C. S. Lewis*, I, 853.
[106] December 26, 1929. See *Collected Letters of C. S. Lewis*, I, 854.

CHAPTER 6

CHECK AND CHECKMATE

"It is emphatically coming home."

—C. S. Lewis, *Collected Letters*

The chess match had reached the end game. God had been closing in, and the Idealist position Lewis had adopted had begun to look more and more like theism. The death of his father had had a profound impact on him, though he only gradually came to realize its significance. Prayer was non-existent in his life, pride was bothering him, his treatment of his father troubled his conscience, he thought his busy schedule bad for him spiritually, he was wondering about the darker side of religion, having just read Bunyan's spiritual autobiography, and he was being challenged to think more highly of myth.

During the period of time late in his pilgrimage, perhaps in 1929, Lewis wrote a poem entitled "Reason," also entitled "Set on the Soul's Acropolis the Reason Stands."[1] This poem wrestles with the relationship between reason and imagination, fitting very well in the period when Lewis began to believe that the imagination could be trusted to discover both meaning and truth (in the sense of spiritual realities—such as angels and God as well as Barfield's spirit guides, intermediate

---

[1] C. S. Lewis, *Poems* (New York: Harcourt Brace & Company, 1964), 1992. The latter title is from King, *The Collected Poems of C. S. Lewis*. King suggests 1929 as the date of composition of this poem.

spirits, and the like—beyond the five senses). The poem reflects Lewis's longing for reason and imagination to reconcile to each other, and it announces that when such a reconciliation occurs, he will be able to say that he believes. That makes the poem fit well in late 1929 or early 1930, not long before he came to believe in God.

1930: COMING HOME

In 1930, C. S. Lewis returned to belief in God, describing his return as coming home.[2] The idea of coming home Lewis owed to G. K. Chesterton's *The Everlasting Man*. In that book, Chesterton wrote that there were two ways of getting home, one of them is to stay there, the other is to walk all the way around the world to return to the same place.[3] Having read widely and pursued a variety of dead ends, Lewis saw himself following the latter method of coming home, a method that he described in his first Christian book, *The Pilgrim's Regress*. Much of the longing he had experienced over the past two decades found fulfillment in the culmination of his spiritual journey from atheism to agnosticism to Realism to Idealism to theism.

Early in the year of his return, the work of his favorite poet, Dante Alighieri, spoke to him of the individual soul, human destiny, sin, and grace. On the second day of the new year, Lewis wrote to Arthur Greeves that he had never really understood Dante before and that the *Paradiso* opened a new world to him. Lewis was probably referring to the spiritual pilgrimage that Dante was describing, how one individual soul fared, and how we all might hope to fare.[4] Lewis no doubt saw himself reaching for that hope. Earlier in that book, he thought, in the *Paradiso*, Dante struck the right note in describing the unfallen Adam.

---

[2] *Collected Letters of C. S. Lewis*, I, 873, where Lewis refers to Chaucer's *Troilus and Criseyde*, V, 1837. This letter, written to Arthur Greeves, is dated January 26, 1930.

[3] G. K. Chesterton, *The Everlasting Man* (San Francisco: Ignatius Press, 1993), xi.

[4] *Collected Letters of C. S. Lewis*, I, 857; Lewis, *A Preface to Paradise Lost*, 132f.

Such a state, Dante implied, was our human destiny,[5] a destiny that C. S. Lewis longed for.

In rereading Dante, Lewis was beginning to see how his own subject area of literature connected with his life. Events were beginning to line up—the remorse he had felt at the death of his father just a few months earlier, the shaking up he would get from Jacob Boehme, the Absolute in Idealism behaving just like God, the continued influence of George MacDonald in *The Diary of an Old Soul*, seeing how a subject needed to be "a way" rather than merely a subject, a reappraisal of the philosopher Berkeley, the mystical view that God—like Shakespeare—could write Himself into His own play, his own unbuckling on top of a double-decker bus (during which he determined to go where the evidence pointed), and an awareness of his own pride. The chess match was taking a much more personal turn.

Three days later, Lewis mentioned in a letter to Arthur that he had written a letter to Alan Griffiths on philosophical subjects. He did not elaborate on the specific philosophical topics he addressed, but he probably wrote to Griffiths about Berkeley's arguments for the existence of God, particularly in the light of what Lewis had read in Dante.[6]

READING JACOB BOEHME

At the same time, Lewis wrote to Arthur about reading the early seventeenth-century German mystic Jacob Boehme's *The Signature of All Things*. He called it "a thunderclap" and wrote that he got "the biggest shaking up" he had received from a book since reading *Phantastes* fourteen years earlier. As a 1932 letter to Warren Lewis hints, probably either his readings in Samuel Johnson or William Law

---

[5] Lewis, *A Preface to Paradise Lost*, 117f. The reference is to the *Paradiso*, XXVI, 83.

[6] Griffiths told his own story in *The Golden String* (Springfield, IL: Templegate, 1980), a story that supports this close relationship between the two men. See p. 56f.

had recommended Boehme to him.[7] That suggests that as a result of this book Lewis was all the more open to the possibility of another world, a spiritual world that was far more real than the imaginative world of *Phantastes*. In addition, however, Lewis's own notes in the margins of his copy include the words "the foundation of hell is manifested, namely, in selfhood and in the false will."[8]

In *The Signature of All Things*, Boehme wrote about creation, the image of God, the nature of sin, the relation of good to evil, the Trinity, the person and work of Christ, time and eternity, desire, the presence of God in nature, and eternal life. In short, as the title indicates, Boehme argued that God's "signature" appears on everything He has made. Boehme did not write conventionally, but mystically, guided by his own unique sensitivity to the divine presence and an awareness of the spiritual, almost sacramental, properties behind nature. Lewis especially appreciated Boehme's description of the mystery of creation, its origin in "the original One," and the One who made "a world and souls and good and evil." Yet he stated that Boehme's writing was beyond him, tantalizing in its description of "something tremendously real."[9] Perhaps Lewis was now aware that coming home was not a purely intellectual exercise; something more, something mystical or experiential, was required.

Two statements from the second chapter of *The Signature of All Things* both distressed and challenged him: "That the nothing is become an eternal life and has found itself, which cannot be, in the Stillness"[10] and "The wrath extinguishes and the turning orb stands still, and instead of the turning a sound is caused in the essence."[11] The first statement insists that "the nothing" cannot be and that it becomes eternal life, and the second affirms the reality of wrath, perhaps as it

---

[7] *Collected Letters of C. S. Lewis*, II, 40.

[8] C. S. Lewis, marginalia in his edition of *The Signature of All Things with other Writings*, Jacob Boehme (London: J. M. Dent & Sons, 1926), 267, cited in Barkman, *C. S. Lewis & Philosophy as a Way of Life*, 347, n. 147.

[9] *Collected Letters of C. S. Lewis*, I, 858f.

[10] Boehme, *The Signature of All Things*, online edition, Chapter 2, para. 18.

[11] Boehme, *The Signature of All Things*, Chapter 2, para. 19.

exists in "the essence," which may be God. Lewis resolved to find a commentator on Boehme's book so he could determine the meaning of those unusual passages. The first of these two quotations appears to be echoed in *The Pilgrim's Regress* in a statement made by a voice that invited the pilgrim John to go down to Mother Kirk, just moments before he dove into the water, no longer trying to preserve himself: "To you I am not Nothing; I am the being blindfolded, the losing all power of self-defense, the surrender, not because any terms are offered, but because resistance is gone: the step into the dark: the defeat of all precautions: utter helplessness turned out to utter risk: the final loss of liberty."[12] By this means the pilgrim came into the Christian faith: "And how John managed it or what he felt I did not know, but he also rubbed his hands, shut his eyes, despaired, and let himself go. It was not a good dive, but, at least, he reached the water head first."[13]

Boehme held to the medieval view that the planets (themselves a reflection of God's influence) influenced the Earth. He believed that seven metals were characteristics of the seven planets. For Boehme and the medievalists, for example, the Sun featured the metal gold.[14] This insight about planetary influence may have affected Lewis, since Boehme wrote about the planets so extensively, and it probably affected the Ransom Trilogy, the Chronicles of Narnia, and other works of Lewis.[15] In fact, Boehme seems to interpret the entire biblical

---

[12] Lewis, *The Pilgrim's Regress*, 164.

[13] Lewis, *The Pilgrim's Regress*, 168.

[14] For example, in a passage dealing with the sun, Boehme wrote, "Gold is nigh to the divine essentiality, or heavenly corporality." Then, later on the same page, he wrote, "Further, we are also to consider of the other metals and minerals, which in like manner do thus take their original" (*The Signature of All Things*, 31). "Mars's metal is iron" (40). Some readers will be familiar with Michael Ward's books *Planet Narnia* and *The Narnia Code* on this topic, which correlate the Chronicles of Narnia with the seven planets of medieval cosmology.

[15] See, for example, this quotation, "Thus Mars clothes all his servants which love him and Saturn with his garment, that they only find the copper of Venus, and not its gold in the copper; the spirit of the seeker enters into Sol, viz. into pride, and supposes that he has Venus, but he has Saturn, viz. covetousness; if he went

narrative from a planetary perspective,[16] but he also takes historical events as types or patterns, interpreting them quite subjectively.[17] While *Phantastes* started Lewis's move toward theism, albeit quite slowly, Boehme's mystical book appears to have accelerated that move, which would culminate in the adoption of theism within the next six months.

Much later, in *Letters to Malcolm*, Lewis wrote that Boehme advised that once an hour we "fling ourselves beyond every creature."[18] Boehme's writing apparently influenced Lewis to consider a bigger, broader picture of the universe than that of pure materialism, but Boehme especially evoked a yearning for something beyond the material, which Idealism had already taught Lewis. In fact, Lewis later echoes Boehme by calling that yearning "the secret signature of each soul."[19] At the same time, he also rejected some of Boehme,

---

forth in the water, viz. in the resigned humility of Venus, the stone of the wise men would be revealed to him" (*The Signature of All Things*, 95, para. 18). Or this, "The mother of all beings is Sulphur, Mercury is her life, Mars her sense, Venus her love, Jupiter her understanding, Luna her corporeal essence, Saturn her Husband" (*The Signature of All Things*, 122, para. 56).

[16] For example, Boehme writes of the connection between Pilate's whipping of Jesus and the influence of Mercury and Mars, thus: "The poisonful rays of Mercury and Mars, which they lay upon the child through the impression of Saturn; as Pilate whipped Jesus" (*The Signature of All Things*, 135, para. 23).

[17] For example, Boehme sees the words of Jesus on the cross to John and his mother as typological for the Christian church. Mary stands for the church, and John stands for the servants of Christ that care for the church, although Boehme does not seem to deny the historical occurrence of that word from Jesus to Mary and John. Instead, he sees at least two levels of meaning, perhaps continuing the pre-Reformation tradition of finding four levels of meaning in a scriptural passage (*The Signature of All Things*, 142f., 52–57). He also compares the three hours of darkness to the sleep of Adam, when Eve was formed, and then to the three days Jesus was in the grave. Then he claims that Jesus was forty hours in the grave, which corresponds to the forty days Adam lived without sinning, the forty days of Israel at Mt. Sinai, the forty years of Israel's temptation in the wilderness, and the forty days between the resurrection of Christ and the ascension (*The Signature of All Things*, 147f., 76–77).

[18] *Letters to Malcolm: Chiefly on Prayer* (London: HarperCollins, 1977), 75.

[19] Lewis, *The Problem of Pain*, 151.

particularly his views that suggested that God created evil and especially Boehme's pantheistic views, which suggested that the human soul would eventually dissolve into the divine soul.[20]

A week after his previous letter, Lewis wrote to Arthur Greeves about his recent change of views, reflecting his reading of Boehme, but he still contended that Arthur had arrived at his picture of Christ by picking and choosing only parts of the Gospels.[21] Lewis was neither a theist nor a Christian at this point, so while he probably read the portions of Boehme's book that focused on Christ, he certainly did not accept them.[22] He wrote to Arthur in the way that one would expect someone to write who read with an open mind, neither dismissing the book nor accepting everything he read.

At this time Lewis probably wrote the poem that reflects Boehme, "Quick! The Black, Sulphurous, Never Quenched."[23] The mystic Jacob Boehme wrote about the power of sulphur, using it as a symbol of one of the three divine essences. When that sulphurous fire is burning, God is at work. *The Signature of All Things* had given Lewis a shaking

---

[20] Downing, *Into the Region of Awe*, 30, 44.

[21] *Collected Letters of C. S. Lewis*, I, 862, January 9, 1930.

[22] For example, p. 202f., para. 27, "Comforting and setting the suffering of Christ in the forefront is not the true faith; no, no, it is only without, and not within: But a converted will, which enters into sorrow for its earthly iniquity, and will have none of it anymore; and yet finds that it is kept back by the self-full earthly lust, and with his converted will departs sincerely out of this abomination and false desire into God's mercy, and casts himself with great anxious [earnest] desire into Christ's obedience, suffering, and death, and in the converted will wholly dies to the earthly lust in Christ's death, which will not depart out of Christ's death, and continually cries Abba, loving Father! take thy dear Son's obedience for me; let me only in his death live in his obedience in thee; let me die in him, that I may be nothing in myself, but live and be in his will, in his humanity in thee; receive me, but wholly in his resurrection, and not in my unworthiness; but receive me in him; let me be dead in him, and give me his life, that I may be thy obedient son in him, that his suffering and death may be mine, that I may be before the same Christ in him who has deprived death of its might, viz. a branch or twig of his life."

[23] Lewis, *The Pilgrim's Regress*, Book Ten, Chapter VII, 188. See *The Collected Poems of C. S. Lewis*, 231.

up at this time because God was at work in his life. The poem is spoken by a man who lives in luxury, and it describes human beings craving the cup of luxury, which, in turn, transforms them into something less than human. They desire more of this luxury, while God seeks to draw them to Him.

Spiritual and Philosophical Meditation

Much was happening in Lewis's life in early 1930. He was rethinking the value of imagination, being challenged by Jacob Boehme, remaining in contact with his chief companion Alan Griffiths, and communicating all this in his letters to Arthur Greeves. In *Surprised by Joy*, Lewis stated that the fourth chess move (which, I will argue, happened just a few months after the third move) happened while he was teaching both philosophy and English,[24] hence, following his appointment to Magdalen in 1925 and probably during his first five-year appointment. Lewis seems to compress these five years at times so that events happening years apart are viewed, in retrospect, as though they happened close together, but still within his first five-year teaching appointment.[25] Lewis himself was not always clear on the precise sequence of events, which he wrote about twenty-five to thirty years after they happened.[26]

Not only was Lewis rethinking the value of imagination, he was also rethinking philosophy. "The fox had been dislodged from Hegelian Wood . . . , bedraggled and weary, hounds barely a field behind."[27] Since Hegel was an Idealist, these words suggest Lewis's dependence on him. Being dislodged from the Hegelian Wood suggests

---

[24] Lewis, *Surprised by Joy*, 222.

[25] Lewis was made a Fellow in 1925, reappointed in 1930 and every five years thereafter.

[26] If we draw once again on Samuel Alexander's distinction between enjoyment and contemplation, Lewis was enjoying the spiritual journey rather than contemplating it. In other words, he was too close to the events themselves to analyze them for date and sequence.

[27] Lewis, *Surprised by Joy*, 225.

that Lewis was thinking Idealism as inadequate to explain his experience. While he had changed his metaphor from a chess game to a fox hunt, the meaning was the same. The Grandmaster was closing in on his chess opponent, the Hunter and foxhounds were closing in on the fox, and the great Angler was playing His fish.[28] The Absolute, the name Hegel gave to reality, was an all-embracing unity which Hegel (who was pantheistic in his thinking) claimed was the only reality. The problem for Lewis was that the Absolute was acting more and more like a person. In fact, Lewis was now thinking more positively of Berkeley, himself a theist, whom he had previously read in 1917 as a student and again in 1924 when he was preparing to lecture on philosophy for Oxford University.[29] He was beginning to see that thinking about an Absolute mind rather than a person was a way of avoiding the personal nature of God. Furthermore, since Berkeley was an Anglican bishop, clearly his Idealism was compatible with the Christian faith.

Alan Griffiths, who described the period from 1929 to 1932 as a time when both he and Lewis were being drawn to the Christian faith,[30] wrote about the discovery of Berkeley's *Principles of Human Knowledge*. Griffiths was reading a lot of philosophy, and Lewis had recommended the book to him. Griffiths was charmed by Berkeley's style, but also by his thought. One passage in particular charmed him, both in style and content, one that described everything existing either in the mind of a person or in the mind of an eternal Spirit.[31]

---

[28] Lewis, *Surprised by Joy*, 211.

[29] Lewis, *Surprised by Joy*, 222f. See also C. E. M. Joad, *Great Philosophies*, 106.

[30] Griffiths, "The Adventure of Faith," *C. S. Lewis at the Breakfast Table*, 11.

[31] This is the exact passage: "Some truths there are so near and obvious to the mind that a man need only open his mind to perceive them. Such I take this important one to be: *viz.* that all the choir of heaven and all the furniture of the earth, in a word all the bodies which compose the mighty frame of the world, have not any subsistence without a mind, that their being is to be perceived and known; that consequently so long as they are not actually perceived by me or do not exist in my mind or that of any other created spirit, they must either have no existence at all or else subsist in the mind of some eternal Spirit." Cited in Griffiths, *The Golden String*, 48.

Griffiths wrote that this passage turned on a light for him. He came to think, as Lewis would later argue, that one could not conceive of things existing without a mind to know them and experience them by the senses and that things were ideas and the ideas came from universal mind or Spirit. He also came to see that "God was a mind, a pure Spirit, and the universe was the thought of his mind, while our own perception of things was simply a limited participation."[32] This insight must have happened between June 1929, when Griffiths completed his degree at Oxford, and April 1930, and it seems highly likely to have been shared with Lewis, with whom Griffiths shared his discoveries, especially since both men were in a similar stage of doubt.[33]

Surprised by Joy contains some confusions in its chronology, because, as stated earlier, Lewis himself did not remember completely the sequence of events and probably for that reason did not include the precise chronology. We have already seen that he dated his conversion to 1929, when it actually took place in 1930. For another example, Lewis wrote about the fourth chess move late in *Surprised by Joy*,[34] then in the next paragraph stated that he then read Chesterton's *Everlasting Man*. But the reading of *The Everlasting Man* took place about four years before the fourth chess move. Lewis probably read Chesterton's *Everlasting Man* in 1926 (the book was published in 1925), soon after his conversation with Harry Weldon about the historical of the resurrection of Jesus, and the conversion to theism, the fourth chess move, i.e., Checkmate, took place in 1930.

By late January, Lewis had a lighter schedule and more time for leisure, for reading, and for spending time with colleagues and friends.

---

[32] Griffiths, *The Golden String*, 48f.

[33] Griffiths, *The Golden String*, 65, who states that he began his experiment in country living in April 1930. This seems to be the latest date for this realization. The earliest date seems to be after Griffiths graduated from Oxford University, which occurred during the summer of 1929. Email from Robin Darwall-Smith, February 19, 2014, on the dates Griffiths took his English exams.

[34] Lewis, *Surprised by Joy*, 222. The Chesterton reading is recorded on p. 223 with the words "Then I read Chesterton's *Everlasting Man*. . . ."

Whereas a year earlier he had only about two free nights each week, Lewis wrote to Arthur Greeves that he now had five free nights a week.[35] This seems to have been an intentional and recent direction he had taken, i.e., to clear his schedule a great deal, or he would not have mentioned it to Arthur. And that meant that he had more leisure time to think, take long walks, and read for pleasure. Such calm and relaxing experiences as his walk with MacFarlane on Boxing Day in late 1929 gave him greater opportunity to allow his reason to affect his imagination and vice versa.

At this time in his life, Lewis ended each day with a cup of cocoa and an excerpt from George MacDonald's *Diary of an Old Soul*. This book contains a calendar of poetic verses, each seven lines in length, one for each day of the year and filled with spiritual insight. The book had been written after the death of two of MacDonald's children. In his letter to Arthur, Lewis wrote this about MacDonald's book: "That is another of the beauties of coming, I won't say, to religion but to *an attempt at religion*—one finds oneself on the main road with all humanity, and can compare notes with an endless succession of previous travelers. It is emphatically coming home."[36] MacDonald is the same man who, in 1916, gave Lewis that sense of holiness in *Phantastes*, even though Lewis did not recognize it as holiness at the time. By March 21, 1930, Lewis had adopted a religious outlook, and he included those topics in a letter to Jenkin.[37] This religious outlook seems to be the same attempt at religion mentioned above, even though Lewis was neither a theist nor a Christian at this time.

Some of MacDonald's verses in *Diary of an Old Soul* give us a perspective on Lewis's religious outlook and growing awareness of his need for a transcendental interferer who would protect him from himself:

---

[35] *Collected Letters of C. S. Lewis*, I, 873. The date is January 26, 1930.
[36] *Collected Letters of C. S. Lewis*, I, 872f. *Troilus and Criseyde*, V, 1837. The date of the letter is January 26, 1930.
[37] *Collected Letters of C. S. Lewis*, I, 887, March 21, 1930.

O Lord, I have been talking to the people;
Thought's wheels have round me whirled a fiery zone,
And the recoil of my word's airy ripple
My heart heedful has puffed up and blown.
Therefore I cast myself before thee prone;
Lay cool hands on my burning brain and press
From my weak heart the swelling emptiness.[38]

Tis—shall thy will be done for me—or mine.[39]

Lord, I do choose the higher than my will.[40]

With every morn my life afresh must break
The crust of self, gathering about me fresh.[41]

These excerpts are a few of the sections that speak about pride, "the crust of self," and the will of God, suggesting that during these days Lewis was becoming more and more aware that he was far too much caught up in himself. A few days after his "attempt at religion" letter of January 26, Lewis wrote to Arthur about things going well for him spiritually, his experience of Joy, his besetting sin of pride, and his sins in general. Because of the lengthy description of his pride in this letter, this was probably the time indicated in *Surprised by Joy*,[42] when Lewis became more aware of the flaws within him.

UNBUCKLING THE ARMOR OF PRIDE

Probably also at this time an unbuckling and melting incident took place while riding on top of an Oxford bus that was traveling up Headington Hill. Late in *Surprised by Joy*, Lewis describes himself becoming aware that he was holding something at bay. He felt he was

---

[38] Italics mine. The entry for January 31 in *The Diary of an Old Soul*, cited in Lewis's *George MacDonald*, 137.

[39] *The Diary of an Old Soul*, 25. The entry is for February 21.

[40] *The Diary of an Old Soul*, 40. The entry is for April 1.

[41] *The Diary of an Old Soul*, 102, cited in Lewis's *George MacDonald*, 138. The entry is for October 10.

[42] Lewis, *Surprised by Joy*, 226.

being given a choice—to unbuckle the armor or to keep it on, to maintain his resistance or to yield. He decided to stop resisting, and when he did, he felt like a snowman beginning to melt.[43] Add to that the fact that he wrote to Arthur Greeves about the seven deadly sins, his own major problem being pride, and you have a man very concerned about his own shortcomings.[44]

Lewis wrote that when he examined himself seriously for the first time, "there I found what appalled me; a zoo of lusts, a bedlam of ambitions, a nursery of fears, a harem of fondled hatreds."[45] Except for his brief time as a sincere Christian during childhood, Lewis had not previously performed such self-examination. He had submerged his feelings of guilt, his lusts, ambitions, fears, deceptions, and hatreds so as to avoid facing these facts. Two weeks later he wrote to Arthur again with a remark about knowing the tune better than knowing the musician, that is, knowing the real life application of ideas rather than the Originator of those ideas. As the last chess move drew near, Lewis wrote introspectively and quite honestly, "Remember, I had always wanted, above all things, not to be 'interfered with.' I had wanted (mad wish) 'to call my soul my own.'"[46]

Two poems date from this period of time and express the pride that the pilgrim John attempted to avoid in *The Pilgrim's Regress*. "I Have Scraped Clean the Plateau"[47] contains the words of Superbia, i.e., Pride, vaunting her own ability to cleanse herself from her sins and not needing another from the outside to do it for her. The next poem, "Because of Endless Pride,"[48] is the song of Vertue, who looks at himself and sings this song, as John and Vertue continue their journey, leaving Superbia (pride) behind. After discussing the value of the self-sufficiency of pride, the Guide counsels them not to confuse

---

[43] Lewis, *Surprised by Joy*, 224f.
[44] *Collected Letters of C. S. Lewis*, I, 882. The date is February 10, 1930.
[45] Lewis, *Surprised by Joy*, 226.
[46] Lewis, *Surprised by Joy*, 228.
[47] Lewis, *The Pilgrim's Regress*, Book Ten, Chapter V, 182.
[48] Lewis, *The Pilgrim's Regress*, Book Ten, Chapter V, 184.

repentance with disgust. He describes repentance as coming from the Landlord and disgust as coming from the Enemy, humility coming from the Landlord and pride from the Enemy. Then Vertue describes gazing into a mirror and trying different postures so that he looks good. He sees pride, like the Greek mythological figure Narcissus, suffering from a stiff neck and self-love which needs to die in recognition of the One who made us.

Years later, shortly after the Russians had been in outer space and remarked that they had not seen God, Lewis wrote an essay entitled "The Seeing Eye." In reflecting on this period of his life, Lewis wrote that his encounter with God came at a time when he was making a serious effort to obey his conscience. He was not searching for God, but, in retrospect he saw that God was searching for him. God was the hunter, and he was the hunted.[49] His effort to live responsibly brought him to an awareness of his inability to live a consistent life that wasn't wrapped up in himself. The unbuckling enabled him to see himself more clearly than he ever had.

Later in life Lewis also wrote about a time when he feared that the arguments and evidence of Christianity were true. He may have been writing about this time in January 1930, when he wrote, "I well remember how eagerly I looked for such arguments when I began to be afraid it was true."[50] His fear that Christianity was true was also very likely one of the results of the remorse he felt after his father's death, a feeling that made sin and sorrow very painful and personal.

Probably around this time, Lewis noticed an inconsistency in his criticism of the universe. As he stated years later in a letter to Griffiths, his error came in asking how he knew the universe to be bad. Where did he get a standard of straightness by which he could judge the world as crooked?[51] In other words, if he considered the universe to be unjust, or even his own actions to be unjust, where had he gotten these

---

[49] Lewis, "The Seeing Eye," *Christian Reflections*, 169.
[50] Lewis, *Mere Christianity*, 216.
[51] *Collected Letters of C. S. Lewis*, II, 747. The date of the letter is December 20, 1946.

ideas of justice and injustice? If there is no right or wrong, no good or evil, there is also no basis on which to complain that some things are unjust.[52] Perhaps, he must have thought, the existence of a standard points to an Originator of the Standard.

One more step that Lewis took was the step from believing in the Absolute to believing in God. He wrote about the steps he had taken from the Absolute to Spirit and from Spirit to God as steps toward the more concrete, hence the more personal, solid, and present.[53] Lewis used the term *Absolute* in his diary on July 23, 1922, and on May 15, 1924, the latter date approximately the time when Lewis became an Idealist.[54] In his letters he used the term *Absolute* on December 26, 1929, so we can read those early dates as the time when he continued to study Idealism and then to adopt it. Idealists use the term *Absolute*, and Lewis's use of the term in late 1929 was one of the last times he used the term before realizing to whom the "Absolute" referred. He used the term *Spirit* on February 3, 1930, and June 7, 1930. This change of terminology can be pressed too far, since Lewis used the terms *Absolute* and *Spirit* almost interchangeably. But he did not use the term *Absolute* after December 26, 1929. The switch, then, between *Absolute* and *Spirit*, the latter a more personal term, probably occurred between December 26, 1929, and February 3, 1930, and the fourth chess move took place a few months after this period of time.[55] In fact, Berkeley, whom Lewis highly regarded, explicitly refers to God as Spirit. However, the third move came first.

---

[52] See Lewis's argument in *Mere Christianity*, 38.

[53] Lewis, *Surprised by Joy*, 237.

[54] Lewis, *All My Road Before Me*, 74 and 323.

[55] The bus ride going up Headington Hill is recounted in *Surprised by Joy* immediately after the T. D. Weldon experience, and we have described the unbuckling, the opportunity to make a free choice, as possibly taking place after the Weldon incident, in January or February 1927. However, in *Surprised by Joy*, Lewis was describing a fifteen-year journey, so it is easy to assume, mistakenly, that events narrated consecutively took place one right after the other. The same is true of the events that here follow.

THE THIRD CHESS MOVE

The third chess move, Check, linked his new understanding about Joy as a pointer to something or someone else with Idealism.[56] This probably happened in 1930, a few months before the fourth and final move, i.e., Checkmate, probably at the time of this comment in a letter to Barfield on February 3: "Terrible things are happening to me. The 'Spirit' or 'Real I' is showing an alarming tendency to become much more personal and is taking the offensive, and behaving just like God. You'd better come on Monday at the latest or I may have entered a monastery."[57] In "Early Prose Joy," Lewis writes, "My old havings-and-wantings began to run together in my mind with my new doctrines."[58] This sentence probably refers to that linking of Joy, the havings-and-wantings, with the Absolute in Idealism. What he really wanted was the Absolute, and the Absolute was actually God. In this havings-and-wantings passage late in "Early Prose Joy," Lewis also writes about the Spirit having rested on his memory of the toy garden, his love of Richard Wagner's music and operas, and the wood beyond the world. This would explain, he thought, why he was unable to satisfy his longing with any of the alternatives to God.[59] Those objects that he thought he desired were merely finite and superficial; his deeper desire was for the infinite. Joy was the Absolute and the Absolute was God, but he had not yet fully accepted that thought.

PHILOSOPHY AS A WAY OF LIFE

In an undated passage in *Surprised by Joy*, probably to be dated February 8–10, 1930, Lewis describes a conversation with Owen Barfield and Alan Griffiths about philosophy as "a way," rather than a subject, for Plato. The Christian philosopher Boethius viewed philosophy in the same way, and at this point Lewis may well have

---

[56] Lewis, *Surprised by Joy*, 221.
[57] *Collected Letters of C. S. Lewis*, I, 882f.
[58] Lewis, "Early Prose Joy," 39.
[59] Lewis, "Early Prose Joy," 39.

remembered how Boethius had respected Plato.[60] The seed planted in his mind by Boethius was continuing to grow.[61] Lewis was thinking of philosophy, including Idealism, as an impersonal subject for him to teach, with an impersonal Mind behind it, and he projected that approach to philosophy onto Plato.

In fact, Griffiths had been an undergraduate at Oxford University until the summer of 1929, when he took exams in English and completed his course of study. He began his study of English under Lewis's tutelage after completing Honour Moderations in Hilary term, 1927.[62] Griffiths would more likely engage in a conversation about philosophy with Lewis and Barfield after, rather than during, his undergraduate years when English was the main subject of interest for Griffiths and Lewis. In *The Golden String*, Griffiths described philosophy at this time as "a matter of passionate interest which I felt to hold the meaning of life for me." This statement from Griffiths coincides with the incident with Barfield, Griffiths, and Lewis, and it was significant enough to be mentioned by Lewis. The story fits well with these last steps in Lewis's spiritual journey to theism. Not only was he learning to live philosophy, he had to learn to live his ideas about God, seeing that philosophy was personal and the Absolute was also.

This is how the incident with Barfield and Griffiths unfolded. February 8–10, 1930, is the only time that both Barfield and Griffiths are mentioned together in Lewis's letters, and, therefore, the most likely time about which he wrote these words:

> The fox had been dislodged from Hegelian Wood and was now running in the open, "with all the wo in the world," bedraggled and weary, hounds barely a field behind. And nearly everyone was now . . . in the pack; Plato, Dante, MacDonald, Herbert, Barfield, Tolkien, Dyson, Joy itself. Everyone and

---

[60] Armstrong, "Boethius, *The Consolation of Philosophy*," *C. S. Lewis's List*, 144.
[61] Armstrong, "Boethius, *The Consolation of Philosophy*," *C. S. Lewis's List*, 145.
[62] Email from Robin Darwall-Smith, Magdalen College archivist, February 19, 2014.

everything had joined the other side. Even my own pupil Griffiths . . . though not yet himself a believer, did his share.[63]

Then Barfield stated that philosophy was not merely a subject for Plato; it was a way of life. Griffiths quickly agreed. Barfield and Griffiths taught him that philosophy needed to be integrated into one's personality, taken personally, and lived, not just taught to students as an academic subject. The story is mentioned in *Surprised by Joy* after the unbuckling during the bus ride incident, when Lewis chose to stop resisting, and it probably happened shortly after that bus ride.[64]

Lewis was beginning to see how personal an academic discipline like philosophy needed to be in order to be fully understood. The same was true of the Christian faith. His adherence to Idealism (the Hegelian Wood, since Hegel had been an Idealist) had been shaken, and he was now able to consider other possibilities for the meaning of life and actually do something about it. He had been dislodged from the wood (i.e., the weakness of his position had been exposed), he was running out in the open, and the other side was fast closing in. He could no longer hide.

---

[63] Lewis, *Surprised by Joy*, 225. The word *wo* probably means both "where" (in German) and "woe." The "where" fits the Hegelian context (Hegel was German; Lewis is escaping the Hegelian Wood) and the "woe" alludes to the story of Diana and Actaeon. In Greek mythology, after Actaeon accidentally came upon Diana, the goddess of the hunt, while she was bathing, he was turned into a deer and then hunted by his own dogs. Lewis, then, is the hunted/the Actaeon figure being pursued by Diana/the Divine. This is classic Lewis: myth and philosophy coming together in a powerful way.

[64] Lewis first mentioned Griffiths in his letters on October 17, 1929, so it is likely that the conversation about Plato took place after that date (*Collected Letters of C. S. Lewis*, I, 834). Griffiths is not mentioned in Lewis's diary, *All My Road Before Me*, which ended in 1927. Since Lewis says that Griffiths was not yet a Christian, this event took place before March 1931, the approximate time when Griffiths became a Christian.

PROBLEMS WITH NATURALISM

Lewis also wrote that during the first week of February 1930 Griffiths stayed with him. Earlier in life, Griffiths had been caught up in naturalism, D. H. Lawrence, and the like, but he was reevaluating those positions and setting aside naturalism, traveling a road quite similar to the one that Lewis was traveling, though Lewis had rejected naturalism long before.[65] Lewis was no doubt able to help Griffiths see why naturalism was a dead end.

Lewis argued that pure naturalism was invalid because it was unable to explain how reason, logic, and inference could arise from chance evolutionary processes. But he could also make the same argument on the basis of ethics and aesthetics—on what basis can any standard of goodness or beauty be anything more than one person's opinion? Based on a pure naturalism, ethics, reason, and aesthetics (or goodness, truth, and beauty) have no standard by which to mark an argument as true or false, a form of behavior as good or evil, or a piece of art as beautiful or ugly. For example, reason must be able to make valid conclusions. If it cannot, then humans cannot even claim any statement to be true. One cannot even argue that one position is better, or more valid, than another. Lewis summarized this position in the following way: "Is the thought that no thoughts are true, itself true? If we answer Yes, we contradict ourselves. For if all thoughts are untrue, then this thought is untrue."[66] An entirely blind, undirected

---

[65] *Collected Letters of C. S. Lewis*, I, 881. Not only did Griffiths travel a similar road, but Lewis's brother Warren did as well. While this can be pressed too far, Warren avoided a church service on board a ship that was taking him to Belfast in April 1930, calling the parts of the service he overheard "lugubrious," according to unpublished diaries of Warren Lewis for the date April 13, 1930. Neither do Warren and his brother Jack attend church on the following Sunday, which is Easter Sunday, by which time Warren has arrived in England. And yet, by June 1930, Warren has a conversation about the resurrection with the craftsmen who are making the stained glass window that was to be dedicated to the Lewis parents and installed in their Belfast church, St. Mark's.

[66] Lewis, "De Futilitate," *Christian Reflections*, 61.

evolutionary process cannot explain how reason arose. Order does not
come from disorder.

Then follows this passage in *Surprised by Joy*, which combines a
concern for ethical behavior with his inconsistent ideas about Idealism
and the Spirit:

> For of course there had long[67] been an ethic (theoretically)
> attached to my Idealism. I thought the business of us finite and
> half-unreal souls was to multiply the consciousness of Spirit.
> ... The way to recover, and act upon, this universal and
> objective vision was daily and hourly to remember our true
> nature, to reascend or return into that Spirit which, insofar as
> we really were at all, we still were. Yes; but I now felt I had
> better try to do it. I faced at last (in MacDonald's words)
> "something to be neither more nor less nor other than *done*."
> An attempt at complete virtue must be made.[68]

Lewis now had to attempt to live his Idealism, because it truly was "a
way."

The Absolute: Personal or Impersonal?

Then Lewis wrote a passage that draws us near to the fourth chess
move and the same perspective as the one he showed when he wrote
to Owen Barfield about the Spirit becoming more personal:

> Of course I could do nothing—I could not last out one hour—
> without continual conscious recourse to what I called Spirit.
> But the fine, philosophical distinction between this and what
> ordinary people call "prayer to God" breaks down as soon as
> you start doing it in earnest. Idealism can be talked, and even
> felt; it cannot be lived. It became patently absurd to go on
> thinking of "Spirit" as either ignorant of, or passive to, my

---

[67] This adjective suggests Lewis was an idealist for years and seems to confirm
Griffiths's assertion that Lewis's *Summa* convinced Griffiths to be an Idealist.
Then Lewis would have been an Idealist in 1928 and probably since 1924.
[68] Lewis, *Surprised by Joy*, 225f.

approaches. Even if my own philosophy were true, how could the initiative lie on my side? My own analogy, as I now first perceived, suggested the opposite: if Shakespeare and Hamlet could ever meet, it must be Shakespeare's doing. Hamlet could initiate nothing.[69]

As Lewis stated in *The Pilgrim's Regress*, "This new and real Landlord must yet be very different from him whom the Stewards proclaimed and indeed from all images that men could make of him. There might still hang about him some of that promising darkness which had covered the Absolute."[70] But who or what was the Absolute?

Lewis once wrote a shorter version of the above passage, stating that it was not possible to explain the Absolute, except as an obscuring of God.[71] At that time Lewis believed, "There was, I explained, no possibility of being in a personal relation with Him. For I thought He projected us as a dramatist projects his characters, and I could no more 'meet' Him, than Hamlet could meet Shakespeare. I didn't call Him 'God' either; I called Him 'Spirit.' One fights for one's remaining comforts."[72] The Absolute did not make any demands on him, acting more like an always approving God than a God who cares about commending the right and correcting the wrong. The Absolute, he wrote, was as different from God as a book is different from a friend, always available but making no demands. It will not bother you.[73] For Lewis, vague spirituality served as a refuge to escape from the divine interferer to whom he might actually be accountable. He explained his frustration with Idealism in this way:

---

[69] Lewis, *Surprised by Joy*, 226f. Barkman states that Lewis was writing about absolute Idealism here rather than subjective Idealism (*C. S. Lewis & Philosophy as a Way of Life*, 51).

[70] Lewis, *The Pilgrim's Regress*, 143.

[71] Lewis, "Early Prose Joy," 34: "The escape from skepticism hung upon the metaphorical passages in which Bradley, despite his own system, filled the Absolute with fugitive and iridescent meanings."

[72] Lewis, *Surprised by Joy*, 223.

[73] Lewis, "Early Prose Joy," 31.

The fourth Move was more alarming. I was now teaching philosophy . . . as well as English. And my watered Hegelianism wouldn't serve for tutorial purposes. A tutor must make things clear. Now the Absolute cannot be made clear. Do you mean Nobody-knows-what, or do you mean a superhuman mind and therefore (we may as well admit) a Person?[74]

A passage from his autobiography describes his move from naturalism to an inconsistent Idealism, inconsistent because it kept God at arm's length:

I had been trying to defend [naturalism] ever since I began reading philosophy[75] . . . but now it seemed to me, I had to give that up. . . . It is astonishing . . . that I could regard this position [i.e., Idealism] as something quite distinct from Theism. I suspect there was some willful blindness. But there were in those days all sorts of blankets, insulators, and insurances which enabled one to get all the conveniences of Theism, without believing in God. . . . The Absolute Mind— better still, the Absolute—was impersonal, or it knew itself (but not us?) only in us, and it was so absolute that it wasn't really much more like mind than anything else. And anyway the more muddled one got about it and the more contradictions one committed, the more this proved that our discursive thought moved only at the level of "Appearance," and "Reality" must be somewhere else. . . . The emotion that went with all this was certainly religious. But this was a religion that cost nothing. We could talk religiously about the Absolute; but there was no danger of Its doing anything about us. . . . There was nothing to fear, better still nothing to obey.[76]

It is no wonder, then, that Lewis later wrote that Idealism, when taken seriously, was actually a disguised theism.[77]

---

[74] Lewis, *Surprised by Joy*, 222.
[75] That is, 1920–22, the years he was reading philosophy as an undergraduate.
[76] Lewis, *Surprised by Joy*, 209f.
[77] Lewis, "Is Theology Poetry?" *The Weight of Glory and Other Addresses*, 105.

SHAKESPEARE, JOHN'S GOSPEL, HISTORY, AND PRAYER

The Christian and pagan mystics helped Lewis across this last gulf between himself and God, since they saw something that Idealism did not, i.e., that God *could indeed* come into the midst of people even as Shakespeare's character was present in Hamlet, Othello, and Iago, which is what God had done in the Incarnation of Jesus Christ. Lewis had thought about the Shakespeare-Hamlet analogy in 1926, but only in 1930 did he conclude that God, like Shakespeare, could write Himself into His own play, on the stage of history. At this point, he was referring to Spirit rather than the Absolute, but he did not name the Spirit as God.[78]

Lewis's reassessment of history—which probably happened between February and June 1930—is a likely time for his writing of the poem "My Heart Is Empty."[79] This poem seems to be directed to God, which is suited to 1930. The author has no desire for anything that God can give. The reference to God who neither slumbers nor sleeps, and to Lazarus, dead in his tomb, is paralleled to the singer of this song, who wants to awaken, but cannot, making the poem suitable to the time leading up to Lewis's adoption of theism. Furthermore, Lewis's new appreciation of the historical nature of the Gospels would have led him into John's Gospel, which contains the story of the death of Lazarus. In fact, when Lewis wrote to Arthur Greeves later that spring, he stated that he had just read the Gospel of John in the original Greek, the very Gospel that had the most influence on him and whose content most clearly showed him the historical nature of the New Testament Gospels.[80]

---

[78] Lewis, "Early Prose Joy," 39.
[79] Lewis, *The Pilgrim's Regress*, Book Eight, Chapter X, 156.
[80] *Collected Letters of C. S. Lewis*, I, 899. For this insight I am indebted to my former student Haley Van Klompenburg. The letter is dated June 1, 1930, so he read John's Gospel in May. See also the essay "Modern Theology and Biblical Criticism," *Fern-Seed and Elephants and other essays on Christianity*, 108, where Lewis calls John's Gospel "reportage."

In *The Pilgrim's Regress*, the main character John has been engaged in a conversation with History and worries about the things he desires, whether they will turn out to be what the Landlord intends for him. Objects are always inadequate to the desire, History states, and perhaps what John truly desires is the One who alone can fulfill this desire. History compares human love with what John truly desires. Then John lies down to sleep, but he hears History sing the poem "My Heart Is Empty."[81] History sings his prayer to God about desire, asking God to desire for him what he was unable to desire. The beauty of this world or that of human love is only a shadow, a copy, or an ectype, of which God's love is the archetype, the original.

At this time, Lewis also struggled with prayer, addressing the Spirit as Thou, rather than thinking of this as prayer to God.[82] He preferred to speak of the Absolute, but he feared the demands of this Absolute, and this fear had prevented Lewis from seeing the Absolute as God. He did not want to face his own failings and the possibility that he might be held accountable for his misdeeds. At the same time, he did not see how he could offer anything but unconditional surrender.[83] And, in fact, though he feared that he might be praying to a myth, Lewis came to believe that God's answer was that He was indeed myth, but true myth, the symbol under which God had offered Himself in history to mankind. All other myths were manmade, but this myth came from God.[84]

The poem "They Tell Me, Lord that When I Seem," written during this year, explores the topic of prayer, which, apparently, someone had suggested to Lewis, is really a person talking to himself, but pretending to talk to God. The author seems to reject that rather simplistic understanding of prayer, but it shows Lewis struggling with the very

---

[81] *Collected Letters of C. S. Lewis*, I, 156.

[82] Lazo, "Correcting the Chronology: Some Implications of 'Early Prose Joy,' " 39.

[83] Lewis, "Early Prose Joy," 38.

[84] See *Collected Letters of C. S. Lewis*, I, 977, for Lewis's explanation of the story of Christ as true myth.

idea of prayer. Such was the case for Lewis during his last days before coming to believe in God.

For Lewis from this time on, diving became a symbol for believing in God. The Latin phrase *Securus Te Projice* ("safely throw yourself in"),[85] which he used in *The Pilgrim's Regress*, refers to learning to dive. As Lewis approached, or was approached by, this Absolute whom he wished to avoid, he realized that he simply needed to lay down his instinct for self-preservation, and diving served as a good metaphor. After all, Barfield had taught him the value of metaphor. In "Early Prose Joy," Lewis compares diving to believing, simply because believing means not preserving one's independence, just as diving means giving oneself up to the water. He became a believer in the same year and the same month that he learned to dive.[86]

THE FOURTH CHESS MOVE: CHECKMATE

Warren Lewis had just arrived home from his service with the RASC in Shanghai on April 16, and only a week later he and his brother traveled to Belfast to settle their father's estate and sell Little Lea. They spoke to various relatives, who would receive some of its contents, visited with Mary Cullen, the housekeeper, did some packing, and buried their childhood toys in the vegetable garden. These final preparations for the disposition of Little Lea undoubtedly brought some closure in their lives, while simultaneously recalling the way in which they had treated their father. This heightened their regret. This visit—on April 23 and 24—was probably the last visit of C. S. Lewis to Little Lea.

One of Lewis's poems dated to 1930, "Leaving For Ever the Home of One's Youth," probably written after the death of Albert Lewis and

---

[85] This Latin phrase appears in *The Pilgrim's Regress* at Book 9, Part IV, 166, the passage where John learns from Vertue and Mother Kirk to dive. It also appears in the second last paragraph of "Early Prose Joy," 40. See St. Augustine, *Confessions* VIII. 11. 27, where the Latin phrase *Securus te projice* appears.

[86] Lewis, "Early Prose Joy," 40. See St. Augustine, *Confessions* VIII. 11. 27, where the Latin phrase *Securus te projice* appears.

the decision to sell Little Lea, perhaps shortly after the events described in the previous paragraph, recalls with some poignancy the days of childhood in that home. His move toward Christianity was causing him to rethink his unkindness toward and impatience with his father. With the recent death of Albert (and Flora's death more than two decades earlier), loneliness pervaded the home more powerfully than would a barren countryside in the midst of winter. Warren Lewis visited Little Lea for the last time on June 3, 1930. The house sold in January 1931. Closing another chapter of life with his parents undoubtedly led Lewis to write this poem, probably in April or May, recalling some events fondly, others with pain, but still others with guilt over the way he had treated his father. Anyone who has ever returned to the home of his childhood knows the emotional impact of that experience.

Sometime during the first six days of June 1930, only a month and a half after Warren Lewis had come home from Shanghai, possibly even while Warren was visiting Little Lea for the last time, C. S. Lewis came home spiritually. Lewis surrendered to the one he most earnestly desired not to meet and became a theist, admitting that "God was God."[87] The man who had avoided the transcendental interferer had recognized that he needed this divine interference. He was no longer the master of his own soul, nor did he want to be, nor had he ever been.[88]

And yet, it is clear Lewis was not a Christian. He wrote to Arthur about the possibility of immortality (not its certainty), and what might

---

[87] Lazo, "Correcting the Chronology: Some Implications of 'Early Prose Joy,'" 58; Lewis, *Surprised by Joy*, 228. I take his June 7 reference to the reading of Coventry Patmore's long poem, *The Angel in the House*, which is about marriage as a mystical image of divine love, as evidence that the conversion to theism had already taken place. Furthermore, on June 7, Frederick Lawson takes him to visit Lawson's father, an experience that pricks Lewis's conscience, something far less likely before an acknowledgment of the existence of God.

[88] Lewis, *The Pilgrim's Regress*, 142.

survive death. Though he wrote about God, he also wrote about religion as though it were something distant rather than personal.[89]

As previously indicated, this surrender did not happen in Trinity term of 1929.[90] One imagines that Lewis was so wrapped up in a rapid series of events that he did not accurately recall the exact sequence in which they occurred, especially since he was writing more than two decades later. To use Samuel Alexander's distinction, he was so caught up in the "enjoyment" of these events that he did not have the opportunity to "contemplate" them. Lewis's letter of December 22, 1929, to Owen Barfield, described above, has confirmed what both Alister McGrath and Andrew Lazo have successfully argued,[91] that Lewis made a mistake of one year, describing as Trinity term of 1929 what should have been identified as Trinity term of 1930.[92] Another reason for Lewis's mistake in dating is that in 1929 he had just emerged from his Great War with Barfield, which had intensified in 1927 and 1928, and from a whirlwind of research, lecture preparation, meeting attendance, and writing. Writing decades later, he did not recall precisely how quickly time had passed between the end of the Great War between Barfield and himself and the end of his war with God. In retrospect, it seemed to be only a few months, but in fact it was more than a year. Furthermore, when Lewis wrote to Arthur Greeves on October 18, 1931, he wrote about what had been holding him back for approximately the last year.[93] This phrase further indicates that his conversion to Christianity took place about a year after his conversion to theism. If he had become a theist during Trinity term of 1929, more than two years would have passed.

Not coincidentally, during the week of June 9–13, Alan Richard Griffiths spent a night with Lewis. Since both men were traveling

---

[89] *Collected Letters of C. S. Lewis*, I, 916f.

[90] Lewis, *Surprised by Joy*, 228.

[91] Alister McGrath, *C. S. Lewis: A Life, Eccentric Genius, Reluctant Prophet* (Carol Stream, IL: Tyndale House, 2013), 139–41; Lazo, "Correcting the Chronology: Some Implications of 'Early Prose Joy,' " 51–62.

[92] The Trinity term of 1930 started on April 23 and ended on July 5.

[93] *Collected Letters of C. S. Lewis*, I, 976.

similar roads (remember that Lewis called Griffiths his "chief companion" on the road to theism and Christianity), they probably talked about the status of their spiritual journeys.

Lewis had just written a poem entitled "Prayer,"[94] a prayer that seems rather sterile, or perhaps only a stumbling first attempt, seeing prayer as an attempt to speak to a Master, but not someone for whom prayer is a personal communication with a loving Savior. As Lewis's problems with prayer had been a factor in adopting atheism, so also was prayer a factor in his adoption of theism. But the very fact that he wrote such a poem suggests that he had recently become a theist, or he would not likely have approached this topic of prayer. After all, when he admitted that God was God, he then knelt and prayed.[95]

Lewis may have written the poem "You Rest Upon Me All My Days"[96] during the first half of 1930, just prior to, or just after, his adoption of theism. In this poem, "You," the "Eye," is watching and making it impossible for this caged bird to escape. At this moment in *The Pilgrim's Regress*, in the chapter entitled "Caught," the pilgrim John has become aware that there is, indeed, a real Landlord. That Landlord sees what he does. John desires to return to his pagan days so that he can escape this divine gaze.

In *The Pilgrim's Regress*, Lewis stated that he moved from "popular realism" to Philosophical Idealism, then from Idealism to Pantheism, then to Theism, and finally to Christianity.[97] "Popular realism" refers to his belief that the world experienced through the five senses is the only reality.[98] He became an Idealist in the mid-1920s, probably in 1924. When was he a pantheist? Lewis had met Pantheism in

---

[94] See Lewis, *Poems*, 122.

[95] Lewis, *Surprised by Joy*, 228.

[96] Lewis, *The Pilgrim's Regress*, Book Eight, Chapter VI, 142.

[97] Lewis, *The Pilgrim's Regress*, 200.

[98] Downing, *The Most Reluctant Convert*, 123. Barkman defines popular realism as "metaphysical realism," which holds to "the existence of real, spatiotemporal objects that exist separately of people's knowledge of them and which have properties and enter into relations independently of the concepts with which people understand them" (*C. S. Lewis & Philosophy as a Way of Life*, 22).

Maeterlinck, Wordsworth, Hegel, Bradley, and Boehme, the last of these especially during the year he became a theist. Since he mentioned it as a stage between Idealism and theism and since his conversion to theism seems to take place directly from Idealism, the most likely explanation is that Lewis found pantheism in one or more of the Idealist philosophers before becoming a theist. In fact, Lewis once described the position of Hegel, an Idealist, as that of pantheism, and this is probably what he meant by tracing Idealism to Pantheism to theism.[99] He also quoted from a pantheistic philosopher in *The Problem of Pain*, words that sound like Idealism,[100] and his words to Barfield during their Great War reflected a similar position, especially when he wrote, "To ask 'Shall I be an element in the goodness of Spirit' is idle. I am that already, and cannot cease to be that for an instant."[101]

David C. Downing argues that the Idealist philosopher F. H. Bradley held positions that were similar to Hinduism. The Universal Soul of Hinduism is similar to the Absolute in Bradley's Idealism, and both are immanent in nature and pantheistic.[102] As Lewis stated elsewhere, "The Pantheist's God does nothing, demands nothing. He is there if you wish for Him, like a book on a shelf. He will not pursue you. There is no danger that at any time heaven and earth should flee away at His glance."[103] That is how Bradley interpreted the Absolute. Late in *The Pilgrim's Regress*, the pilgrim John identified himself with the eternal Spirit that was driving him on his journey, and yet he was having difficulty maintaining that he was part of that Spirit (which is

---

[99] Lewis, *Mere Christianity*, 36.

[100] Lewis, *The Problem of Pain*, 42: "When the Absolute falls into the sea it becomes a fish." Lewis also once compared a Western Idealist to an Oriental Pantheist. See Lewis, "De Futilitate," *Christian Reflections*, 59. See also, however, Lewis's words in "Christianity and Culture," *Christian Reflections*, 22, where he speaks of a Wordsworthian contemplation of nature that allows one to realize that there is something outside ourselves. This awareness would undoubtedly have come during Lewis's Idealist phase in the mid- to late 1920s.

[101] *De Bono et Malo, The "Great War" of Owen Barfield and C. S. Lewis*, Inklings Studies Supplement No. 1, 142.

[102] Downing, *The Most Reluctant Convert*, 129.

[103] *Miracles: A Preliminary Study* (New York: Simon & Schuster, 1996), 124.

what Idealism holds) rather than distinct from it. As a result, John began to ask for help from Someone, or Something, outside himself, and he realized that he had been praying.[104] He had not been praying to a metaphor, but to Someone capable of providing help.[105]

THE NEW MAN

On July 8, Lewis wrote to Arthur about absolute chastity, finishing the *Paradiso* with Barfield, and also swimming with Barfield. Lewis was reading a little of Thomas Traherne's *Centuries of Meditations* each evening, and he praised the merits of these spiritual meditations while thinking that Traherne underestimated the problem of evil. He told Arthur about his recent time in June and early July with Barfield, including learning to dive and diving having important religious meaning.[106] He also wrote, "I don't remember for many years to have felt so disposed for new reading as I do now, and specially poetry. Everything seems—you know the feeling—to be beginning again and one has the sense of immortality."[107] With his new outlook on life, he felt like life was starting over.

On August 3, Lewis wrote to Arthur that he felt young again,[108] frequently one of the results of belief in God, which enables a person to make a new beginning. Later that same month, Lewis wrote to Arthur about having written a few religious lyrics in the past year, undoubtedly including "Prayer"; the letter contains several other references to God.[109] Not only does this hint at his conversion to theism, it actually shows that he had been moving in that direction long before he actually came to believe in God.

Lewis had become a theist. Checkmate.

---

[104] Lewis, *The Pilgrim's Regress*, 137f.
[105] Lewis, *The Pilgrim's Regress*, 140.
[106] *Collected Letters of C. S. Lewis*, I, 915.
[107] *Collected Letters of C. S. Lewis*, I, 915.
[108] *Collected Letters of C. S. Lewis*, I, 921.
[109] Lewis suggests that Arthur read the Christian apologist Friedrich Von Hügel for his religious outlook (*Collected Letters of C. S. Lewis*, I, 932).

CHAPTER 7

FROM THEISM TO CHRISTIANITY

"This is not 'a religion,' nor 'a philosophy.' It is the summing up and actuality of them all."

—C. S. Lewis, *Surprised by Joy*

Since Lewis discovered the writings of William Morris in 1914, Morris had been one of his favorite authors. On July 1, 1930,[1] Lewis wrote to Arthur Greeves about a visit he had made to see Owen Barfield. He told about having read William Morris's play, *Love is Enough*, and he saw for the first time that the light of holiness shone through Morris's play. Then he writes, "I have the key now and perhaps can stand the sweetness safely."[2] The key, of course, was the understanding that God truly exists. That explains why he also wrote to Greeves about eternal values and being rooted. The holiness in Morris was the same holiness that Lewis had seen fourteen years earlier in George MacDonald's *Phantastes*. This time he recognized holiness when he saw it, but for *Phantastes* he saw it only in hindsight. He wrote to Arthur about what he saw in Morris's *Love is Enough*:

---

[1] Lewis actually dates the letter June 31, incorrectly. It should, of course, be dated July 1, since June has only thirty days (*Collected Letters of C. S. Lewis*, I, 910).
[2] *Collected Letters of C. S. Lewis*, I, 911. This is the July 1, 1930, letter to Arthur Greeves.

I always thought Morris the most essentially *pagan* of all poets. The beauty of the actual world, the vague longings wh. it
excites, the inevitable failure to satisfy these longings, and over
all the haunting sense of time & change making the world
heartbreakingly beautiful just because it slips away. . . . All
this, I thought, he gave to perfection: but of what this longing
really pointed to, of the reason why beauty made us homesick,
of the reality *behind*, I thought he had no inkling. . . . For the
first . . . time the light of *holiness* shines through Morris'
romanticism.[3]

A week later, Lewis wrote again to Arthur about going swimming
with Barfield. "Here I learned to dive which is a great change in my life
& has important (religious) connections."[4] As stated in the previous
chapter, that event, his conversion to theism, occurred during the first
six days of June 1930. Lewis wrote about his conversion to theism in
Surprised by Joy in the following terms: "My conversion involved as
yet no belief in a future life. I now number it among my greatest
mercies that I was permitted for several months, perhaps for a year, to
know God and to attempt obedience without even raising that
question."[5] During that year, he was not acknowledging God because
of some hoped-for eternal reward. Lewis was thankful that he knew
God's invitation to trust Him before he knew God's power.[6]

In a long narrative poem, written shortly after his conversion to
theism, but still a year away from his conversion to Christianity,[7] Lewis
told the story of a sailor, perhaps reflecting both on his reading of the
journeys of Homer's Odysseus and his spiritual journey over the past
decade and more. The poem was called "The Nameless Isle," (also
known as "In a Spring Season I Sailed Away"). The poem expresses a

---

[3] *Collected Letters of C. S. Lewis*, I, 910f.
[4] *Collected Letters of C. S. Lewis*, I, 915. The letter is dated July 8, 1930.
[5] Lewis, *Surprised by Joy*, 231. Note that the phrase, "perhaps for a year," fits well
with the gap between June 1930 and September 1931 for Lewis's conversion from
theism to Christianity.
[6] Lewis, *Surprised by Joy*, 232.
[7] The poem is dated to August 1930 by Walter Hooper and Roger Lancelyn Green.

yearning for home reminiscent of Lewis's description of his conversion to theism in what Joe Christopher calls "a rehandling of motifs from Mozart's *Magic Flute*."[8]

The poem describes the sailor shipwrecked in a storm and coming to rest on land. On that nameless isle the sailor meets a woman, a "witch-hearted queen," who is also a "nobly fashioned" woman. She has been separated from her daughter and offers her love to the man who would return her daughter to her. The sailor agrees to rescue the daughter from a wizard, who has stolen both her daughter and a magic flute. The sailor enters the forest, and he comes to the place where the wizard lives.

After finding the lost flute, he meets a group of stone soldiers and a live dwarf. The soldiers are the sailor's British shipmates. The sailor promises to help the dwarf, who also informs him that the queen has the power to turn living creatures to stone, and she has bewitched the other half of the sailors. The sailor travels with the dwarf until he finds the Queen's daughter, also turned to stone. He is drawn to her and kisses her, but this sleeping beauty does not awaken. Then the wizard invites the sailor to consider how becoming stone might draw him to the beautiful daughter and insulate him from the trials of life. The wizard reveals the fact that the daughter is his daughter also and that he has turned her to stone to save her from the queen.

The queen had stolen the flute, but she threw it away some time ago as she fled from the wizard. The dwarf then pulls the flute from the pouch of the sailor and begins to play. The flute charms the wizard, transforms the dwarf, and awakens his British shipmates. The daughter of the queen also awakens. The wizard, also changed, decides to search for his wife, the queen. Love brings about the reconciliation of the queen with the wizard, and it brings the sailor and the daughter together. At the conclusion, the wizard magically builds a ship for the sailor, the maiden, and the dwarf, who sail away to England. The end of the poem compares their journey to that of Israel coming out of Egypt to their own country.

---

[8] Joe R. Christopher, *C. S. Lewis* (Boston: Twayne Publishers, 1987), 4.

The poem leaves the reader wondering who the wizard and the queen represent, why the sailor and the maiden sail away, why the queen threw the flute away, and what role the dwarf plays in this narrative. Was the sailor a self-portrait? What do the flute and its music represent, and how does it bring about reconciliation? Did Lewis intend that music be held up as the key to life, love, and reconciliation? Is the trip to England at the end of the poem Lewis's way of describing his "coming home"? While the poem leaves us with unanswered questions, the dwarf bears some resemblance to the dwarf in William Morris's *The Wood Beyond the World*, which Lewis had read by this time, but the dwarf is transformed for Lewis's purposes. The work of the magic flute brings about restoration between the queen and the wizard and between the sailor and the maiden, as Lewis himself would have hoped for with his father (who was no longer living at this time), but the concluding journey reflects the yearning of the sailor for his home.

During autumn of 1930, though not a Christian, Lewis wrote, "I thought one ought to 'fly one's flag' by some unmistakable overt sign."[9] As a result, he began attending Holy Trinity Church, Headington Quarry, on Sundays and Magdalen College chapel on weekdays. Several months later, the Lewis brothers agreed that Holy Trinity, Headington Quarry, would be their church,[10] and then, a few weeks after that, we have the first clear indication that Lewis was attending Magdalen chapel regularly.[11] Just the previous month Lewis had had a dream about speaking with his father and had written to Arthur Greeves about the fear of dying, both topics that suggest the need for resolving the problem of his flawed human nature. That same letter to Arthur described his recent moral history as deplorable.[12]

---

[9] Lewis, *Surprised by Joy*, 233.

[10] *Brothers & Friends*, 69, a diary entry dated October 12, 1930.

[11] *Collected Letters of C. S. Lewis*, I, 942, in a letter to Arthur Greeves dated October 29, 1930.

[12] *Collected Letters of C. S. Lewis*, I, 942.

The next four poems in *The Pilgrim's Regress* seem to come from the time shortly after Lewis's conversion to theism. All four of the poems appear in the book after the pilgrim John has crossed the chasm, diving into the water of the canyon—Lewis's picture of conversion—and coming to Mother Kirk. The first post-diving poem that Lewis wrote was entitled "Thou Only Art Alternative to God."[13]

In this poem, the Guide has led John and Vertue back across the canyon, not long after John has safely thrown himself in, dived into the water, let himself go, and come to believe in the Landlord. Although the pilgrim John says that he thinks that Mother Kirk (the Church) treats them poorly, the Guide asserts that security remains our enemy. Then Vertue sings this song, or poem. In the mouth of Vertue, Lewis describes Satan as the only alternative to God. One chooses Heaven or Hell, God or Satan. It is far better to choose the former than the latter.

Then Lewis wrote "God in His Mercy Made."[14] This poem expresses the idea that God made Hell because of His mercy. In response to Vertue's description of those who have desire without hope, the Guide states that people condemn themselves to a life of hopelessness and that Hell was made to place limits on that condition. This poem must have been written after June 1930, the time of Lewis's conversion to theism. Then Lewis wrote another poem with similar content, "Nearly They Stood Who Fall."[15] This poem, sung by the Guide, seems to say that those who look both backward (to see where they might have made a misstep) and forward (to see where they may fall) should not look back at the past. The black hole exists, but it exists as a tourniquet on a wound, placing limits on the despair that evil can cause.

---

[13] Lewis, *The Pilgrim's Regress*, Book Ten, Chapter I, 176.

[14] Lewis, *The Pilgrim's Regress*, Book Ten, Chapter IV, 181.

[15] Lewis, *The Pilgrim's Regress*, Book Ten, Chapter III, 179.

Finally, Lewis wrote "Iron Will Eat the World's Old Beauty Up."[16] John, Vertue, and the Guide continue their journey. This poem contains biblical imagery, reflecting both on Adam's original sin and the bondage of Israel in Egypt. Though the world destroys the beauty and wisdom of the world with its machines, God sees beyond the end to the resurrection. The poem reflects Lewis's dislike of much that is modern. The Lewis who, before his conversion, had preferred the newer to the older, adopted the completely opposite position, preferring the older to the later, old ideas to modernity, an ancient God-made nature to newer manmade machines.

Alan Richard Griffiths was now also a theist, having come to believe in God at about the same time as Lewis.[17] At this time, Griffiths and Lewis were reading and recommending to each other some of the same works that they found helpful. On May 18, 1931, Lewis wrote to Arthur Greeves about having read William Law. This is probably the time when he and Griffiths shared with each other Law's *A Serious Call to a Devout and Holy Life*, which both of them read during this period of reading Christian masterpieces.[18] He may also have read English clergyman and philosopher Joseph Butler's *The Analogy of Religion* around the same time, since Griffiths read it and probably shared it with Lewis.[19] Butler (1692–1752) argued that a return to the orthodox Christian religion, a personal religion, was superior to the impersonal tenets of deism. Then, shortly thereafter, Lewis read William R. Inge's *Personal Religion and the Life of Devotion*, another book that showed the superiority of personal religion over impersonal religiosity.

In fact, Griffiths stated this about his connection with Lewis:

---

[16] Lewis, *The Pilgrim's Regress*, Book Ten, Chapter VI, 186. This poem could be dated to the time when Lewis, Barfield, Harwood, and Field composed a poem on the Fall, i.e., April 6, 1930. See *Collected Letters of C. S. Lewis*, I, 895.

[17] Lewis, *Surprised by Joy*, 234f.

[18] Griffiths, *The Golden String*, 48.

[19] Griffiths, *The Golden String*, 48.

While I was reading philosophy I kept up a constant correspondence with him, and it was through him that my mind was gradually brought back to Christianity. During the following years [i.e., after Griffiths had graduated in 1929] we pursued the study of Christianity together, and first one of us and then the other would make the discovery of some masterpiece of Christian thought which we had not known before. I remember in particular how the discovery of William Law's *Serious Call* and Butler's *Analogy of Religion* excited us both. An unseen hand seemed to be leading us both to the same goal.[20]

Later Lewis would call Law and Butler "two lions,"[21] that is, two authors who were not safe, but still powerful, and he subsequently chose a quotation from Law's *Serious Call* to place on the title page to Book Ten, "The Regress," of *The Pilgrim's Regress*, which commented on the usefulness of the knowledge we gain from our senses.[22]

In Lewis's thinking a lot was changing, including a reappraisal of the reliability of the New Testament. Although Lewis had earlier adopted some of the positions of historical criticism, a position that takes the Gospels as generally historical, but embellished and dramatically changed by the early church, he had changed his view by the late 1920s. This change occurred largely as a result of his extensive reading of English literature, which enabled him to distinguish between history and myth,[23] even though both history and myth can have the same themes and the same sequence of events. He also

---

[20] Griffiths, *The Golden String*, 48.

[21] Lewis, "On the Reading of Old Books," *God in the Dock*, 204.

[22] Lewis, *The Pilgrim's Regress*, 173.

[23] Lewis, *Surprised by Joy*, 236. See Lewis's essay "Fern-seed and Elephants," originally titled "Modern Theology and Biblical Criticism," for a full explanation of his position. See also my article about that essay on the Marion E. Wade Center website: " 'Modern Theology and Biblical Criticism' in Context," a supplement to vol. 31 of *VII*: www.wheaton.edu/wadecenter/Journal-VII/Contents/Online-Articles.

changed as a result of conversation with Harry Weldon and a reread-ing of the Gospel of John.

Regarding the conversation with Weldon, which took place in 1926, Lewis wrote, "The real clue had been put into my hand by that hard-boiled Atheist when he said, 'Rum thing, all that about the Dying God. Seems to have really happened once'; by him and by Barfield's encouragement of a more respectful, if not more delighted, attitude to Pagan myth. The question was no longer to find the one simply true religion among a thousand religions simply false. It was rather, 'Where has religion reached its true maturity? Where, if anywhere, have the hints of all Paganism been fulfilled?' "[24]

The historical nature of Christianity influenced Lewis a great deal, especially now that he had revised his understanding of the New Testament Gospels. Later he wrote that faith flows from historical events, and that these historical events, to be fully understood and explained, require the existence of a Supreme Being.[25] He saw historical events as the foundation of faith, but events that are more than mere events.

Lewis was aware not only of the role of history, but also the role of myth in the Christian faith. He now began to think of myth as capable of conveying truth about spiritual realities. He also thought of certain concepts as capable of being both history and myth at the same time, that is, as true myth. He later wrote about Jesus of Nazareth,

> If ever a myth had become fact, had been incarnated, it would
> be just like this. And nothing else in all literature was just like
> this. . . . And no person was like the Person it depicted; as real,
> as recognizable, through all that depth of time, as Plato's
> Socrates or Boswell's Johnson . . . , yet also . . . lit by a light
> from beyond the world, a god. . . . Here and here only in all
> time the myth must have become fact; the Word, flesh; God,

---

[24] Lewis, *Surprised by Joy*, 235.
[25] Lewis, "Is Theism Important?" *God in the Dock*, 175.

Man. This is not "a religion," nor "a philosophy." It is the summing up and actuality of them all.[26]

It was not a subject, as Griffiths and Barfield had agreed, but a way of life.

After Checkmate

Warren Lewis was already at the position where his younger brother would arrive in September 1931. In January 1931, Warren commented to his brother that the religious view of things seemed to him to be true.[27] Several months later, Warren attended worship at Salisbury Cathedral on April 19, 1931, two weeks after Easter, writing favorably about the sermon on the resurrection. On May 9, about four months before his brother became a Christian, Warren began to pray again and returned to the Christian faith, describing his spiritual journey as indifference, skepticism, atheism, agnosticism, and then Christianity.[28]

While serving the RASC in Bulford, England, Warren wrote in his diary, between June 11 and 13, 1931, about a discussion regarding the stained glass window that he and his brother had commissioned for their Belfast church, St. Mark's, Dundela, to honor their parents. The diary entry was about the reasoning of the firm creating the window, namely that the resurrection was not a topic that should be relegated to a side aisle, which is where the Lewis window was to be placed. For Warren this made sense, and his brother agreed. This, of course, implies that the Lewis window was originally going to have the resurrection built into it and that it was going to be placed in a side aisle. Consequently, since the side aisle was destined to be the location of the window, the Lewis brothers agreed to change the design to put St. James in the central panel of the window, flanked by St. Mark and

---

[26] Lewis, *Surprised by Joy*, 236.
[27] *Collected Letters of C. S. Lewis*, I, 948. On January 10, 1931.
[28] From the unpublished diary of Warren Lewis, April 19, 1931 and the published excerpts, *Brothers & Friends*, May 13, 1931.

St. Luke. Warren took the lead in this discussion, probably because he had already become a Christian, while his younger brother went along.

On Saturday night, September 19, 1931, Lewis had a lengthy conversation with Hugo Dyson and J. R. R. Tolkien until 3 a.m., and, after Tolkien had left, he continued until 4 a.m. with Dyson. Lewis later described that conversation in detail.[29] That night Lewis came to see myth as a "gleam of divine truth falling on human imagination."[30] Very possibly on that night Lewis described myth to Tolkien as "lies breathed through silver."[31] Tolkien and Dyson must have shown Lewis that the historical nature of the Gospels must be reckoned with, even while allowing myth to remain myth. God's myth had come into history, and the New Testament Gospels could no longer be dismissed. Lewis's introduction of a hermit, whose name was History, as a character in *The Pilgrim's Regress* seems to confirm the importance of history and the historicity of the Gospels. The hermit understands and explains the various characters and locations in the land,[32] providing perspective and context. Lewis must also have seen that myth, in pagan stories, was God expressing Himself through the minds of these pagan poets, with God using the images of the language of the poets, but he began to see that Christianity was God expressing Himself through real things, particularly the historical events of the death and resurrection of Christ.[33]

On October 18, 1931, Lewis wrote that the death and resurrection of Christ had really happened.[34] How did he reach this position? On September 28, 1931, the Lewis brothers traveled to the newly opened

---

[29] He described this in a letter to Arthur Greeves on September 22, 1931.

[30] Lewis, *Miracles*, 134.

[31] See the poem "Mythopoeia," by J. R. R. Tolkien. Donald T. Williams thinks Lewis made that comment on the night of the midnight conversation on Addison's Walk between Lewis, Tolkien, and Hugo Dyson, September 19, 1931 (*C. S. Lewis's List*, 34).

[32] Lewis, *The Pilgrim's Regress*, 143. See all of Chapters VII through X in Book Eight.

[33] *Collected Letters of C. S. Lewis*, I, 977.

[34] *Collected Letters of C. S. Lewis*, I, 977.

Whipsnade Zoo on Warren's motorcycle as part of a family outing.[35] Warren drove, and Lewis rode in the sidecar. Lewis later wrote, "When we set out I did not believe that Jesus Christ is the Son of God, and when we reached the zoo I did."[36] He had solved the problem of an internal zoo of lusts during an external trip to a zoo of animals.

While George MacDonald described the conversion experience this way: "*Open your hand, and you will sleep indeed—then wake indeed*,"[37] Warren described it another way:

> This seemed to me no sudden plunge into a new life, but rather a slow steady convalescence from a deep-seated spiritual illness of long standing—an illness that had its origins in our childhood, in the dry husks of religion offered by the semi-political church-going of Ulster, in the similar dull emptiness of compulsory church during our schooldays.[38]

The Bible is full of conversion stories, and God seems to reach people in a variety of ways. To Zacchaeus, the lonely tax collector, Jesus was hospitality personified (Luke 19), to the love-starved woman at the well he was love personified (John 4), to the man born blind (John 9) he was a miracle-working wise man, to the bereaved Mary and Martha he was the conqueror of death (John 11), and to the religious leader Nicodemus he was an intellect capable of answering his questions (John 3). For Lewis, conversion was far more like that of Nicodemus than that of Zacchaeus, the blind man, Mary and Martha, or the woman at the well. No two people come to believe in the same way, but for an intellect like Lewis we should not be surprised that the

---

[35] The zoo is still in operation today in Dunstable, Bedfordshire, England, about forty miles east of Oxford.

[36] Lewis, *Surprised by Joy*, 237. Surely his letter to Sister Penelope on August 9, 1939, claiming that he had been a Christian for twelve years, is evidence that Lewis confused dates rather than evidence for an earlier conversion (*Collected Letters of C. S. Lewis*, II, 263f.).

[37] Cited by Lewis in *The Pilgrim's Regress*, 159.

[38] Warren Lewis, "Memoir of C. S. Lewis," in *Letters of C. S. Lewis*, revised Harvest edition (1993), 39.

event was fifteen years in the making (after all, Warren had called it a "spiritual illness of long standing") and that it was far more intellectual than emotional.

CHAPTER 8

THE RETURN TO CHRISTIANITY IN OVERVIEW

REASONS FROM AN UNSCRUPULOUS GOD

"Here and here only in all time the myth must have become fact; the Word, flesh; God, Man."

—C. S. Lewis, *Surprised by Joy*

The journey from atheism to Christianity took C. S. Lewis fifteen years, and this chapter provides a summary snapshot of that fifteen-year journey. Much of the journey was intellectual (Lewis himself once described his conversion as almost purely philosophical[1]) and much of it imaginative, but there were also social factors, personal tragedy, introspection, a new appreciation of the historical nature of the New Testament Gospels, a touch of mysticism, an awareness of personal shortcomings, a reappraisal of myth, a better appreciation of nature,

---

[1] C. S. Lewis, "Autobiographical Note," prepared by the Macmillan Company (1946), 1. Cited in Barkman, "Rudolf Otto, *The Idea of the Holy*," *C. S. Lewis's List*, 113, n. 2. See also Alan Jacobs, *The Narnian*, xviiif. See also *Collected Letters of C. S. Lewis*, II, 568, where he calls his background mixed up with "technical philosophy," and page 575, where he writes that the details of his conversion story were "technically philosophical."

questions about the place of longing in our lives, and an honest openness. The loss of his parents served as catalysts in his spiritual journey, the death of his mother a major cause of his atheism and the death of his father a key turning point in his return to Christianity.

The earliest movement toward belief in God came from a sense of longing, arising during childhood experiences of beauty. That sense of longing, Lewis later contended, had been put in him by God Himself, almost as a time release capsule that delivers its medicine to the body over a period of time rather than as an injection that delivers the medicine all at once.

In the midst of Lewis's rather unimaginative childhood, he unexpectedly experienced longing, "the memory of a memory,"[2] which prepared him for his return to theism and Christianity, even before he left. This longing was further spurred by Beatrix Potter's children's story, *Squirrel Nutkin*, John Tenniel, and the idea of Autumn. The toy garden that Warren brought to his younger brother, later seen as a pointer to God, was C. S. Lewis's first experience of beauty. Beauty, great music, great poetry, story, art, and nature—whose various objects he once called "magnificent symbols of Divinity"[3]—also awakened this longing. Likewise, marriage, travel, and learning awakened longings, but they ended up as pointers to something else.[4]

The Lewis brothers grew up with what Warren Lewis called the dry husks of religion and compulsory church attendance. Rather than experiencing a vibrant Christian faith and spiritually mature adult mentoring, Warren and Jack experienced nominal Christianity, a Christianity confined largely to Sunday morning. Nor was there much community; the two boys had very few friends outside of the family circle.

---

[2] Lewis, *Surprised by Joy*, 16.

[3] C. S. Lewis, *Reflections on the Psalms* (New York: Harcourt Brace Jovanovich, 1958), 81. On nature and art as pointers, see *Collected Letters of C. S. Lewis*, III, 583f.

[4] Lewis, *Mere Christianity*, 135.

After Lewis's adoption of atheism in 1912, the reading of George MacDonald's *Phantastes* in 1916 started his long return to theism and then Christianity. Although Lewis did not realize it at the time, *Phantastes* reflected in its pages a quality of holiness, or goodness, redirecting his imagination toward good rather than evil. In the next several years, when Lewis was attracted to some aspects of the occult world, MacDonald proved to be a hedge against those influences. From this time on, MacDonald would be one of Lewis's favorite authors, so much so that he once described MacDonald as his master and once said that he did not think he ever wrote a book in which he did not quote MacDonald.[5] The writings of George MacDonald provided him with a spiritual mentor, something his father had failed to provide. George MacDonald's other writings were also influential on Lewis, some for their spiritual and devotional quality and others for the imaginative story. *The Diary of an Old Soul* was one of those devotional writings, and Lewis found the imaginative and engaging story in *Lilith*, *The Princess and the Goblin*, *Sir Gibbie*, and *The Golden Key*. Even Owen Barfield's children's story, *The Silver Trumpet*, helped in the awakening of his imagination. Other books by MacDonald, such as *Unspoken Sermons*, provided a mature influence much later in life.

Even before MacDonald, the stories of William Morris and Sir Thomas Malory as well as the poetry of W. B. Yeats appealed to Lewis for many of the same reasons. Lewis did not at first recognize Morris's writings as pointers to a supernatural world, thinking that the longing itself was what he wanted. Eventually he came to see Morris as one whose writings elicited a desire for something that nothing in this world could satisfy. Morris was such a captivating writer for Lewis that he wrote papers about him, both pre- and post-conversion, defending Morris to an Oxford literary society, the Martlets, and including an essay about him in his 1939 collection of essays, *Rehabilitations*.[6]

---

[5] Lewis, *George MacDonald*, xxxii.
[6] See my article, "C. S. Lewis and the Martlets," www.cslewis.com/blog/lewis-and-martlets.

Lewis discovered Morris during his years at Great Bookham with his atheistic tutor Kirkpatrick. His time studying with Kirkpatrick (1914–17) did not cause his atheism, because he was already an atheist when he arrived. Kirkpatrick did provide some support for Lewis's atheistic position, especially through the works of Frazer, Schopenhauer, and Nietzsche, all of whom Kirkpatrick admired. More important, however, was the fact that Kirkpatrick taught him thinking skills that later enabled him to set aside his objections and consider theism and the Christian faith fairly and objectively.

Except for one late night conversation in 1931, we do not know to what extent Lewis's Christian friends, especially Nevill Coghill, J. R. R. Tolkien, and Hugo Dyson, spoke with him explicitly about the Christian faith. They certainly drew on their faith to speak, teach, and write from a depth of personal acquaintance with God and an appreciation of myth. Since conversation for Lewis was almost always a summons to disputation,[7] we can assume there was much give and take between Lewis and these friends. The same was true of his contact with other friends, especially Arthur Greeves, Owen Barfield, and A. C. Harwood. They challenged his assumptions, even as he challenged theirs. In the case for Christianity, Lewis lost one of the few debates of his adult life.

Many Christian authors also influenced Lewis, who did not hesitate to read these authors even when he rejected their central premises. Among the works that most influenced his conversion, he read G. K. Chesterton's *The Everlasting Man*, John Milton's *Paradise Lost*, George Herbert's poetry, Edmund Spenser's *The Fairie Queene*, Jacob Boehme's *The Signature of All Things*, and George Berkeley's *Principles of Human Knowledge*—whose writings he once described as unanswerable.[8] Their writings served as a contrast with those atheistic authors whom he should have enjoyed, but whose writings appeared thin to him. His intellectual honesty allowed him to read with an open mind what those writers had to say.

---

[7] Note Lewis, *Surprised by Joy*, 136, to see where Lewis learned this tactic.
[8] *Collected Letters of C. S. Lewis*, II, 702f.

When in 1923 Owen Barfield and A. C. Harwood, both of them non-Christians, became Anthroposophists, Lewis's world was shaken. By their conversion to Anthroposophism, they rejected naturalism and demonstrated an openness to other worlds, especially a spiritual world beyond the five senses. Much as the deaths of his mother and father profoundly affected Lewis in opposite ways, the change in these two close friends also affected him, challenging him to think about life beyond the material universe.

The stark grimness of materialism, especially as exemplified in the writings of atheists Friedrich Nietzsche and Arthur Schopenhauer, "the great pessimist," affected Lewis in the late teens and early 1920s. In 1914, he had read about Nietzsche as the indirect author of the war, and in 1924 he read Nietzsche's *Beyond Good and Evil*. He read Schopenhauer in 1915, while studying with Kirkpatrick, in 1918 after his return from the war, and again in 1922 while he was holding to atheistic materialism. In 1918, he wrote to Arthur Greeves favorably about Schopenhauer's thoughts on the origin of love, admitting that he had often dipped into Schopenhauer while living with Kirkpatrick. Lewis's exposure to the writings of Schopenhauer and the mind of Kirkpatrick undoubtedly entrenched him in atheism, as did his reading of Sir James Frazer's *The Golden Bough*, which described Christianity as just another mythology.

Lewis had returned from the war determined to live a consistent materialism. The difficulty of doing so, however, helped him to see the inadequacy of Realism, based on the difficulty of materialism to explain valid standards of right and wrong (goodness, or ethics), the origin of valid reason (truth), and objective beauty, or the idea that goodness, truth, and beauty were anything more than subjective opinions. Furthermore, he had to deal with occasional bouts with depression and oppression, some of which were spurred on by the strange madness of Doc Askins, who thought he was being dragged to Hell.

In 1924, Lewis lost his two bishops in his chess game with God. The first loss came while reading Euripides's *Hippolytus*. With that reading he recovered the Joy, or longing, which he had attempted to shut out of his mind for years in his futile attempt to live a completely materialistic life. He lost his second bishop as a result of his reading of Samuel Alexander's *Space, Time and Deity*, a book that convinced him that Joy was a pointer to something outside himself rather than something within, which was causing this sense of longing. This enabled him to adopt Idealism, which he had reconsidered as a result of being hired to teach philosophy at Oxford University during the 1924–25 school year, but also as a result of the flaws in materialism. Idealism held to an idea—the Absolute or Spirit—which functioned like a mind behind the universe and in which each person somehow participated. During this Idealist period, Lewis adopted the pantheistic idea that many Idealists held, namely that the individual soul emerges from Spirit of which it is a part.

He eventually set aside Idealism as an inadequate approach to life, in part because one cannot live it, in part because he had to make it clear to his students, but especially because the Absolute seemed to him simply a way to avoid talking about God. Nevertheless Idealism was an important step in Lewis's life since it moved beyond materialistic philosophy, enabling Lewis to see meaning, design, and purpose in the world around us.

If anything is true of Lewis, it is this: C. S. Lewis honestly grappled with the truth. As the Greek philosopher Socrates had encouraged people to follow the argument wherever it led,[9] so also did Lewis, both in his academic work and in the later stages of his search for meaning in life.

One example of this openness to an alternative view occurred in 1926. During April of that year, Lewis heard a candid appraisal from a hostile source, i.e., Harry Weldon's comment that, given the Gospels, it almost looked as if the resurrection had happened once. Weldon had apparently read at least one of the four Gospels, probably the Gospel of John, and then expressed that opinion one evening in Lewis's rooms at Magdalen College. This estimate, expressed by a man whom Lewis

---

[9] Lewis, "The Founding of the Oxford Socratic Club," *God in the Dock*, 126.

considered hostile to the Christian faith, greatly surprised Lewis. As a result of Weldon's comment, Lewis began to read the Gospels, hear them read in chapel services, and see them in a different light. This event probably took place soon after Lewis had read Chesterton's *The Everlasting Man* and, with Chesterton's help, led him to the conclusion that the Christian outline of history made more sense than the secular and atheistic version given by H. G. Wells. Chesterton paved the way for Weldon's comment to have a much stronger impact.

With the help of Owen Barfield and J. R. R. Tolkien, Lewis came to a new opinion about the value of myth. Barfield's *Poetic Diction* taught him that all language is metaphorical, which built on what he had learned earlier, that the Christian metaphor, or story, was at least as good as any other metaphor. His Great War with Barfield had been about the nature of the imagination, i.e., whether or not it was capable of conveying truth. For Lewis at this time, myth conveyed meaning, but not truth about the external world. Near the end of that Great War, Lewis read Andrew Lang's *Myth, Ritual and Religion* in the summer of 1929, learning from Lang that religious beliefs existed at the beginning of each culture and that degeneration happened thereafter, the very reverse of what he had previously believed. He began to think that the shape of the events of the life of Jesus of Nazareth—God incarnating Himself in His creation—may have been prefigured in the myths of various religions, thereby making paganism a preparation for Christianity. He also began to think that the story of Jesus' dying and rising was a true myth with similarities to other myths, except that this one actually happened.[10] Without this change in his thinking, which came far more as a result of his years-long argument with Barfield in their Great War than as a result of reading Lang, Lewis would not have been able to see that the Incarnation of God in Jesus Christ was both myth and history.

Although it was not clear at the time, Albert Lewis's death on September 25, 1929, had a profound impact on both Lewis brothers. Lewis, especially, felt remorse over the way he had treated his father.

---

[10] *Collected Letters of C. S. Lewis*, II, 977.

Though the brothers had reasons for their attitude toward their father, they both felt his absence after Albert's death and both felt guilt for their contempt toward their father, for their deceit in hiding information from him, for their derogatory reference to him as the Pudaitabird or the O.A.B. (Old Air Bag), and for their avoidance of his company. In *The Pilgrim's Regress*, the pilgrim's words about his now deceased parents undoubtedly expressed the thoughts and feelings of Lewis, "I had much I would have said to them."[11]

Late in the journey toward theism, Lewis became aware of the moral law within him and his personal "zoo of lusts." His father's death was one of the reasons for this new introspection, especially when he compared his own treatment of his father with the way a friend treated his father. He saw pride, rather than sins of the flesh, as his besetting sin and blamed himself for his arrogant postures in letters to his lifelong friend Arthur Greeves. Later he would write that spiritual sins are far worse than the sins of the flesh[12] and that a prostitute might be far closer to heaven than a self-righteous prig who regularly attends church.[13] Having been guilty of both sins of the spirit and sins of the flesh, he knew from experience which was worse.

Lewis also had a profound respect for mystical writers, one of whom, Jacob Boehme, wrote a book that impressed him late in his spiritual journey. That book, *The Signature of All Things*, gave him "the biggest shaking up" that he had received from a book since he read *Phantastes*. Prior to Boehme he had read about St. Francis, whom Chesterton had described as a mystic,[14] and he had read Dean Inge, especially his essay "Institutionalism and Mysticism." In 1924, he had read Henry More's *Defense of the Cabbala*, a Jewish mystical work. He came to believe that God could actually write Himself into the Gospel story, much like Shakespeare could write himself into one of his plays. Later in life he read and enjoyed such mystical writers as Julian of

---

[11] Lewis, *The Pilgrim's Regress*, 197.
[12] Lewis, *Mere Christianity*, 102. In this, Lewis is agreeing with Dante's *Purgatorio*.
[13] Lewis, *Mere Christianity*, 103.
[14] Chesterton, *Life of St. Francis*, Chapter I, "The Problem of St. Francis."

Norwich, Teresa of Avila, and Walter Hilton. His good friend and former student Alan Griffiths, his chief companion on the road back to God, had a similar respect for mysticism and undoubtedly influenced him in the books he recommended and the conversations they shared, especially during those last months before he became a Christian.

The third chess move brought Joy and Idealism together, allowing Lewis to see that his longing, or Joy, was a longing for the Idea behind Idealism, what Idealists called the Absolute, which was something very like a mind. In other words, what he had truly longed for during all of those years was this Mind. As he read Bradley and Berkeley, the difficulty in explaining the Absolute led him to the conclusion that the Absolute was a convenient way of talking about God without becoming accountable to Him. When he wrote to Owen Barfield on February 3, 1930, about entering a monastery, he had just come to the conclusion that the object of his longing, Joy, was a longing for the Absolute, or a Mind, and that Mind just might be God.

Lewis increasingly came to see the weaknesses of his own position, which criticized the Christian view of the world. One major weakness was the realization that he needed to have a standard of straightness by which to determine that the world was crooked, a ruler by which to measure the unruly. In that realization, he saw that he was using the Christian understanding of morality as a basis for criticizing that same morality. In short, this was the problem with the problem of pain: "If the universe is so bad, or even half so bad, how on earth did human beings ever come to attribute it to the activity of a wise and good Creator?"[15] He concluded that among the solid reasons for this attribution were the testimony of Scripture, the logical consistency of Christian ethics, the widespread acceptance of morality among nearly all peoples, the historical events of the Incarnation, death, and resurrection of Jesus, the sense of longing for something that this life could not provide, and the reality of human guilt.

---

[15] Lewis, *The Problem of Pain*, 3.

Ironically, his willful desire for autonomy, the ability to be the master of his own fate, which was his central reason for adopting atheism, was also one of the reasons for his return to the Christian faith. Once he recognized his willfulness for what it was, he had recognized the enemy within and could do something about it. The longing pointed to something or someone out there, not in here, i.e., to God, while the enemy was in here, not out there, and he was his own worst enemy. Lewis had deliberately kept God at arm's length for years in order to maintain his personal autonomy. He eventually saw his own desire to live his life without any interference as rebellion against the One who had made him. In this he was only seeing what happens in everyone's life, i.e., a desire to be one's own person, whether it appears in a two-year-old, a thirty-two-year-old, or an eighty-two-year-old. He also saw that God makes a person more fully a person when one gives oneself up to God.

CHAPTER 9

C. S. LEWIS ON ATHEISM

"I would gladly believe that many atheists and agnostics care
for the things I care for."

—C. S. Lewis, "Lilies that Fester"

C. S. Lewis once wrote that atheism was as old as the Greek philosopher Epicurus, who lived in the fourth century B.C.[1] Lewis had a lot to say about atheists and atheism. He mentioned the topic at least seventy-eight times in at least thirty books and essays. Having been an atheist himself, he understood Christianity from—as he put it—the outside. He had held many of the same positions that atheists held in the teens and 1920s for many of the same reasons, and many of those reasons still influence people today. Although Lewis did not make any sort of systematic description, definition, or formal reaction to atheism, we can glean a great deal from his writings. The following paragraphs describe atheism according to C. S. Lewis.

LEWIS'S ENCOUNTERS WITH ATHEISTS

Perhaps most important of all, Lewis knew quite a few atheists and avoided making generalizations about all atheists. He knew how different they were from one another. Generalizations do not apply to individuals, and people become atheists for a wide variety of reasons.

---

[1] *Collected Letters of C. S. Lewis*, II, 633.

Apart from himself, the atheist he knew best was William T. Kirkpatrick, his tutor at Gastons in Great Bookham, Surrey. Kirkpatrick taught Lewis how to think, but he did not cause Lewis's atheism.[2] Lewis was already an atheist before he arrived at Great Bookham, though he gained additional support from Kirkpatrick for his atheism. Kirkpatrick's rationalistic atheism, was "chiefly of the anthropological and pessimistic kind,"[3] the same type of atheism Lewis had adopted. This apparently meant not only that Kirkpatrick was pessimistic about human nature, but also that he failed to see evidence that human beings were made in the image of God. Kirkpatrick was convinced that *The Golden Bough* had explained the origin of religion in the ancient mythologies,[4] and Lewis adopted a similar position.

During his undergraduate years, Lewis was influenced by Dr. Frederick Macran,[5] the Irish priest, whose unusual atheism, mixed with a desire for immortality, motivated Lewis to avoid anything that might lead him to desire immortality, as though it were some kind of reward or bribe. In addition to Macran, his undergraduate friends A. K. Hamilton Jenkin,[6] R. M. S. Pasley, and George Arnold Rink[7] were atheists with whom he frequently socialized. And, of course, his own brother Warren described himself as an atheist at one time.[8]

Lewis's convictions about atheists flowed from his experience with these and many other atheists, both past and present, whom he knew, socialized with, corresponded with, read (some of whom he met, others of whom he only read), and mentioned in his writings. These included the English novelist Arnold Bennett,[9] the English literary

---

[2] C. S. Lewis, "Fern-seed and Elephants," *Fern-Seed and Elephants and Other Essays on Christianity*, 122.
[3] Lewis, *Surprised by Joy*, 139.
[4] Lewis, *Surprised by Joy*, 139.
[5] *Collected Letters of C. S. Lewis*, I, 547.
[6] *Collected Letters of C. S. Lewis*, II, 241.
[7] Lewis, *All My Road Before Me*, 189, February 1, 1923.
[8] *Brothers & Friends*, 80, May 13, 1931.
[9] *Collected Letters of C. S. Lewis*, II, 240.

critic I. A. Richards,[10] his former student Alan Richard Griffiths, the biologist J. B. S. Haldane,[11] the philosopher C. E. M. Joad, philosopher Antony Flew, poet and novelist Kathleen Nott, the essayist Matthew Arnold (whom he read but never met),[12] the artist Wayland Young,[13] several of his colleagues at Magdalen College,[14] probably including philosopher T. D. Weldon and historian A. J. P. Taylor,[15] an Oxford undergraduate named Edwards,[16] and literally scores of others in Oxford and elsewhere.[17] Those would include Thomas Hardy, the novelist, and the poet A. E. Housman, two writers whom he read but never met.[18] He met and corresponded with former atheists, such as Margaret Gray, to whom he recommended books for reading.[19] He also corresponded with and met another of his atheistic contemporaries, science fiction writer, Arthur C. Clarke, who wrote to Lewis about Lewis's own fictional story, *Perelandra*.[20] Lewis even married a former atheist, Joy Davidman. His contact with so many atheists led Lewis to make few assumptions about an atheist's beliefs, apart from some fundamental convictions, which follow.

---

[10] Lewis, "Christianity and Culture," 12.

[11] Haldane addressed the subject of "Atheism" at the Socratic Club on November 15, 1948 (Roger Lancelyn Green and Walter Hooper, *C. S. Lewis: A Biography*, revised edition [A Harvest Book, 1974], 217).

[12] Brown, *A Life Observed*, 6.

[13] "Chronologically Lewis," February 23, 1952. See also *Collected Letters of C. S. Lewis*, III, 167f.

[14] *Collected Letters of C. S. Lewis*, II, 495; III, 521.

[15] See Kathleen Burk, *Troublemaker: The Life and History of A. J. P. Taylor* (New Haven: Yale University Press, 2000).

[16] See "Chronologically Lewis," May 19, 1917. Edwards's first name is unknown.

[17] "Interim Report," *Present Concerns*, 95.

[18] Lewis, *The Problem of Pain*, 93.

[19] He wrote to her on May 9, 1961 (*Collected Letters of C. S. Lewis*, III, 1264).

[20] See especially *Collected Letters of C. S. Lewis*, II, 593f., for a letter written by Lewis on December 7, 1943, in response to Clarke's letter.

LEWIS ON THE ASSUMPTIONS OF ATHEISM

The most fundamental assumption of atheism appears in the definition of the word *atheism*: God does not exist.[21] In this, wrote Lewis, atheists assume that most of the human race is now wrong, and has always been wrong, about the existence of God.[22] The vast majority of human beings, well in excess of ninety percent, believe in God, whether the God of Christianity, Judaism, Hinduism, Islam, or one of the lesser known religions. But an atheist, then as well as now, has to believe that the majority is wrong on this topic.

Lewis also thought that his Christian view of other religions was preferable to the view he had when he was an atheist. He wrote, "When I was an atheist I had to try to persuade myself that most of the human race have always been wrong about the question that mattered to them most; when I became a Christian I was able to take a more liberal view."[23] As a Christian he could accept the theistic position of most people, setting aside his narrow view of theists, and he could even accept the truth of the moral law, which, he argued in *The Abolition of Man*, has been common to most religions throughout history. He did not have to think that all religions were completely wrong about their most basic affirmation.

Later in life, in *Letters to Malcolm: Chiefly on Prayer*, Lewis wrote, "We may ignore, but we can nowhere evade, the presence of God. The world is crowded with Him. He walks everywhere *incognito*. And the *incognito* is not always hard to penetrate. The real labor is to remember, to attend. In fact, to come awake. Still more, to remain

---

[21] Many distinguish between positive atheism (affirming the non-existence of God) and negative atheism (the failure to affirm the existence of God). Lewis was a positive atheist, and most of what he wrote addressed positive atheism. An atheist can also be wide or narrow, in the former case denying that any god exists and in the latter case denying the existence of a specific deity. Lewis was a wide atheist. These distinctions will not be made in the chapter, especially since Lewis thought about particular atheists whom he had met rather than atheism as a whole.

[22] Lewis, *Mere Christianity*, 35.

[23] Lewis, *Mere Christianity*, 35.

awake."[24] God is present in the world of Nature, in the ebb and flow of the seasons, in the longing for something beyond this material world, in the distant stars and planets, in the beauty of art, the rapture of music, the love of the beloved for the lover, the sexual embrace, the writings of pagan poets, and even in the awareness that something is desperately wrong with the world.

Lewis thought that atheists "see through" the imaginative and mythological, confident that they see life as it really is because they adopt a scientific understanding of the world.[25] A scientific understanding is good, Lewis thought, as far as it goes, but it deals with nature and does not address whether or not something can exist beyond nature. Many atheists regard the existence of man and the other animals simply as the result of other biological facts.[26] In other words, man is an accidental product of natural selection, random chance, and vast amounts of time. Man is merely a more advanced evolutionary product, no more valuable than any other form of life.

While atheism can lead us down dark and depressing paths, atheism at times may allow the sensitive atheist "to enjoy the aesthetic trappings of Christianity" in a way that Christians cannot.[27] One example Lewis used was that of Lucretius, the first-century BC Roman poet and philosopher, also an atheist, who was better able than many of his pagan contemporaries to see the beauty of the gods, in particular their eternity, their peace, and their remoteness.[28] Likewise, without any commitment to preserving the truth of some part of Christianity, the modern-day Matthew Arnold could admire the beauty of the gothic cathedrals and medieval art while denying the existence of God.

Most atheists reject the Fall of Adam and Eve into sin, in part, because they underestimate the reality of sin.[29] Sin is out there, in other

---

[24] Lewis, *Letters to Malcolm*, 75.
[25] Lewis, *Surprised by Joy*, 204.
[26] Lewis, *The Problem of Pain*, 142.
[27] Lewis, "Is Theology Poetry?" *The Weight of Glory and Other Addresses*, 93.
[28] Lewis, *The Allegory of Love*, 83.
[29] Lewis states this, not just of atheists, but of everyone in "The Poison of Subjectivism," *Christian Reflections*, 78.

people, cultures, societies, systems, but not in here, in my own person. It was not until Lewis looked inside himself and saw a "zoo of lusts" that he understood the impact of sin on himself and those around him. He learned about the problem of personal failings, but he seemed unable to do anything about it.[30] One of the consequences of the underestimation, or rejection, of the Fall, according to Lewis, is an overestimation of the value of education. Often atheists assume that, since evil is either non-existent or minimally invasive, mankind can be put right by education.[31]

In his essay "Religion and Rocketry," Lewis also wrote about two equal and opposite scientific proposals: one, that life only began on earth with the rarest of accidents, and another, proposed by Cambridge astronomer Sir Fred Hoyle, that life probably began in many places. Both positions, Lewis wrote, claimed to show the absurdity of the Christian belief that God created the universe and that God became man in the Incarnation of Christ. One argues "mere one-time accident," and the other argues "probably happened many times." The odd thing is that arguments from two diametrically opposed positions would both be used to attack Christianity. Lewis concluded that "those who do not find Him on earth are unlikely to find Him in space."[32]

Another assumption by some atheists, Lewis believed, is that the vast size of the universe in comparison with the relatively small size of the Earth invalidates Christianity.[33] In comparison with space itself, some atheists claim, the stars and planets that move in this space are so few and so small that it is hard to believe that life is more than a byproduct.[34] For Lewis, however, the size of our planet and the vastness of space tell us nothing about the existence of God. Blaise Pascal drew a similar conclusion: "Through space the universe grasps

---

[30] Lewis, "The Poison of Subjectivism," *Christian Reflections*, 79.
[31] Lewis, "Revival or Decay," *God in the Dock*, 252.
[32] Lewis, "The Seeing Eye," *Christian Reflections*, 171.
[33] Lewis, *Miracles*, 73.
[34] Lewis, *The Problem of Pain*, 1.

me and swallows me up like a speck; through thought I grasp it."[35] While Lewis did not explain why size and vastness tell us nothing about God, he thought that planet Earth below and the heavens above are part of our natural order, whereas the existence of God is a question about the supernatural order, i.e., the order that is "supra" or "above" the natural. The heavens and the Earth are physical realities, while God is a spiritual reality.[36]

Lewis also wrote about the position of atheists on animals. He believed that atheists regarded the coexistence of mankind and animals as a mere biological fact. Thus, for some atheists the taming of an animal by humans is an arbitrary interference of one species with another—the natural animal is the wild animal, while the tame animal is unnatural. Christians, however, think that God appointed mankind to have dominion over the beasts, and every way in which people interact with animals is either a proper exercise or an improper abuse of that God-given authority.[37]

LEWIS ON THE CAUSES OF ATHEISM

The immediate reason for writing his autobiography, *Surprised by Joy*, appears in the Preface, where Lewis stated that he had received requests to tell how he traveled the road from atheism to Christianity. *Surprised by Joy* provided the answer to those requests. As a result, his autobiography contains a good deal of information about the reasons he became an atheist as well as the reasons he left atheism.

Many of the reasons for which Lewis adopted atheism are the same reasons he thought others had given in making the same choice. Both the frailty of the world and the argument from undesign were among those reasons. Nature behaves badly,[38] and if God is the creator of Nature, then either God is evil or a poor Designer. Perhaps He is not

---

[35] Blaise Pascal, *Pensées*, trans. A. J. Krailsheimer (New York: Penguin Books, 1966), #113, 59.

[36] See, for example, Lewis, *Mere Christianity*, 17f.

[37] Lewis, *The Problem of Pain*, 142.

[38] Lewis, *Miracles*, 155.

good. Perhaps He is not all-powerful. Perhaps He simply does not exist. Later Lewis would argue that the selective or undemocratic quality in Nature is neither good nor evil,[39] believing that pain and death in the natural world are the result of the historic Fall of Adam and Eve and not the fault of God. The corollary to this misbehaving Nature for him was that the argument from design was a very weak basis for theism.[40] Had the current findings of microbiology about the vast complexity of the inner workings of an individual cell been available to Lewis, he might have considered the argument from design to be far weightier. Later he would argue that attributing certain behaviors to instinct, for example, in the world of insects, comes from the refusal to recognize design in that behavior.[41]

The fact that human beings had an inherent vanity, that life preyed on life, and that beauty and happiness were produced only to be destroyed were hard pills for Lewis to swallow. Furthermore, Lewis noted that reason enables mankind "by a hundred ingenious contrivances to inflict a great deal more pain than they otherwise could have done," and the history of mankind is "largely a record of crime, war, disease, and terror."[42] Lewis also wrote about his own pessimism as a contributing cause of his atheism,[43] undoubtedly pessimism caused by the suffering, pain, and death he saw around him, especially the death of his mother. As we have seen, elsewhere he indicated that the loss of his mother, unhappiness at school, the memory of the First World War, and his experience of that war had all led to his pessimistic view of existence and either caused or confirmed his adoption of atheism.[44]

---

[39] Lewis, *Miracles*, 155.

[40] *Collected Letters of C. S. Lewis*, II, 747.

[41] Lewis, "On Ethics," *Christian Reflections*, 49.

[42] Lewis, *The Problem of Pain*, 2.

[43] Lewis, *Surprised by Joy*, 190. See also *Collected Letters of C. S. Lewis*, II, 747.

[44] Letter to Bede Griffiths on December 20, 1946 (*Collected Letters of C. S. Lewis*, II, 747).

One of the more telling comments Lewis made in one of his letters was the fact that many atheists came from pious homes.[45] The type of religious education some atheists received was one of the factors leading to their atheism, and he advocated a different approach to the Christian faith, one that showed the power of the Christian faith.[46] He was referring to the superficial Christianity he had received at home and the harsh legalism of Ulster Christianity.[47] In addition, Lewis argued that the positions of theological liberalism, especially the higher critical theories of some New Testament scholars, at times drove people to atheism.[48]

Lewis argued that some atheists hold to their atheism because they want it to be true, just as some might adopt Christianity because they want it to be true. But nothing can be proven, Lewis argued, by merely wanting or wishing.[49] Just as Freud thought that religious people imagined a father figure who was far better than their earthly father, so Freud—Lewis maintained—could have denied the existence of God and an after-life because he wished not to be held accountable in the next life.[50] In fact, there is no need to conclude that either side is operating irrationally; there is evidence on both sides.

---

[45] *Collected Letters of C. S. Lewis*, III, 506.

[46] *Collected Letters of C. S. Lewis*, III, 506. See especially Lewis, "Sometimes Fairy Stories May Say Best What's to Be Said," *Of Other Worlds*, 35–38.

[47] On the legalism of Ulster Christianity, see Lewis, *The Pilgrim's Regress*.

[48] "Modern Theology and Biblical Criticism," *Fern-seed and Elephants*, 105.

[49] "On Obstinacy in Belief," *The World's Last Night and Other Essays* (New York: Harcourt, Brace and Company, 1952), 19f. Strange though it may seem, Lewis actually wrote, "A man may be a Christian because he wants Christianity to be true. He may be an atheist because he wants atheism to be true. He may be an atheist because he wants Christianity to be true. He may be a Christian because he wants atheism to be true."

[50] Lewis, "On Obstinacy in Belief," 19. See, for example, American philosopher Thomas Nagel, who writes, "I am talking about . . . the fear of religion itself. . . . I want atheism to be true and am made uneasy by the fact that some of the most intelligent and well-informed people I know are religious believers. It isn't just that I don't believe in God, and naturally, hope that I am right in my belief. It's that I hope there is no God! I don't want there to be a God; I don't want the universe to be like that" (*The Last Word* [New York: Oxford University Press,

LEWIS ON THE CHARACTERISTICS OF ATHEISM

One of the chief characteristics of atheism, Lewis wrote, is the fact that some atheists both deny the existence of God and are angry with God for not existing.[51] Lewis claimed that it was not uncommon to find atheists "perpetually angry with God for not being there."[52] The major reason for such anger is the difficulty in making sense of suffering and the problem of existence. This was the case with the atheist Thomas Henry Huxley, whom Lewis commended for his serious attempt to make sense of the problem of suffering.[53] One of the other contradictions in Lewis's "whirl of contradictions"[54] is the fact that atheists frequently sense the approach of God. That was certainly the case during the last days of his atheism. Whenever he had a moment's leisure he felt "the steady, unrelenting approach" of the One whom he did not want to meet.[55]

As he indicated in his series of poems, *Spirits in Bondage*, atheists are often ambivalent in their denial of the existence of God. As a Christian, Lewis candidly admitted, he at times had moods when his Christian views looked improbable. On the other hand, when he was

---

2000], 130). See also "On Obstinacy in Belief," *The World's Last Night and Other Essays*, 19.

[51] Lewis, *Surprised by Joy*, 115. See also Lewis, *The Problem of Pain*, 93.

[52] *Collected Letters of C. S. Lewis*, II, 223f. The letter is dated April 18, 1938. Some years ago Julie Exline, Case Western Reserve University psychologist, reported that college students, atheists, and agnostics were angrier with God than were religious people. In this study, Exline and her co-researchers studied people who were angry with God because of bereavement and cancer. They also found young people, even young atheists, more likely to be angry with God than older people (J. J. Exline, et al., "Anger toward God: Social-cognitive predictors, prevalence, and links with adjustment to bereavement and cancer," *Journal of Personality and Social Psychology*, 100 [2011]: 129–48).

[53] *The Problem of Pain*, 93. While Lewis does not indicate which Huxley, he probably meant Thomas Henry Huxley, who was known as "Darwin's Bulldog."

[54] Lewis, *Surprised by Joy*, 115.

[55] Lewis, *Surprised by Joy*, 228.

an atheist he had moods when Christianity looked quite probable.[56] Moods do not determine truth; they are an unreliable basis for deciding what is true.

As Lewis wrote in a letter to Alan Griffiths, he knew the universe to be bad. But he asked himself where he got a standard of straightness by which he could judge the world as crooked.[57] Atheists seek justice, whether it be for the environment, the migrant worker, the child caught in human trafficking, or the pet that is abused by its owner. But if certain positions are wrong, where does the idea of right and wrong come from? If all of life is relative (an idea that especially flows from the lack of divine authority), the product of random chance, natural selection, and vast amounts of time, then there is nothing that can be considered objectively right or wrong. No position has more right to be considered valid than another. And yet, when he was an atheist, Lewis considered some positions to be objectively wrong and thereby caught himself in a contradiction.

To say my idea of justice is just my private idea rather than something based on objective truth, Lewis argued, is to turn my position into a subjective opinion that is no more valid than anyone else's opinion. To say my idea of justice is universal—i.e., that everyone ought to agree—is an appeal to a standard. But if there is no such thing as God, and no objective standard of right and wrong, why should my private idea be any more correct than another person's idea? But if the idea of justice is sensible, then there is meaning to the universe.[58] Then right and wrong have a much more valid foundation. If the universe had no meaning, he wrote, we would never have learned that it has no meaning.[59] Or as atheist J. B. S. Haldane candidly wrote in a passage Lewis cited, "If my mental processes are determined wholly by the motions of atoms in my brain, I have no reason to suppose that my

---

[56] Lewis, *Mere Christianity,* 140. See also Lewis, "Religion: Reality or Substitute?" *Christian Reflections,* 41.

[57] *Collected Letters of C. S. Lewis,* II, 747. The letter is dated December 20, 1946.

[58] Lewis, *Mere Christianity,* 38f.

[59] Lewis, *Mere Christianity,* 39.

beliefs are true . . . and hence I have no reason for supposing my brain to be composed of atoms."[60] The idea of rational inquiry assumes there are truths to discover. If, however, the universe has no meaning, there is only nonsense and there are no truths to discover. Therefore, the idea of rational inquirers discovering the truth that the universe has no meaning contradicts itself.

But finally, atheists are also human beings, wired in many of the same ways that others are wired. "I would gladly believe," Lewis wrote, "that many atheists and agnostics care for the things I care for."[61] And undoubtedly they do.

Relating with Atheists

Lewis had respect for those good atheists[62] who honestly grappled with the apparent problems of theism and Christianity. When he invited Jenkin, an atheist, to join him and his friends on a multi-day country walk, Lewis told Jenkin that his friends would respect Jenkin's position.[63] He respected the legitimacy of Jenkin's concerns, since Lewis himself had been in a similar position for many years. Two of Lewis's fellow students, Edwards[64] and Butler, as well as Alan Richard Griffiths, the latter a student of Lewis's, moved from atheism to Christianity, as, of course, have millions of others through the centuries.[65]

The one place where Lewis interacted most with atheists was at the Oxford Socratic Club, where he and many Oxford undergraduates invited intelligent atheists to come and speak—men such as Antony Flew, Archibald Robertson, C. E. M. Joad, and J. B. S. Haldane. These atheists were treated with respect. Respect, for Lewis, meant seriously

---

[60] J. B. S. Haldane, *Possible Worlds*, 209, cited in *Miracles: A Preliminary Study* (New York: Simon & Schuster, 1996), 24.
[61] C. S. Lewis, "Lilies that Fester," *Christian Reunion and Other Essays* (Glasgow: William Collins Sons & Co., Ltd., 1990), 44.
[62] Lewis, "De Futilitate," *Christian Reflections*, 70.
[63] *Collected Letters of C. S. Lewis*, II, 241.
[64] See "Chronologically Lewis," May 19, 1917.
[65] *Collected Letters of C. S. Lewis*, I, 307.

considering the positions they held and discussing them with an open mind. He critiqued their views when they had finished speaking, sometimes settling into an impromptu debate. He had no difficulty understanding a position he had once held and discarded, but he also treated atheists with the respect that he would have wanted for himself.

C. S. Lewis knew many an atheist, understood many of their reasons for adopting atheism, identified with their ambivalence, and respected both their position and—if present—their honest attempts to grapple with the problems of suffering and injustice. However, he fundamentally disagreed with them, arguing that the atheists assumed the validity of reason in adopting their position, which was not possible in a purely naturalistic world. And in their complaints about the problem of evil or Christian moral teaching, they also assumed the existence of an objective moral standard. According to Lewis, the atheists were cutting off the branches they were collectively sitting on.

Conclusions

"You are no longer faced with an argument which demands your assent, but with a Person who demands your confidence."

—C. S. Lewis, "On Obstinacy in Belief"

About C. S. Lewis's Atheism

C. S. Lewis was one of the twentieth century's most famous atheists. Then, after the invasion of the supernatural into his life, he became one of the twentieth century's most famous Christians. Lewis did not willingly turn his mind to belief in God nor did he believe that which he wished to be true; he believed reluctantly. As Lewis stated in one of his essays, he was decided upon.[1] God had told him to put his gun down so they could talk.[2] Lewis was not wishing for a glorified father figure, even though his father had many failings. He was actually wishing that God did not exist, believing that God did not exist, and angry with God for not existing. Like everyone else, he was looking for autonomy. God had to have been involved in Lewis becoming a theist, and then a Christian, since Lewis was heading in the opposite direction. He was not going to come to God on his own. But then again, we understand that situation because we know what it means to want our own way.

Early in 1930, in the experience he described as unbuckling, the lowering of his defenses, Lewis determined that he would follow the evidence wherever it led.[3] That commitment served him well for the

---

[1] Lewis, "Cross-examination," *God in the Dock*, 261.

[2] Lewis, "Cross-examination," *God in the Dock*, 261.

[3] Remember that he had stated, "I had learned something from Kirk about the honor of the intellect and the shame of voluntary inconsistency" (Lewis, *Surprised by Joy*, 173).

rest of his life, but it also brought him to a point where he was able to face the possibility of God. Finally, Lewis was convinced only because he came into contact with strong evidence for God, particularly in the longing for something or someone else beyond this world. That happened because God was on the offensive. Lewis wrote, "To believe that God—at least *this* God—exists is to believe that you as a person now stand in the presence of God as a Person. What would, a moment before, have been variations in opinion, now become variations in your personal attitude to a Person. You are no longer faced with an argument which demands your assent, but with a Person who demands your confidence."[4] God, whom Lewis kept at a distance through his adoption of Idealism, with its impersonal conception of a Mind behind the universe, broke through that philosophical smog and showed him that the idea at the center of the universe was truly like a mind, but more than a mind, in fact both a Person and more than a Person.

Lewis had avoided this Person even up to the last several months of his pre-theistic life, preferring to refer to that ultimate being as "the Absolute" or "Spirit," but not God. Finally, when he looked closely at that "Absolute" and when he tried to explain it to his students, he realized that he was cloaking the reality of God behind words in an attempt to avoid God's claim on his life. The Divine Interferer that he had previously avoided now interfered in good ways, providing direction for life, freedom from guilt, and hope to replace his pessimism.

ABOUT THE ATTITUDES
AND ASSUMPTIONS OF ATHEISTS

Atheists often honestly attempt to explain inconsistencies and tragedies in the world around us. That is why Lewis once called such a person a "good atheist."[5] The world contains too much suffering, many think, for this world to be the creation of a good, all-powerful, and loving God. And they would be right, if there had never been a

---

[4] C. S. Lewis, "On Obstinacy in Belief," *The World's Last Night and Other Essays* (New York: Harcourt, Brace and Company, 1952), 26.
[5] Lewis, "De Futilitate," *Christian Reflections*, 70.

Fall, or corruption, of this world. At the same time, however, the Christian answer for suffering makes a great deal more sense than the atheistic answer. For Christians, another life exists beyond this life, and the scales are in some sense balanced and wrongs made right. For the atheist, a life of suffering often starts in tragedy, is led in tragedy, ends in tragedy, and there is no such balancing now or ever. Even if the Christian answer to suffering is not fully satisfactory, often because of God's hiddenness and our limited thinking, it addresses the question of suffering more substantively and more satisfactorily than any other way of thinking. Eternity balances the scales.

At times atheists adopt what Lewis called "a whirl of contradictions,"[6] such as the position that complains about injustice in the world without realizing where the ideas of justice and injustice come from. At times atheists ask honest questions and make honest conclusions. The world is full of pain and suffering, so why does God not step in and fix it? That is an honest question. And the honest answer is, "Well, He has." He stepped into a suffering world and suffered in the person of Jesus Christ, both providing comfort to the afflicted and making some sense out of the suffering, usually even bringing good from the suffering without justifying the suffering, One who has "borne our griefs" and "carried our sorrows" (Isaiah 53:4).

As the English philosopher C. E. M. Joad, who read Lewis[7] and was once invited to speak at the Oxford Socratic Club,[8] thought was true of himself, atheists also sometimes underestimate the problem of evil and overestimate the value of education and human nature. Although Joad once thought that there was "no fundamental and incurable wickedness in human beings"[9] and that "calamity and suffering have

---

[6] *Surprised by Joy*, 115.

[7] Joad mentioned reading Lewis's *The Abolition of Man* and *The Screwtape Letters*. See Walter Hooper, *C. S. Lewis: A Companion & Guide* (New York, 1996), 276 and C. E. M. Joad *God and Evil* (London, 1942), 298.

[8] See my article "From Vocal Agnostic to Reluctant Convert: The Influence of C. S. Lewis on the Conversion C. E. M. Joad," *Sehnsucht*, Vol. 3 (2009).

[9] C. E. M. Joad, *The Testament of Joad* (London: Faber & Faber, 1937), 13. See also Joad, *The Book of Joad*, 88, where he wrote, "It is not because men are bad at heart,

no purpose whatever,"[10] George Bernard Shaw's expression of human evil eventually seemed to Joad to be "intolerably shallow."[11] Reports about the Nazi death camps probably affected Joad. After the conviction, drawn from his observation of World War II, that mankind is evil, came the conviction that evil was resident also in himself.[12] And that conviction, coupled with reading Lewis, eventually led Joad to conclude that taking seriously the facts of moral experience required a supernatural view of life.[13] In addition, Joad began to notice that others possessed something that he did not, something he would like to have.[14] He claimed, "I would like to cultivate virtue and to be a better man, but I simply do not know how to do it."[15]

Joad later wrote, "I was for years baffled by the problem of pain and evil; in fact, it was this problem that for years denied belief in the Christian religion."[16] Joad learned, as Lewis had, that Christianity "creates, rather than solves, the problem of pain, for pain would be no problem unless, side by side with our daily experience of this painful world, we had received what we think good assurance that ultimate reality is righteous and loving."[17]

Often the atheist is ambivalent about God. The atheist thinks there is no God, but then complains about God's apparent inaction. The atheist denies the existence of God and then is angry with God for not existing, or at least angry with people who believe in a God the atheist is convinced does not exist. Lewis admitted that there were times when he doubted the truths of the Christian faith he had just defended, just

---

but because they are weak in the head that they so harry and torment one another and make their world a hell."

[10] Joad, *The Testament of Joad*, 68.

[11] C. E. M. Joad, *The Recovery of Belief: A Restatement of Christian Philosophy* (London, 1951), 63.

[12] Joad, *The Recovery of Belief*, 64, 76. He does not tie this conviction to any particular event or series of events.

[13] Joad, *The Recovery of Belief*, 78.

[14] Joad, *The Testament of Joad*, 89.

[15] Joad, *The Testament of Joad*, 102.

[16] Joad, *The Recovery of Belief*, 23.

[17] Lewis, *The Problem of Pain*, 14.

as there were times when, as an atheist, he had similar doubts about his atheism. In fact, he also saw Christianity as "an immensely formidable unity" when he was outside the Christian faith, even in spite of Christendom's divisions.[18]

ABOUT GOD

God's ways truly are not our ways (Isaiah 55:8), so it comes as no surprise that we cannot fully comprehend a divine being. God cannot be fully understood, but He can be known in part (1 Corinthians 13:9). If we were able fully to understand God, then He would actually be less than God. Nor can God be put in a box, treated like a slot machine, outmaneuvered or outguessed. The wind blows where it will, and so also does the Spirit of God (John 3:8). When Jesus compared the work of the Spirit to the wind, He highlighted the Spirit's invisibility, power, and unpredictability. As Lewis himself suggested in *The Lion, the Witch and the Wardrobe*, He is not a tame God.

Few people will walk such an intellectual path as did Lewis, because God comes to human beings in different ways. At the same time, however, God does not easily take "no" for an answer. He loves His creation, especially the human part of that creation, since the first human beings were created in God's image at the high point of the creation week, a day described in Genesis in much more detail than any other day—the sixth and last day of creation. He loves persistently, never withdrawing that love until the human being closes the door and says, "My will be done, not Yours." And God provides many ways for His creation to be aware of His presence, from the nearly infinite and multi-layered design and complexity of our DNA to the vast distances and awesome majesty of distant galaxies (Psalm 19:1) and everything in between.

As Ravi Zacharias has written and Lewis learned, "The naturalist has no intelligent cause to look to, no moral law to point to, no essential meaning to cling to, and finally, no hope to look forward to for his

---

[18] Lewis, "On the Reading of Old Books," *God in the Dock*, 204. See also a letter to Dorothy L. Sayers in *Collected Letters of C. S. Lewis*, II, 730.

destiny."[19] But, in reality, God is the intelligent cause, the author of the moral law, the one who gives meaning and purpose to life, and the source and end of an eternal future.

Former atheist Lee Strobel once admitted,

> Essentially, I realized that to stay an atheist, I would have to believe that nothing produces everything; non-life produces life; randomness produces fine-tuning; chaos produces information; unconsciousness produces consciousness; and non-reason produces reason. Those leaps of faith were simply too big for me to take, especially in light of the affirmative case for God's existence and Jesus' resurrection (and, hence, his divinity). In other words, in my assessment the Christian worldview accounted for the totality of the evidence much better than the atheistic worldview.[20]

The best way, however, that God can be known is in His Word, the sixty-six complex and interrelated books of Old and New Testaments that speak to people's hearts from a consistent perspective and fulfill our deepest desires. In that Word, God's love is demonstrated not only in the words, but especially in the Word (John 1:1, 14), that is, in the person of His Son, Jesus, He who conquered mankind's greatest enemy—death. And for Lewis, death, a defeated enemy, was the doorway to life: "Submit to death, death of your ambitions and favorite wishes every day and death of your whole body in the end: submit with every fiber of your being, and you will find eternal life."[21]

---

[19] Ravi Zacharias, *A Shattered Visage: The Real Face of Atheism* (Grand Rapids: Baker, 1990), 156f.

[20] www.patheos.com/blogs/friendlyatheist/2009/01/02/lee-strobel-answers-your-questions-part-1/

[21] Lewis, *Mere Christianity*, 227.

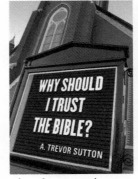